WASHINGTON

FROM

THE

GROUND

UP

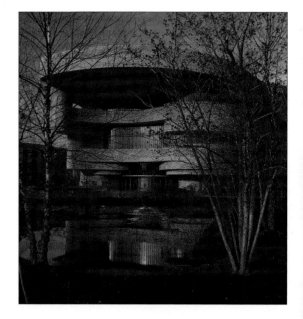

WASHINGTON FROM THE GROUND UP

JAMES H.S. MCGREGOR

THE BELKNAP PRESS OF

HARVARD UNIVERSITY PRESS

Cambridge, Massachusetts

London, England   2007

Library of Congress Cataloging-in-Publication Data

McGregor, James H. (James Harvey), 1946–

Washington from the ground up / James H. S. McGregor

    p. cm.

Includes bibliographical references and index.

ISBN-13: 978-0-674-02604-9

ISBN-10: 0-674-02604-7

1. Washington (D.C.)—Description and travel.

2. Washington (D.C.)—History.

3. City planning—Washington (D.C.)—History.

4. Historic buildings—Washington (D.C.)

5. Washington (D.C.)—Buildings, structures, etc.

I. Title.

F194.M+   917.5304'4—dc22

2007001445

In memory of my parents,

James Harvey McGregor and Mary Twigg McGregor

CONTENTS

WASHINGTON

FROM

THE

GROUND

UP

INTRODUCTION

Two centuries after its founding, Washington remains
at heart what it was intended to be, a city of monumental symbols driven by a desire to explain itself—to
body forth democratic power and to show its contours
and aspirations. The city's history illustrates the work-
ings of the Rube Goldberg machine that is the democratic political process.
Through a compromise that may have saved the early republic, George
Washington was empowered to choose the capital site. But no single intelli-
gence combined the architectural ability, political savvy, and sheer
endurance required to guide the city's development from site plan through
finished construction.

Pierre Charles L'Enfant, who laid out the streets and sited the monuments, did not survive the partisan process long enough to design its two
central buildings, the President's House and the Capitol. William Thornton,
who won the hastily scheduled contest to design the Capitol, lived to see his
design altered and his creation—still incomplete—burned by British troops
during the War of 1812. After the fire, the Capitol was restored by a man
who vilified Thornton and canceled nearly every feature of his original plan.
A favorite of Thomas Jefferson, that architect—Benjamin Latrobe—himself
came to grief in James Monroe's administration and was replaced by a

Bostonian, Charles Bulfinch. Cherished by urban planners as an example of the power and influence of their profession, Washington DC is also a cautionary tale about the unending struggle between the creative imagination and an intractable client.

The client is sometimes a single-minded chief executive, but more often it is the polycephalic Congress. Occasionally, the whole government, embroiled in the unending tug of war among rival branches, becomes involved. No idea comes through this skirmish in its original form. At the same time, no idea ever dies completely. The political machine grinds up proposals while it tries, sometimes over decades, to make up its mind. When resolution finally comes, government tends to favor projects for reasons and in forms remote from any first design or guiding principle.

The Washington Monument is a good example of this byzantine, geologically paced process. The Continental Congress voted an equestrian monument to Washington in 1783. In 1790 L'Enfant drew the still uncommissioned memorial on his plan near the present site of the Washington Monument. As Congress continued to shilly-shally beyond the centenary of the first president's birth in 1832, a private organization took over. The design they chose set the monument—now a chariot drawn by a team of horses with a toga-draped Washington at the reins—on an elevated platform, ringed the platform with a colonnade, and marked it with an obelisk 600 feet tall.

After a few decades of desultory building interrupted by political misdeeds of an unusually low order, the government finally stepped in. Officials scotched the colonnade, the chariot, and the horses—thus completely ignoring the founders' resolution—reduced the obelisk to 555 feet, and brought the project to completion. It is hard to argue that this is a rational way to do business or a process that an aspiring designer or individual legislator might hope to weather, let alone control. It is also hard to argue that the result is a failure. What the Continental Congress had in mind was too small to hold its own in the key spot L'Enfant had set aside. Certainly the grandiose project envisaged by the monument committee would have been a monstrosity. The process that eventually brought the memorial to completion was grotesquely inefficient, but it produced one of the most impressive and well-known monuments in the world.

The same political machine that torpedoed L'Enfant and Latrobe buoyed the dreams of men who knew how to manage power. Washington and Jefferson disagreed on many features of the new national government, but they shared a vision of the federal capital. The two political leaders—both skilled architects—and the men they appointed created a thread of common thought and practice that laid the strongest and deepest foundations for the city.

Washington chose the site and, with his secretary of state, Jefferson, agreed on the general outlines of a modest town. Then, in a surprising change of heart, both men allowed themselves to be persuaded of the superior merit of someone else's idea. L'Enfant laid out a federal city many orders of magnitude greater than anything the two founders had imagined. To their credit, both saw that L'Enfant's projected city would better suit the expanding nation they believed would come. Even after being forced to fire their designer, they carried on the building of a city that he, rather than they, had envisaged.

Washington died before the new national government moved to the site that bore his name. Five years later, Jefferson moved into the President's House and began again to assume direct political and artistic control over the construction of the capital. Jefferson's legacy lasted long after his own administration. The most important architects involved in the creation of federal buildings—the volatile Latrobe and the savvy Bulfinch—shared Jefferson's neoclassical ideals. If Jefferson and Washington and the architects they inspired are the key figures in shaping the city, the pervasive American belief that neoclassicism was a fundamentally democratic building style has guided its subsequent growth. Though the city has endured periods of reaction against neoclassicism—most notably in the aftermath of the Civil War and in the second half of the twentieth century—the neoclassical sensibility, which is now in its Postmodern phase, has exerted a strong and consistent power.

In L'Enfant's design, which is still intact in the city center, the connection between his abstract pattern of streets and the natural topography it overlay is easy to miss. But L'Enfant himself was very aware of the contours of the land, and the city he outlined reflected them. Pennsylvania Avenue, which links the Capitol and White House, follows the course of a road already in use in the eighteenth century. Called the Georgetown Ferry Road, it skirted marshy lowlands to the south as it followed the edge of solid ground from the Potomac River on the west to the Anacostia River on the east. Farther north, Florida Avenue, where L'Enfant's plan abruptly ends, was another old roadway that ran along the base of a steep rise in ground level. With the accuracy of a contour line on a map, this curving avenue marks the boundary between the tidewater plain and the interior piedmont.

Between the marshy areas south of Pennsylvania Avenue and the heights beyond Florida Avenue, the ground was solid, relatively flat, and a more or less uniform eighty feet above sea level. L'Enfant's plan concentrated on this homogeneous tract of land, and development of the city before the Civil War was confined to it. Further south, an area of similar height and composition at the confluence of the Anacostia and Potomac rivers was built up at the same time. But development along the Mall did not begin until the land was drained and the soil consolidated, a slow process that began in the middle of the nineteenth century.

In the early 1800s, when the federal government was small and legislators tended to be itinerant—boarding in town while Congress was in session and then returning home for the bulk of the year—the city had little motive or ability to grow. The Civil War brought its first great surge in population. Army camps and hospitals for the wounded mushroomed at the edges of the thinly settled central area. The government expanded tremendously and did not shrink when the war was over. The spread of public transportation pushed population away from the center, along farm roads and into old piedmont estates, which quickly became housing developments. Massive increases in government jobs during and after the two world wars pushed the city's population to an all-time high in the 1950s.

Then, in a pattern that was repeated throughout America, Washingtonians began to leave the heavily urbanized center for suburbs beyond its boundaries. Long-distance commuting by car replaced generally shorter commutes by public transportation. In leaving the city limits, commuters also left behind its urban services and the property taxes that supported them. Ringed by wealthy suburbs whose residents held the lion's share of government jobs, the city center struggled with high unemployment and increasing crime. And slowly but inexorably, the racial composition of the city shifted from majority white to majority black.

Situated on the frontier between North and South, the city had always been a mecca for African Americans, who first fled the subjection of slavery, then the rigors of Jim Crow, and finally the collapse of the South's cotton economy. More insistently than the promise of employment, Washington offered blacks the promise of freedom and equality. That promise has always been equivocal and haphazardly fulfilled. Lincoln's Emancipation Proclamation changed Civil War aims from preservation of the Union to black liberation. But this policy, welcomed by abolitionists, enraged the Confederacy, and it caused riots as far north as New York City, where some African Americans were lynched. The assassination of Martin Luther King Jr. in 1968 led to riots in Washington that destroyed the economy of black neighborhoods while leaving the rest of the city terrified but untouched.

The crack cocaine epidemic that began in the late 1980s decimated neighborhoods already driven down by despair. Corrupt local politicians channeled resources meant to ease poverty and its effects into the pockets of depraved administrators. For many years the capital was two cities—Washington, which was official, affluent, and white, and DC, which was impoverished, hopeless, and black. Since the mid-1990s, however, that rift has been healing, and the twin cities have found grounds of rapprochement in a local government that has won the respect and support of both communities.

Contemporary Washington presents itself as a city of small neighborhoods with distinctive characteristics which, together, host the national government at their center. This image is the creation of a newly self-

conscious, largely black, though increasingly multiethnic city government. Communities such as Adams Morgan, Meridian Hill, LeDroit Park,
Cleveland Park, Chinatown, Georgetown, and Petworth—each with its
individual flavor—make the city a patchwork of identifiable communities
like London or Toronto. The building of the Metro system and its Green
Line extension through the center-city Shaw neighborhood, along with the
opening of two downtown convention centers and the Verizon sports and
entertainment complex, have revitalized neglected neighborhoods. Racial
and economic divides persist, but their worst effects are disappearing.

This relatively open, cosmopolitan, and comfortable city plays host to
a deeply troubled guest. The World Trade Center and Pentagon bombings
of September 11, 2001, have alarmed official Washington to an unprecedented degree. Public access to public buildings has been severely
restricted and in many cases eliminated. Metal detectors guard the
entrance to every museum. Bags and backpacks are inspected at every
public doorway. A subterranean Visitor Center on the east side of the
Capitol, scheduled for completion in 2008, aims not only to organize
tours of the Capitol (a requirement for entry) but to substitute didactic
exhibits for the building itself. The same is true of the White House,
where public tours are even more restricted. Other national landmarks
such as the Supreme Court, the Justice Department, and the Eisenhower
Executive Office Building can be visited only on scheduled guided tours.

This concern for security is understandable, but it is also deeply disturbing. Democratic institutions do not thrive in the absence of the people. A didactic exhibit, or the blinkered lens of a C-Span camera, is no
substitute for seeing Congress or the Supreme Court in session. The

insistent and unapologetic degradation of a citizen to a mere onlooker—a visitor—threatens the democratic process itself. A republic that is insulated from public view but not from the pressures and allurements of powerful interests assumes a risk much greater than any that terrorism can impose.

Chapter One

DIAMOND CITY

Washington DC sits in the Y-shaped intersection of the Potomac River to the west and the Anacostia River to the east. Between these two waterways, not far from the present site of the White House, a stream once flowed into the Potomac. Originally called Goose Creek, this swampy channel was renamed Tiber by Francis Pope, the first English owner of the land. He named his estate Rome, which made him Pope of Rome—a joke not to go unnoticed in the Catholic colony of Maryland. Of course Rome must have its Tiber, and so Pope renamed Goose Creek.

Just north of Tiber Creek, the terrain rises gently to a broad plateau before making a second much sharper ascent. At this second height of land, the tidewater plain ends and the piedmont hills begin. Georgetown, a mile up the Potomac, and Bladensburg, four miles up the Anacostia, sit at this topographical boundary. Like these towns, Washington DC stands at the western edge of America's longest-settled geologic province and takes one tiny step into the uplands that formed the eighteenth-century frontier. In 1623 Captain Henry Fleete sailed up the Potomac to the Indian settlement of Tahoga at the fall line to trade for corn. His crew were killed by the Anacostan Indians, and Fleete was held captive for many years. Spanish explorers may have visited the area long before Fleete, but they left no physical mark.

In 1790 this site stood at the geographical center of a train of seaboard states that made up North America's young republic. Councils of representatives from the newly minted states, and those of the confederacy that preceded the drafting of the Constitution, had met in a number of American cities, from Annapolis to New York, with stops of various lengths in Lancaster, Philadelphia, and Princeton. Philadelphia and New York were both in contention to become the permanent seat of the federal government, along with two new towns soon to be created along the Delaware River. By adding his weight to a complex political deal, George Washington succeeded in placing the capital along the river he cherished and in whose development he and his family had long been heavily invested.

The Constitution drafted in 1787 created a federal government where none had existed before. By its terms, a national bicameral Congress, a national judiciary, and a president held powers not forwarded to them by state governments but delegated directly by the people of the United States. This new government with its unique powers promised to remedy the lack of coordination among states that had plagued the union under the Articles of Confederation. It also created great uncertainty and considerable unease about the exact nature and limitations of federal power. A group of states that had labored together to free themselves from what they regarded as tyranny were understandably gun-shy about exposing themselves to the ambitions of strong national leaders. In addition to their fear of tyranny, legislators faced the challenge of an untried form of government. No one was clear about what this new political union might be expected to achieve or exactly how it might function.

Almost as soon as the Constitution was ratified, Alexander Hamilton, a
New Yorker and partisan of a strong central government, argued for the
formation of a national bank. In the minds of many legislators, particularly those from the South, this move raised grave fears of economic
domination. Hamilton sweetened the deal when he proposed that a
national bank, once created, would assume the debt that individual
states had incurred while fighting the Revolutionary War. But from the
South's point of view, even the substantial benefits of debt assumption
could not outweigh the disadvantages of a national bank, which promised
gains to New Yorkers and little but hardship for cash-poor plantation owners whose wealth was frozen in land and slaves and whose incomes
depended on the vagaries of the market for tobacco, indigo, and rice.

The regional split on the question of a national bank created an
opportunity for a political trade on the location of a federal city. A capital
on the Potomac was appealing to southerners, and especially to Virgini-
ans, who had played such a large part in the Revolution and the founding
of the republic. A capital somewhere between Philadelphia and New York
would do nothing to ease the misgivings of southern states. In a series of
informal talks, Hamilton and Jefferson, both members of President Washington's cabinet but men with opposite views on federal power, worked
out the details of a trade between support for a national bank by southerners and support of a southern capital by northerners.

The site that Washington chose, though virtually unpeopled in 1790,
was linked by land and water to both the North and the South. Three
nearby deep-water harbors—Alexandria in Virginia, along with Georgetown
and Bladensburg in Maryland—accommodated coastal freighters and
packets that made port in each of the original thirteen states. Today, we
regard water transportation as secondary, but colonial travelers from

Savannah to Boston preferred it to the hardships of existing roads. Primitive though they were, the few highways that linked the North and South also passed through or near the new federal district. Ferries across the Potomac funneled overland traffic from Williamsburg and points south to Annapolis and points north through the general area that would become the District of Columbia.

The early development of the United States was not just a story of North and South, however. President Washington was well aware of a perpendicular axis of travel passing through the future capital; and if there is any hint of self-interest in his support for a Potomac site, it reflects that awareness. In the 1740s a group of Virginia investors, which included Washington's older brother, formed the Ohio Company to promote and profit from settlement in the inland region drained by the Ohio River. This area had been only sketchily explored, but the river was known to be navigable for most of its length, to carve a wide swath through rich country, and to flow into the Mississippi River.

Unfortunately, the territories of the Ohio and Mississippi rivers were claimed by the French. And rather than have their colonial possessions nibbled away piecemeal by American colonists, the French were determined to defend them. During the French and Indian War, the young George Washington had fought first in the service of the Virginia colonial militia and then as an aide-de-camp to Major General Edward Braddock, supreme commander of British troops in America. In 1755 Braddock's regulars were ambushed and slaughtered at Fort Duquesne (now Pittsburgh), near the three-river junction of the Ohio, Allegheny, and Monongahela—a deeply shocking event that ultimately fueled Americans' hopes of defeating the fabled British army in their own war for independence.

Washington returned to service in the Virginia militia before again joining a British force in a successful march against the French stronghold.

Once the Ohio Valley was cleared of French troops, settlers poured into the region. The Indian allies of the French resisted, and they were joined by the Delaware and Susquehanna, who had once been at peace with the colonists. South of the Ohio River, Indian resistance was quickly overcome. Daniel Boone, who had helped cut the wilderness road toward Fort Duquesne that Braddock's troops had followed, opened the way to settlement in Kentucky, which became the fifteenth state in 1792. Despite the Ohio Company's evident success in opening former French territory to British settlement, it dissolved with little profit to its investors. George Washington, however, continued to believe in the benefits of a Virginia-based opening toward this rich new territory beyond the Appalachian mountain range.

The long coastal plain that forms the eastern seaboard of the United States is hedged in by a belt of mountains almost equally long. From north Georgia to Maine and on into maritime Canada, the spine of the Appalachians created a rough barrier to westward expansion during the colonial period. In 1763 the British drew a line of demarcation along this natural feature and declared it the boundary to British colonization. Everything west of this line would remain Indian land in perpetuity; territory to the east fell within the economic sphere of Great Britain. This Proclamation of 1763—a reaction to the high cost and low benefit to the mother country of the French and Indian War—spurred widespread opposition in the colonies and was added to the growing list of grievances that Jefferson would spell out in the Declaration of Independence.

In Washington's mind, and in that of many men and women to follow, the Potomac promised to be a gateway through the mountains and the beginning of a great highway west. Washington himself had traveled the river by boat many times. Though he knew that difficult terrain separated the Potomac and Ohio rivers and that they flowed in opposite directions (the Potomac to the east and the Ohio to the west), he believed that one of the larger Potomac tributaries could be developed into a navigable link. Washington founded the Patowmack Improvement Company in 1785 to make the Potomac useful for year-round two-way commerce. It was reliably navigable only in spring floods, and even then in only one direction.

Britain had started to industrialize in the second half of the eighteenth century, and in the 1780s had begun to use steam to power machinery. But mass production required the efficient transportation of raw materials and finished products. British roads were every bit as poor as colonial roads at this time, making overland freight transfer slow and expensive. Canals were the best alternatives to these clogged, inefficient highways, and soon Britain was crisscrossed by a webwork of waterways that brought coal to factory furnaces and carried finished goods to market. Benjamin Franklin, a colonial representative in London from 1765 to 1775, was well aware of the success of England's canals and their potential benefits for America. In a letter to Samuel Rhoads written from London in August 1772, he recommended hiring British engineers with experience in canal building, and he also cautioned, "Here they look on the *constant Practicability* of a Navigation, allowing Boats to pass and repass at all Times and Seasons, without Hindrance, to be a Point of the greatest Importance."

Obstacles to year-round two-way navigation of the Potomac were not

confined to the mountain country far to
the west. Just beyond Georgetown and
the site of the new capital, the soft
substructure of the coastal plain gave
way, and the bedrock of the piedmont
rose to the surface. Nine miles above
the city, in a series of cascades
stretching less than a mile, the
Potomac River dropped nearly eighty

1

feet. The stairlike structure of these falls meant that no individual cascade was more than twenty feet high—puny by the standards of Niagara
or Victoria. (1) Still, the effort of canal builders to circumnavigate the
Potomac Falls was a feat of engineering on a scale never before
attempted in America. With cooperation from Virginia and Maryland—the
two states that owned the river—and with an agreement from all thirteen
states to coordinate trade regulations, the Patowmack Company, with
George Washington as its president, began work in 1785.

Some seventeen years later, a mile-long canal around the Great Falls,
with five locks for lifting and lowering boats, was complete. Much of the
canal had to be cut through hard metamorphic rock. The precarious solution was blasting with black powder, a new technique in the eighteenth
century. During the same period, dredging and channeling the Potomac
made the waterway passable to vessels that varied from crude log rafts to
twenty-ton barges. The earliest cargoes were flour, whiskey, tobacco, and
iron from farms and villages upstream. Eventually, building stone for the
federal city would also be transported down the river.

While thousands of boats traveled in both directions on the improved river and new canal, the venture was a financial failure. The Patowmack Company declared bankruptcy in 1828, and the infrastructure it had created at such tremendous cost passed on to the Chesapeake and Ohio Canal Company, which in 1830 abandoned a river route altogether and began construction of a canal running alongside the Potomac. "Success to the navigation of the Potomac," Washington's frequent toast at banquets, was not to be achieved in his lifetime. The C&O Canal was completed as far as Cumberland, Maryland, in 1850. Work ended there, and Washington's vision of joining the Potomac and the Ohio by water was never realized.

In 1802, during Jefferson's second term, Congress authorized a more modest attempt to link the two rivers: the creation of a national road between Cumberland and the Ohio River. Work began in 1811, and the new road, which followed Braddock's and Washington's route, reached the Ohio River in 1818. But the job of opening the West to commerce through the Potomac Valley fell mostly to the railroad. The Baltimore and Ohio Railroad Company, chartered in Maryland and Virginia in 1827, reached Cumberland eight years before the canal did, and it arrived at its Ohio River terminus—Wheeling, West Virginia—in 1852. The railroad bypassed Washington altogether.

If the inland opening of the Potomac lay in an indefinite future far beyond the limit of Washington's lifetime, an opening to Atlantic sea lanes was longstanding. The history of the area at the confluence of the Potomac and Anacostia rivers had been tied to the plantation culture of the Chesapeake region since earliest colonial times. In its economic development and pattern of land-holding, Maryland was more or less indistinguishable from its southern neighbor, Virginia. Its one distinctive

feature was religious toleration. Virginia followed English law in restrict-
ing the civil rights of Roman Catholics, but in Maryland Catholics could
practice their religion freely.

Throughout the Chesapeake, colonists established a way of life that
was rooted in the socioeconomic system of British manors. Many
colonists were men of high social rank who were deprived of wealth by
the English law of entail that favored primogeniture and kept large
estates intact by passing them entirely to the eldest son. Gentlemen who
saw their fathers' estates fall into the hands of their elder brothers could
console themselves with manors of their own in the colonies, where land
was plentiful and cheap. A colonial estate was also an engine for producing wealth, since agriculture was the economic backbone of the British
nobility, and would remain so until industrialization replaced it in the late
eighteenth century. The key to transforming land into wealth in both the
New World and the Old was the same—labor.

In the densely populated British Isles, villages on the periphery of
estates provided agricultural laborers for manors. British peasants rotated
crops from year to year and let fields lie fallow to restore the soil. In the
New World, Native Americans practiced subsistence farming—growing
corn, beans, squash, and tobacco as needed year by year and producing
little surplus. When the soil in one area became exhausted, Indians simply moved their villages. But a land grant from the king could not be
moved from place to place as soil became unproductive, and so laborers
had to be found to work these vast estates year in and year out.

Maryland's proprietors tried to trade American land for British labor,
by keying the size of land grants to the number of additional colonists a
prospective landowner could resettle. A grantee who paid the resettle-

ment costs of five colonists would receive two thousand acres of land at a modest price. But before the seventeenth century ended, this system was already ineffective. Within the first decades of the colony's life, settlers had to be supplemented by indentured laborers. Indentures were contracts between a colonial landowner and a British worker. In exchange for passage and maintenance, the indentured laborer was bound to his employer for a fixed number of years. At the end of the term, the emancipated worker was free to establish whatever form of tenancy or labor contract he could negotiate.

The plantation system consumed workers at an extraordinary rate. But the demand for labor in the Chesapeake region was especially high because eighteenth-century tidewater planters cultivated one crop to the virtual exclusion of everything else: tobacco. In addition to requiring a very long growing season, tobacco is a thirsty, tender, disease-prone, soil-devouring plant. Work on a tobacco plantation began in February with the cultivation of seedlings. Late in March the seedlings were transplanted one by one to carefully prepared fields. Throughout the spring and summer, the crop required frequent cultivation to destroy competing weeds; when rains failed in the hot summer, the tender plants needed watering. In an era before irrigation, water by the bucketful had to be carried to the fields. The leaves were harvested by hand in the late fall, bundled, and hung in curing sheds to dry. Then they were packed in hogsheads and rolled overland to ships. Because of the demands that tobacco made on the soil, fields were quickly depleted of nutrients, and new ones had to be opened for cultivation every few years. The labor of clearing fields in virgin country was backbreaking.

Despite the efforts tobacco cultivation required, the global demand for this product made it profitable. In 1620 (the year the Pilgrims landed at Plymouth Rock), Virginia colonists shipped some twenty pounds of tobacco to England. The overall demand for tobacco during that year was considerably greater, however, and most of it was satisfied by Spain, where the crop was a government monopoly. As smoking grew in popularity, the value of the colonial crop increased. By the beginning of the eighteenth century, the demand for agricultural workers in Virginia and Maryland was insatiable, and it was clear that neither colonists nor indentured laborers could meet that demand. Felons and prisoners of war were transported to the Chesapeake. Kidnapped agricultural workers in Britain were another labor source; they frequently arrived in Virginia in chains. Simply getting a laborer to America did not end the difficulties, however. Once they arrived in the colonies, indentured workers, both free and coerced, often escaped to the frontier and claimed land of their own.

In 1619 a Dutch ship short on supplies landed in Jamestown, Virginia. The master of the vessel traded twenty African captives for ship's biscuit, flour, and salt pork before resuming his voyage to the West Indies. The twenty Africans were put to work in the tobacco fields as indentured servants. In the next decades, as the number of African field hands in Virginia and Maryland increased, their status declined from that of indentured workers, more or less on a par with Europeans, to the category of slaves. As early as the 1640s, Virginia law treated indentured Africans as property.

By the 1660s, Virginia statutes began to mimic the well-codified laws of the Roman Empire that considered the offspring of a slave to be a slave. In 1682 the legislature declared that "all servants which shall be imported into this country either by sea or by land, whether Negroes, Moors, mulattoes or Indians who and whose parentage and native countries are not Christian at the time of their first purchase by some Christian and all Indians, which shall be sold by our neighboring Indians, or any other trafficking with us for slaves, are hereby adjudged, deemed and taken to be slaves to all intents and purposes any law, usage, or custom to the contrary notwithstanding."

Under Roman law, slavery was an extreme civil disability—a kind of social death—that was first incurred by right of conquest. Justinian's *Institutes,* a textbook for beginning lawyers written in the sixth century AD, explained that "slaves are called *servi,* because generals pre*serve* their captives, and do not put them to death. Slaves are also called *manicipia,* because they are taken from the enemy by a strong hand *[manus]*" (I.iii.3). Whether born of a slave mother, abandoned as a child, stolen by pirates, or captured in warfare, all slaves were, in the eyes of Roman law, prisoners whose lives had been spared by their captors. In exchange for commutation of their death sentence, captives ceded all personal rights. Captors were free to dispose of slaves in any way they chose, and their absolute power over them could be transferred to another by gift or sale. That is more or less the situation the Virginia law of 1682 imagined. In the early years of slavery, Christian baptism emancipated a slave, but that escape clause was repealed in 1667; even slaves who converted to Christianity remained in bondage.

Every seventeenth-century Virginia legislator knew the contrary traditions of slavery that are described in the Bible. The Jews, like the Egyptians and the other nations they bordered, kept slaves, but in the Biblical tradition slavery came about more commonly through debt than conquest. Unlike the Romans, the Israelites were careful to limit the term of involuntary servitude, because, as Deuteronomy 15:15 says, "Thou shalt remember that thou wast a slave in the land of Egypt." But in the codification of slavery law in the North American colonies, the pragmatic prevailed over conscience and religious tradition, and over the emerging sense within the very same legislators that British rule of American colonists was tyrannical. The terrible and unfathomable paradox of American history is the evolution of slavery in the same assemblies that argued repeatedly for the innate equality of all men and their inalienable rights to life and liberty.

2

At tremendous individual and social cost, slavery evolved during the seventeenth century to supply the labor necessary to sustain the plantation economies of Virginia and Maryland. Sixty-seven thousand slaves entered the Chesapeake region directly from Africa between 1698 and 1774. Births and slave trade within the colonies increased that number dramatically. The slave population of Virginia and Maryland, as counted in the first United States Census of 1790, was 395,663. In that year slaves outnumbered free males by more than three to one. (2) By the mid-eighteenth century, approximately half of the enslaved Africans in America lived in the Chesapeake region, where they made up the majority of the population.

In addition to land and labor, the other requirement of the plantation economy was international transport. Tobacco was of no economic value unless it could reach the world marketplace. British colonial policy in the wake of the French and Indian War was very attentive to the peculiar conditions of tidewater life, and for obvious commercial reasons (and more occult political ones) did everything in its power to sustain them. The Chesapeake Bay and the tidal reaches of the Potomac, Rappahannock, and James rivers, together with their major tributaries, form an interior coastline many thousands of miles in length. The major colonial plantations were set along these shores, and merchant ships from England served every plantation individually.

Tobacco was collected at the plantation dock and loaded aboard a British merchant vessel. British mercantile policy made sure that whatever the plantation owners could not produce at home was delivered to them in a British ship. Wines from France, sherry from Spain, clothing and furniture from London, medicines, eyeglasses, nails and planes, surgical instruments, sextants and compasses were off-loaded, as tobacco barrels rolled onboard. Tobacco producers with inland farms, and families who cultivated only a few acres, sold their tobacco either to brokers in the waterside towns or to large plantation owners, who acted as both brokers and producers.

The advantages to the British economy were obvious. Wealthy colonists provided a market for British manufacturing and luxury goods. British ships carried these products west and shipped raw materials east.

British banks provided the credit
that made the system work. For
over a century, most tidewater
estate owners—directly linked to
the mother country by a secure
chain of supply—had little interest
in land beyond the mountains and
little incentive for political union
with other colonies. Town life was

3

very active in the North, but towns in Virginia and Maryland were small
and widely scattered. The plantation was the center of society.

President Washington's own Mount Vernon was more or less typical of
a tidewater estate. He inherited the plantation, some two thousand acres
in extent, from his half-brother Lawrence in 1761. He quickly increased
his holdings to eight thousand acres, which he organized into five farms.
He set aside the five-hundred-acre Mansion Farm along the Potomac—
and the house now called Mount Vernon—to be developed as a country
estate rather than a working farm. (3) On the rest of his land, Washington's more than three hundred slaves planted a variety of crops. Flour
ground in the gristmill on the site and packed in barrels made by Washington's slaves was loaded directly onto ocean-going ships. Washington
also owned a distillery that produced whisky for consumption and sale.

In 1790 Washington set out from Mount Vernon to tour prospective
sites for the federal capital. Once he settled on the area at the confluence of the Potomac and Anacostia rivers, he met with the owners of the
land in Georgetown in January 1791 and negotiated terms for cession to

the new government. Maryland, which donated the majority of the land, and Virginia, which added a smaller share, voted modest funding for the district's development as well. Each state believed that their cessions and contributions would pay dividends when the new capital was established. The same logic guided Washington's proposal to owners of the land that would be occupied by the new city. The landowners would cede the acreage required for roads and government building sites at no cost. Since their holdings would gain considerable value in the process, they could share profits with the government and still come out ahead. The logic of Washington's argument was convincing, and the landowners agreed to his terms.

Pierre Charles L'Enfant, an amateur architect and designer, offered to lay out the new federal city. Son of an artist attached to the French court at Versailles, L'Enfant had trained at the Royal Academy of Painting and Sculpture in Paris, where his father was an instructor, rather than at the Royal Academy of Architecture, which might have better suited his talents. L'Enfant came to America in 1776 or soon after and joined the Revolution. He served in various theaters of the war. Though the details of his military service are unclear, he was probably involved in the design of camps and fortifications. At the war's end he was promoted to the rank of major of engineers.

When the federal government moved to New York City in 1787, L'Enfant supervised the transformation of the old city hall into Federal Hall. He arrived in Georgetown in March 1791, where he met the team of surveyors already laying out the district's boundaries. The team was headed by Andrew Ellicott, who was assisted by a self-taught mechanical engineer and mathematician named Benjamin Banneker. Banneker, a free

black man, was the grandson and namesake of an African slave called
Banne Ka.

The federal district was a square ten miles on a side, positioned so
that each of its corners pointed in one of the cardinal directions. It
looked like a diamond balanced on its southern tip. Though abstract, this
superimposed geometry bore some relationship to the contours of the
land. The bottom half of the diamond framed the two rivers; its southern
apex was an idealized confluence and its south-facing sides paralleled
the Potomac and Anacostia. The points of the diamond formed a skeletal
compass rose that summed up the broader geography of the site and the
rationale for its choice: set at the dividing line between North and South,
the city was also linked to the westward inclination of
the expanding nation. In 1790 Paris lay on the zero
meridian, and nautical charts reflected this in their
measure of longitude. It was only late in the nineteenth
century that the Greenwich meridian became the world
standard. By emphasizing the cardinal directions in the
design of the federal district, the founders may have
been staking some claim to the creation of a rival zero-
degree longitude line for the new nation.

The center point of this idealized hundred-mile area
lay on the northern bank of the Tiber near its junction
with the Potomac (just south of where the White House
sits today). Both Washington and Jefferson, who as

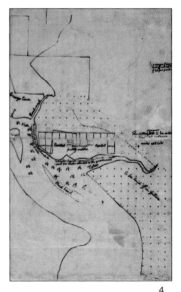

4

secretary of state was directly responsible for the project, were in agreement about the site and the size of the future capital. In 1791 Jefferson
sketched a map of a modest capital along the Potomac directly north of

Tiber, at the site of an earlier projected town to be called Hamburg or Funkstown. (4) The equally spaced dots of his street grid continued south of Tiber, but he added a note that this area was "to be laid off in future." Jefferson devoted a space eleven blocks by three immediately above the creek to a capitol building and a presidential residence. Along the creek he set aside an open area for what he called "public walks."

Washington and Jefferson both believed that it was important to keep their plan under wraps. They realized that once their preferences became known, speculators in Georgetown would try to grab up the blocks designated for federal buildings and push land prices to levels that the young government could not afford. In a fit of cleverness uncharacteristic of both men, they decided to mislead speculators by spreading the rumor that they preferred a site for the capital along the Anacostia rather than the Potomac. To give their scheme more credibility, they urged L'Enfant to begin his survey in that part of the new federal district and to postpone examination of the area they had already chosen.

L'Enfant played along, carefully exploring the areas that were not going to be part of the capital his clients had in mind. It was a cold and rainy March when he set to work. The tobacco fields were still unplanted and the wheat fields unplowed. Even in the best weather there was little enough to see in the way of houses or farm buildings. The boggy soil along the rivers was pitted here and there with shallow pools and spiked with clumps of reed and willow. But north of the creek, where the land began its first gentle rise, the soil was firm and dry. A road from Georgetown to the Anacostia ferry traced the southern edge of this higher ground just beyond the limits of the marshland. A second road joined Georgetown and Bladensburg. Not far from the point where the Tiber nar-

rowed and turned sharply north, L'Enfant rode up Jenkins Hill, a modest
plateau well above the marshy creekside. It struck him as "a pedestal
looking for a monument."

As he explored the land between the rivers day after day, L'Enfant
came to believe that Washington and Jefferson had chosen the wrong site
for their capital and that the scale they had in mind was too modest.
What the two leaders imagined was little more than another river town
like Bladensburg, Georgetown, or Alexandria. Except for a small government center, nothing would distinguish it from these earlier settlements.
L'Enfant proposed that the center of the new capital be shifted east,
toward the Anacostia River, and that the project be expanded. The city he
envisaged was twenty times bigger than the one Jefferson had drawn.
Though the size of L'Enfant's grid exceeded what his clients had outlined, all three men were optimistic about the potential expansion of the
United States, and a capital city that fit the scale of the nation they
imagined was bound to appeal to them. To their enormous credit, both
the president and the secretary of state adopted the new plan and
quickly abandoned their own.

Once L'Enfant revised the site for the federal city, its coordination
with the diamond-shaped federal district became a problem. Jefferson's
little town would have evolved on both sides of the district's center point,
and perhaps over time it would have grown toward the district's edges,
along the west bank of the Potomac and the east bank of the Anacostia.
L'Enfant's plan bore a more complex relationship to the hundred-square-
mile diamond. (Map 1) The city he designed was slightly off axis with the
District as a whole. Instead, it was anchored in both the small- and large-
scale geography of its site. Jenkins Hill served as the pedestal for L'En-

fant's Capitol building, while the firm ground above the junction of the Tiber and the Potomac would hold the President's House. The northern limit of his city was a semicircular road called Boundary Street (now Florida Avenue) that skirted the steep hillside at the edge of the piedmont. The Georgetown Ferry Road (Pennsylvania Avenue), which traced the limits of firm ground on its way from Georgetown to the ford over the Anacostia, became a major axis in L'Enfant's plan.

While favoring these small-scale natural features, L'Enfant gave prominence to the largest scale geographical feature of the region, the Y-shaped river confluence. He imagined the city growing within the space naturally defined by the two branching rivers. L'Enfant transformed a plan in which the two rivers served as links among nearby communities into one in which the rivers served as boundaries of the capital city. The effect of this shift has been profound and prolonged. Virginia ultimately took back from the federal government the land along the west bank of the Potomac because none of it had been developed. The area south of the Anacostia, though still in the District, has been marginalized throughout its history, in part because L'Enfant left its development out of his urban scheme.

Though he replaced the president's preferred site with a larger one to the east, L'Enfant retained Jefferson's proposal for a Capitol building. The House of Representatives and the Senate would meet in a central structure standing on Jenkins Hill, at a distance from the chief executive's house. The Capitol and the President's House would be linked by both a wide avenue (Pennsylvania) and an expanded version of Jefferson's public walks (now the National Mall). Tiber, its channel deepened and its sides confined by embankments, would create a practical and picturesque waterway along this promenade avenue, and a canal would extend it to join the Anacostia.

In Jefferson's sketch and in L'Enfant's plan, Francis Pope's joke had taken a serious turn. It is hard to look at the core of the federal city and not think of Rome. Jefferson himself had not visited that city, but he knew it from eighteenth-century maps and engravings. (5) There is no evidence that L'Enfant had traveled to Rome either, though as a student at the Royal Academy of Painting and Sculpture he would have heard a great deal about it. The Prix de Rome—a three-year resident fellowship at the French Academy—was the goal of every ambitious student there. Despite uncertainty about the genesis of L'Enfant's plan for the federal city, an association between the complex of government buildings he imagined and the center of government that had evolved by the eighteenth century in Rome is inescapable.

The ancient Forum was the seat of power in the Roman republic and the meeting place of the Senate. This busy area butted up against the steep Capitoline Hill on the northwest, which was the site of temples to three of the most important deities of the state, Jupiter, Juno, and Minerva. In the first century BC, Augustus established an empire that soon replaced republican rule, centered in the Senate, with a single leader. To assert his omnipotence, Augustus laid the foundations for a grand imperial residence and government center on the

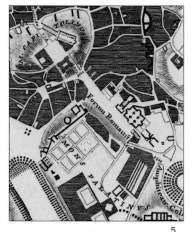

5

Palatine Hill to the southeast of the Capitoline. The word "palace" takes its name from these structures, whose opulence overshadowed the ancient Forum.

When the Roman Empire fell in the fifth century AD, the old Forum became increasingly overgrown, and by the eighteenth century it was a park strewn with picturesque ruins. During the Middle Ages and Renaissance, the Capitoline Hill housed the limited local government that the ruling papacy conceded to the Romans. When Michelangelo reorganized the Capitoline in the sixteenth century, he created buildings for both the single Roman senator and an assembly called the Conservators. Today, these buildings house one of Rome's principal museums, but the Palazzo Senatore is still the seat of government; the mayor of Rome has his office there. In its evolution from a religious to a government center, the Capitoline Hill gave its name to both "capital" cities and "capitol" buildings.

So by the eighteenth century, the Roman Capitoline was a center of government; the Forum was a low-lying rectangular promenade; and perpendicular to the long axis formed by these two structures stood the ruins of a palace that represented the authority of a single leader. In L'Enfant's plan for Washington, these three features are linked in much the same pattern. Of course their significance was very different in the federal city. The Capitol in Washington was a legislative center, and the palace was a mere house. In eighteenth-century Rome, the Forum was a park with no surviving political identity, while in Jefferson's drawing the analogous "public walks" may have, in some general way, represented the people who unite to form the federal government.

Around this L-shaped core, L'Enfant cast two webworks of streets. One was a grid that divided the city into rectangles and squares like those

envisaged in Jefferson's plan—though L'Enfant's blocks were of various
dimensions and proportions. The second network was a spider web of
diagonal avenues that radiated from key monuments. Eight avenues
sprung from the Capitol site like spokes of an eccentric wheel. Six
avenues began at the President's House. Secondary sites in the plan also
served as hubs of radiating avenues. Two long avenues unconnected to
major sites ran diagonally across the city, roughly parallel to the Georgetown Ferry Road.

These radiating avenues are the most striking feature of L'Enfant's
plan and the one to which he gave a great deal of attention. They remain
a defining characteristic of Washington today. According to the designer's
notes on his plan, these "lines or Avenues of direct communication have
been devised to connect the separate and most distant objects with the
principal, and to preserve through the whole a reciprocity of sight at the
same time. Attention has been paid to the passing of those leading
Avenues over the most favorable ground for prospect and convenience."
The grid Jefferson devised—the common plan for American towns in the
eighteenth century—was adequate for a small town, but L'Enfant's much
larger city would have been impossible to negotiate without the long diagonal streets he constructed. They gave additional prominence to the principal buildings of the city and eased travel among them. A trip between
the Capitol and the President's House along the avenue that replaced the
Georgetown Ferry Road would have been fifty percent longer on a grid of
perpendicular streets and would have required many turns.

In L'Enfant's words, both "prospect and convenience" lay behind the
rationale for the avenues. By prospect, he meant the creation of a viewpoint or vista along the wide avenue toward some distant monument.

Street design of this kind was pioneered in the Renaissance by urban planners and theatrical designers, who in many instances were the same person. By the eighteenth century, theatrical backdrops imitated real streets, and urban avenues in turn reflected the skill of designers attuned to scenic balance, harmony, and drama. These combined traditions were publicized in urban views like those of Canaletto in Venice, which were immensely popular in Britain and widely known through engravings by Antonio Visentini.

L'Enfant projected his serviceable roads on a very large scale. "Every grand transverse Avenue, and every principal divergent one, such as the communication from the President's house to the Congress house, &c., are 160 feet in breadth"; lesser streets were to be between 110 and 130 feet wide. While these long avenues were the antithesis of those Jefferson had projected in his modest sketch, the secretary of state became their champion. He made finished drawings of three different ways of combining carriageways and walkways between the Capitol and the President's House, and he encouraged the planting of tress. Many scholars believe that Jefferson was responsible for naming principal avenues after states of the union, though how the street connecting the capital's two major buildings came to be called Pennsylvania Avenue remains a mystery. Probably at the suggestion of his clients, L'Enfant named his perpendicular streets with letters and numbers instead of names.

The greatest thoroughfare in the city would be the "Grand Avenue, 400 feet in breadth, and about a mile in length," that would subsume Jefferson's public walks. This wide open space is now called the National Mall. L'Enfant intended it to be bordered with gardens throughout its whole length. Three fourths of it would form a "well improved field," probably something like a sheep's meadow or vast lawn—the ceremonial equivalent of the commons found in colonial towns such as Boston. It also owed a debt to the Champs Elysées in Paris, laid out a few years before L'Enfant left that city. Around this great open area at the capital's center were building lots "which command the most agreeable prospects, and which are the best calculated for spacious houses and gardens, such as may accommodate foreign Ministers." In letters to President Washington, L'Enfant suggested that this Grand Avenue might also be suitable for a public theater, for the exhibition of curiosities, and for other entertainments.

The avenue began at the Capitol and ended at a slope leading up to the grounds of the President's House, which was, like the imperial palace on the Roman Palatine, near but not on the great forumlike open area. On the Grand Avenue itself, the office of president would be represented symbolically by "the equestrian figure of George Washington," a monument voted in 1783 by the Continental Congress. In the nineteenth century, the Washington Monument as we know it today replaced this equestrian statue. Because of unstable ground at the actual meeting point of a line drawn from the center of the White House and the center of the Mall, the monument was shifted to a firm site a little to the southeast.

In his notes to the plan, L'Enfant counted up fifteen major squares where radiating avenues met, and he linked them to the fifteen states that then existed. These squares were "to be divided among the several States in the Union, for each of them to improve . . . The center of each Square will admit of Statues, Columns, Obelisks or any other ornaments, such as the different States may choose to erect; to perpetuate not only the memory of such individuals whose Counsels or military achievements were conspicuous in giving liberty and independence to this Country; but also those whose usefulness hath rendered them worthy of general imitation; to invite the Youth of succeeding generations to tread in the paths of those Sages or heroes whom their Country has thought proper to celebrate." The state squares complete the capital's representation of the organization of American government. The constellation of state squares, bound together by the avenues radiating from the central buildings, represent the United States as a confederation.

Just as each state would create a shrine in the national capital to honor its local heroes, the capital would also set aside a place to honor the heroes of the nation as a whole. L'Enfant provided space for a "Church . . . intended for national purposes, such as public prayer, thanksgivings, funeral Orations . . . and assigned to the special use of no particular Sect or denomination, but equally open to all. It will be likewise a proper shelter for such monuments as were voted by the late Continental Congress, for those heroes who fell in the cause of liberty and for such others as may hereafter be decreed by the voice of a grateful nation."

L'Enfant's annotations to his plan make no mention of the third branch of the federal government, the Judiciary, though in a letter to George Washington the designer mentions the Supreme Court along with the national bank. Historians believe that Jefferson intended the Court to be housed in what is now called Judiciary Square near Fourth and D streets. Like the Capitol and the President's House, the Court would occupy a small promontory.

L'Enfant was not designing just a symbolic city, but one in which the needs of the population would be met. At a large square in the eastern

end of the city, framed by the two east-west avenues that begin at the
Capitol (Constitution and Independence avenues today), L'Enfant placed
a city hall. A central market, served by the Tiber canal, would supply the
citizens who were expected to live and work in this part of town. Public
entertainment would be assured by a playhouse and exhibition spaces.
Fortifications would defend the city. A dock and mercantile exchange at
the confluence of the rivers would serve as the point of exchange for
goods traveling down the Potomac and those coming upriver on ocean-
going ships. Like the three towns that already controlled commerce in the
area, the federal city would thrive on trade. The public walks would welcome all the citizens of the nation, while Pennsylvania Avenue would
serve as both a national parade route and a local main street.

Despite the brilliance of his plan and the support it won from Washington and Jefferson, L'Enfant was fired in early 1792, less than a year
after his arrival in the federal district. There were several sources of dis-
satisfaction. When the plan was first presented to the landowners, they
quickly discovered that of the six thousand acres making up the new city,
more than three thousand would be taken over by roads and public buildings. This reduced the salable property and anticipated profits by half
and nearly caused the landowners to back out of the deal. L'Enfant
weathered this crisis and the next one, which involved his failure to provide an engraved map at the time of the first sale. But the action that
spelled his downfall was a bold intervention to save his ideal city from
encroachment by a landowner secure in his property rights.

When Daniel Carroll, lord of Duddington manor, the largest holding in
the federal district, began work on a new mansion, he chose a site
directly on axis with the Capitol at the spot L'Enfant had set aside for city

hall. When Carroll refused to build elsewhere, L'Enfant sent a crew of workers to demolish the unfinished house. Despite the president's evident belief in the wisdom, if not the propriety, of what L'Enfant had done, Washington was forced to fire the man who had designed the nation's capital. L'Enfant was offered a building lot near the President's House and twenty-five thousand dollars for his plan, both of which he refused. He resided in nearby Maryland until his death in 1825 but had no further part in the development of the federal district. In 1909, after his long-neglected plan had become the foundation for a massive renewal of the city, L'Enfant's body was disinterred and lay in state in the Capitol Rotunda before being reburied, as a celebrated hero, at Arlington National Cemetery.

Chapter Two

A CAPITOL BY DESIGN

The firing of L'Enfant created enormous problems for Washington and Jefferson. The designer had been a quick study and an even quicker worker. His survey of the site and initial schematic design for the city had been finished in less than five months. But this essential work was just the first stage of a master plan for the city and its most significant buildings. With L'Enfant fired, who would design the Capitol and President's House? In March 1792 Jefferson drafted an advertisement offering five hundred dollars and a choice building lot for the winning entrant in a contest to design "a CAPITOL to be erected in this City."

The ad specified that the building was to be of brick and to contain "a Conference Room and a Room for the Representatives both capable of accommodating three hundred persons." The building program included a Senate Room of twelve hundred square feet, a lobby or antechamber for each of the two legislative branches, and twelve rooms of six hundred square feet each for committees and clerks' offices. "Drawings will be expected of the ground plats, elevations of each front, and sections through the building in such directions as may be necessary to explain the internal structure; and an estimate of the cubic feet of brick-work completing the whole mass of the walls." Qualifying entries were to be submitted by the middle of July, four months later.

6

Jefferson's advertisement spells out the functional elements of the design, but it gives no hint of the structural
feature that has been the most potent symbol of the
building since its inception. A political cartoon in the
Boston Sentinel of August 1789 pictured ratification of
the Constitution by the state of North Carolina as the
"erection of the Eleventh Pillar of the great National DOME." As he had
done for the layout of the federal district, Jefferson drew his own sketch
for the Capitol, based on a cherished classical model, the Pantheon in
Rome. That cylindrical temple with its hemispherical dome was designed
by the Emperor Hadrian in the second century AD. In 609 it was sancti-
fied as a Christian church dedicated to the Virgin Mary. Almost alone
among Rome's monuments, the Pantheon survived intact into the eighteenth century, and it is still visited by tourists today.

Jefferson knew the building through some of the many drawings and
descriptions of it that were published from the Renaissance on. (6) He
adapted it in the façade and dome of his piedmont home, Monticello. In
Jefferson's first drawing of the Capitol, the inner edge of the circular
ground plan was strung with three elliptical meeting rooms and an elliptical entryway. (7) The rooms were labeled Senate, House of Representatives, and Courts of Justice. A rectangular cham-
ber labeled "passages and stairs" filled the
central space. Never adopted for the national
Capitol, Jefferson reworked this plan for the interior of the rotunda at the University of Virginia.

Jefferson drew a second sketch of the Capitol
that extended the very confined space of the first. His new design began

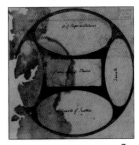

7

with another Pantheon-shaped structure, from which four wings radiate at

right angles. (8) Though it is hard to be certain of details in the hasty

sketch, the wings appear to be structured like Greek or Roman temples,

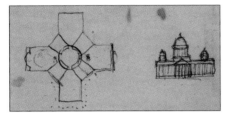 though two of them have small

domes above them. Three of the

wings could have been devoted

to the branches of government,

while the fourth could have

8 served as an entryway to the complex. The rotunda from which all the

wings radiate would have united them as a hub rather than as an overar-

ching form.

The winning design, submitted by William Thornton, a physician and

amateur architect from the Virgin Islands, came in late. Thornton, who

had studied medicine in Scotland and traveled in Europe, emigrated to

Philadelphia and became an American citizen in 1787. Both Jefferson

and Washington found his design

more harmonious and more practi-

cal than any of the other submis-

sions, and Thornton won the prize.

In some of its features, the build-

9

ing Thornton designed was calculated to appeal to Jefferson as well as

Washington. A tripartite building with wings devoted to the House and

Senate, his Capitol is a two-dimensional version of Jefferson's radiating

structure. (9) Thornton's central section is an imitation of the Pantheon

that has been raised on an arcaded and rusticated basement. His reduc-

tion of the building's wings from four to two required that two of the

three functions of the federal government be combined. Since the Senate and Supreme Court were smaller than the House of Representatives, they were grouped together in the north wing of the Capitol.

Stephen Hallet, the runner-up, who may have had more practical experience as a builder, was put in charge of construction, and Washington himself laid the cornerstone of the Capitol in 1793. As work got under way, Thornton continued to perfect his design. A major revision in 1797 added a feature that had been called for in Jefferson's advertisement but not included in Thornton's original plan. At Washington's urging, Thornton added a semicircular bulge to the west side of the building; this exedra was surrounded and topped by a second dome raised on a colonnaded drum that soared over the original rotunda. In plan, this structure formed one half of a great circular space labeled "Conference." The conferences it would host were very particular ones, however. In Washington's vision, whenever the president came to the Capitol to address the legislators, the senators and representatives would gather outside their own assembly rooms in what amounted to a presidential audience chamber. This plan suited the temper of Washington's presidency, but it had no appeal for antifederalists like Jefferson who mistrusted his regal style.

The center section of Thornton's revised plan contained the most symbolic and the most controversial parts, and those that would be the most challenging to build. To a government set to arrive in the federal district by 1800, this section also offered the least practical benefit. For those reasons, Thornton put aside the center section and began work on the Senate and Court wing at the north end of the building. Instead of the classical temples in Jefferson's sketch, Thornton found his source for the Senate and House chambers in Renaissance domestic architecture. In the process he changed the Capitol from an idealized temple of liberty like the one Jefferson imagined into a building more in tune with the contemporary palaces of Europe.

Thornton's building corresponds to a type invented in Rome in the second decade of the sixteenth century. Donato Bramante, the first architect of the new St. Peter's Basilica, and Raphael Sanzio, the celebrated painter, pioneered this style in a house, now destroyed, which they designed for Raphael. Based on principles laid out by the Roman architect Vitruvius and on the example of ancient buildings still standing in Renaissance Rome, Bramante and Raphael created a pattern for palaces that remained influential three centuries after their deaths. This style dictated a clear distinction between the lower story of the building, which in the Renaissance was often used for workshops or stores, and the upper floors, which were reserved as the residence of a noble family. They chose rusticated walls of heavy rough-cut blocks for the lower story. Columns or pilasters and ornamented windows distinguished the main upper story or stories.

10

Thornton planned identical façades for the east and west sides of the Capitol's two wings. Each wing combined a large independent main block and a smaller passageway (now subsumed by the center section) subordinated to the rest of the building by simplified decoration and a slight setback. (10) In each wing, above a small platform, or plinth, rusticated piers in the lower story bracketed five rectangular recesses. The center bay framed a fictive doorway, and the side recesses contained rectangular windows. Eight Corinthian pilasters on small pedestals that sprung from the rusticated shafts in the first story divided the upper level into five bays. Double pilasters at the outer corner marked the break between this structure and the passageway. Each side bay enclosed a window with rounded lintel supported on brackets and a square mezzanine window above it. In the center bay a shallow arch that reached the full height of the story embraced an arched opening with an ornamental frieze beneath it and a round window above. Thornton also designed a projecting porch for the end of each block, but these porticoes disappeared in the mid-nineteenth-century extensions of the building.

When the federal government arrived in cargo holds and wagon loads in the late fall of 1800, only the Senate wing on the north side of the building was finished. An improbable and very unsatisfactory temporary structure was thrown up on the site of the House wing, and a low enclosed portico—something like a sheltered construction-site walkway— temporarily linked the two. The first meeting place of the House of Representatives was an oval stack of hastily laid bricks shored up by pilings. A rounded roof with skylights and a central lantern topped off a building that was half Pantheon and half beaver lodge. Hideous to look at, the building was remarkably uncomfortable. It quickly became known as the Oven. Representatives were forced to endure it and other temporary quarters until the House wing was finally ready for use in 1807.

Following the administration of John Adams, Jefferson was inaugurated as the nation's third president in the spring of 1801, just months after the federal government moved to its rough-hewn new home. Having overseen the city's conception as secretary of state, he was now responsible for its transformation from a theoretical capital into a functioning center of government. For two years he worked without a professional partner. But in 1803 the situation changed dramatically when Jefferson appointed Benjamin Latrobe architect of the Capitol.

Latrobe, who came to America from Britain in 1795, was the first man in that position to be professionally trained. Educated on the Continent, he had studied both engineering and architectural design before accepting private commissions in the 1780s. Like Jefferson, Latrobe was a skilled draftsman and an enthusiastic imitator of classical ideals. His practical skills exceeded those of the president, who often found his way to a technical or aesthetic resolution by constructing full-scale buildings and then tearing them down. Soon after Latrobe was put in charge of the Capitol, he began a two-pronged attack both on Thornton's plans and on the way they had been carried out by a series of short-term political appointees.

Latrobe began by making a complete survey of the half-built structure under his charge. In eighty pages of drawings and notes, he identified what he saw as egregious flaws in Thornton's design and its execution. Latrobe stayed on the attack throughout Jefferson's presidency, pillorying Thornton as an individual and a designer. Eventually Thornton sued for libel. In his first assault against his *bête noir,* Latrobe detailed the leaky roof, cracked plaster, bent and rotting beams, and settling foundations in a building not even ten years old. If the Capitol were to last, he argued, immediate and extensive structural repairs to the Senate wing were essential. The situation in the House wing was even worse; in Latrobe's view, construction would have to be started afresh, with proper foundations and materials that were well chosen and correctly combined.

The new architect did not limit himself to criticizing the quality of the work that had been carried out, however. He was also fiercely critical of Thornton's arrangement of the interior spaces. One of the things that galled Latrobe and provoked his most savage attacks against Thornton was the vertical organization of the Capitol interior. Latrobe understood that the rusticated lower story in the kind of building Thornton had designed should be devoted to utilitarian spaces—all those secondary rooms for clerks and files and committee meetings that Jefferson had spelled out in his original advertisement. In ignorance or in defiance of this tradition, Thornton had placed major assembly rooms on the ground floor of the building and the secondary rooms above. Latrobe corrected Thornton's inversions where he could, but he was unable to rescue the Supreme Court from its basement meeting place.

With Jefferson's blessing, Latrobe's redesigned Capitol did away with Washington's conference room, the feature of Thornton's design that was most objectionable to the new populist president. Meanwhile, Jefferson himself intervened to change the east façade of the building. He designed a portico to run along the face of Thornton's passageways, framing the temple front Thornton had designed and also thrusting it forward. This remarkable revision expanded the space of the rotunda, made room for a larger and more impressive dome, and gave the façade a more obviously classical character. Most important, by having the pediment step forward, Jefferson gave the building a stronger central focus than Thornton had imagined and subordinated his Renaissance-inspired wings. In Jefferson's redesign, the Capitol's symbol of sacred liberty—its temple front—gained prominence, and the dominance of the center block over the wings asserted the theme of unity from diversity.

The House and Senate wings were nearly completed in accord with Latrobe's revised plan by the time James Madison became the fourth president in 1809. The middle section of the building remained incomplete, and Jefferson's design for the center bay of the east front existed as merely an idea on paper. In the last two years of Madison's first term, the War of 1812 against Britain broke out. With its murky origins and unclear objectives, this war at first remained far from Washington, but in August 1814 a British fleet sailed into the Chesapeake Bay. Americans assumed that Baltimore—already a major port and a storehouse of strategic materials—was the target. Instead of attacking that well-defended city, however, the British fleet remained in the bay while a small force sailed up the Patuxent River.

After a slow march overland in the sultry August heat, a combined force of marines and army regulars made their way toward the Anacostia River. Bridges linking Washington and Maryland along the river's lower stretches had already been destroyed by the Americans. But the bridge at Bladensburg had been left standing, and the British focused their attack there. Opposing them on the west side of the river was a hastily assembled and poorly coordinated American force. When the British attacked, the American militiamen quickly bolted. Because of their rapid withdrawal, the battle was later referred to as the Bladensburg Races. Unchallenged, British troops marched down the Bladensburg Road to the capital. President Madison, along with most of the city's residents, fled in panic. Retreating sailors torched the Navy Yard in a last-minute effort to prevent capture of strategic supplies.

To avenge American raids on Canadian cities, the British troops decided to destroy government buildings, though they spared most private structures. The President's House was set on fire and severely damaged. An equally determined effort was made to burn the Capitol. Rockets were fired at the iron roof of the House. Documents and furniture were gathered in heaps in the House chamber, mixed with gunpowder, and set ablaze. The heat drove the soldiers from the building before they could set similar fires in other rooms in the House wing. In the north wing, which housed the congressional library along with the Senate and Supreme Court, combustible material was more plentiful and destruction more complete. Marble columns in the Senate chamber burned to lime; the outside walls of the building, which in the House wing suffered minimal damage, were weakened. The destruction might have been worse except for a freak storm the following afternoon that put out some of the fires. Having succeeded in teaching the Americans a lesson, the British forces, fearful of a counterattack, returned to their ships. A month later, Baltimore's Fort McHenry was bombarded by British cannon, but as Francis Scott Key celebrated in "The Star Spangled Banner," the attack was repelled.

Government workers returned to a gutted capital. While the President's House was being rebuilt, the president and Mrs. Madison moved into Octagon House on Eighteenth Street, which had also been designed by Thornton. Congress met for awhile in the Patent Office between Seventh and Ninth streets, and there was considerable pressure to move the government back to Philadelphia. A group of prominent Washington citizens, fearing the loss of their livelihood if the capital should be moved, paid for the quick erection of a building across First Street from the ruined Senate chamber, on the site now occupied by the Supreme Court.

Called the Brick Capitol, the building was ready for use at the beginning
of the legislative session in 1815. Congress met there for four years
while the Capitol was repaired and redesigned.

Latrobe was called back for the rebuilding. He worked under the
supervision of a retired military engineer with a keen sense of discipline
and little understanding of personnel management or architecture. The
architect took advantage of the widespread destruction to rethink the
wings he had already redesigned once. (11) While resistance to Latrobe's
vision for the Capitol still existed in some quarters, the grounds of opposition had shifted. Thornton's original design had received George Washington's blessing, and as long as the memory of the first president was
still fresh, his choice had great authority. But by the end of the War of

1812, the influence of Washington's
legacy, in practical terms, was quite
reduced.

11

Latrobe's real constituency was
now the powerful House and Senate.
Without respect for the chain of com-
mand that had been imposed on him, members of each chamber vied for
the architect's attention. Each legislative body wanted to ensure that its
wing would be the first to be returned to service. Meanwhile, President
Monroe, who took the oath of office in front of the Brick Capitol in March
1817 and had no interest in architecture, simply pressed the designer to
complete the restoration quickly and cheaply.

Latrobe found himself unable to serve all his masters, and in an
unfortunate confrontation in Monroe's presence, the architect came close

to striking his immediate superior. He had no choice but to resign. Despite everything he had endured, however, Latrobe succeeded in redesigning both the House and Senate wings along lines that suited his own sensibilities, and his intentions were carried out faithfully by his successor, Charles Bulfinch. Born in Massachusetts in 1763, Bulfinch was a member of a prominent Boston family with a history of involvement with architecture. After graduating from Harvard in 1781, Bulfinch traveled for two years in Europe. While in Paris, he met Jefferson, who encouraged his architectural interests and advised him to visit classical monuments in southern France and Italy.

After returning to Boston, Bulfinch began designing both public and private buildings. These included a house for Joseph Coolidge Sr., whose son married Jefferson's granddaughter. He is best known for his design of the Massachusetts State House on Beacon Hill in Boston. In 1817 Bulfinch succeeded Latrobe, whose work he admired, as Capitol architect, and for the next thirteen years he supervised the restructuring of the two wings of the building. He also redesigned and supervised construction of the long-planned center bay, with its Rotunda and dome. Nurtured by Jefferson in Paris, Bulfinch was the ideal architect to bring to completion the parts of the Capitol most sacred to the former president.

In the changing political climate of the 1820s, however, Jefferson's preferences carried even less weight than those of George Washington, still the acknowledged patriarch of the republic. To congressmen greedy for space, the undeveloped center bay seemed like virgin territory waiting to be conquered, rather than a national monument long overdue for completion. Bulfinch was under immediate pressure to scrap the long-standing plans for a Rotunda—something the legislators were inclined to dismiss as an oversized lobby—and fill the center bay with committee rooms and cubby holes for clerks. To assuage his powerful clients, Bulfinch scaled back the Rotunda and found more space within the original center for utilitarian rooms.

He also found two extraordinary new ways to satisfy the legislators' demands. On the west side, he extended the end of the center bay to the edge of the existing level ground of the Capitol, creating more space. He then took advantage of the slope to create a sub-basement story, which he walled with even rougher and more heavily rusticated stone than Thornton's original first story. These innovations mollified his immediate constituents and left Bulfinch free to create the grand Rotunda that had been the building's focus from the start. It also allowed him to complete Jefferson's colonnade and portico on the east side and add a set of stairs leading up to it. The stairs returned the focus of the building toward its center bay but also helped to erase the final effects of Thornton's misunderstanding of his rusticated first story. A great stairway leading to a pedimented portico which was in turn overshadowed by a dome created a single monumental entryway to the building. The many ground floor entrances in Thornton's plan were now completely gone. (12)

Much of the central building's exterior as Bulfinch completed it in 1829 is still visible today. But changes to come would be significant: pushing forward Jefferson's neoclassical porch and colonnade, to counterbalance new Senate and House wings that would be added in the 1850s, with their rival pediments and

12

redundant external stairs; replacing Bulfinch's relatively modest, somewhat bulbous dome with a soaring structure during the Civil War; enlarging the eastern façade of the center bay between 1958 and 1962; and constructing a subterranean Visitor Center in the new millennium.

From 1825 to 1828, near the end of Bulfinch's tenure, an Italian-born artist, Luigi Persico, created a sculptural group for the east pediment. Called the *Genius of America,* this allegorical work clusters three human figures and an eagle in the center of a vast and otherwise unpopulated space. Under the peak of the pediment roof, lifted up on a dais, stands the classically draped female figure who represents America. She is crowned and armed with a spear. Her shield, emblazoned with the letters USA, rests on a wreathed Roman altar inscribed with the date July 4, 1776. An American eagle at her feet looks back toward her. With her left arm, America gestures across her body toward a personification of Justice. That figure, who is without a blindfold, holds her scales in one hand and a scroll with the word "Constitution" and the date of its adoption by the Constitutional Convention, September 17, 1787. Turning away from Justice, America looks toward a figure of Hope, who is identified by the huge naval anchor on which she leans. This thoroughly insufficient scene was originally carved in sandstone. When the pediment was moved forward in 1959, the unadventurous piece of sculpture was faithfully reproduced in gleaming marble.

After the fire of 1814, Latrobe refurbished the Supreme Court room but made only minor changes. When the Senate moved into its third (and current) quarters in 1859, the Court relocated to the former Senate chamber, and its old courtroom in the basement was turned into a law

library. **(Map 2)** During renovations of the Capitol for the nation's bicentennial, the basement courtroom was restored as nearly as possible to its
original condition. Lintels and Doric columns of Virginia sandstone support an arcade with three openings along the flat end of the room. Semicircular cornices outline a fictive oculus in the dome, and the heavy
stone ribs of its scalloped fabric spread outward and down to an arcade
supported by piers. **(13)** Latrobe substituted these piers for the columns
that had been in place before the fire. Lit from behind by three windows,
the justices sat immediately in front of the arcade. Clerks sat to either
side of them; tables for the litigants occupied the center of the room. A
vaulted extension made room for a small audience.

The ceiling of the Supreme Court chamber is unique among Latrobe's
Capitol designs. In both the House and Senate chambers, half domes are
indented by shallow box-shaped depressions called coffers. Latrobe used
coffers in the vaults of the arches at the flat end of the Supreme Court

chamber, but his roof is
shaped something like a
parachute, with the
lighter-colored ceiling billowing up from darker
stiff ribs. The Roman
emperor and architect
Hadrian was fond of

13

domes of this sort. His detractors mocked them as pumpkin domes, but
they were probably based on the billowing awnings that shaded many
Roman structures. Some examples survive at Hadrian's villa in Tivoli and

in other Roman ruins. Despite their distinguished parentage, however, these domes were seldom imitated by neoclassical architects.

Latrobe thought of his semicircular domed rooms as theaters. This was not because he saw the action of government agencies as essentially dramatic; he favored rooms of this kind because of their acoustics. Greek and Roman theaters were D-shaped, with banks of seats climbing into their rounded edge. Because classical theaters were open to the sky, hearing the actors was often a problem. When theaters were revived during the Renaissance in Italy, they were generally covered by roofs. Renaissance theaters were designed not just for dramatic presentations but also for staging dissections, which became an increasingly important part of medical education in Europe in the late seventeenth century.

The Romans created D-shaped spaces with half-domed roofs that bulged outward from the flat ends of large audience halls. A figure of authority like an emperor or judge would sit on an elevated throne in this space, called an apse, which directed the audience's attention toward him. The curved sides of the apse and its semidomed ceiling reflected the sound of his voice. For the Romans, the apse was both a symbol of authority and an amplifier of the voice of authority. When the Roman emperors began to sponsor the building of Christian churches in the fourth century, they borrowed this form from large Roman assembly halls. The apse, which both represented authority and focused sound, became the center of worship and the area reserved for the clergy and choir.

Latrobe closed in the flat end of the free-standing apses he created. And in complete contradiction to the Roman tradition, he placed figures of authority along this flat wall in the place where the Roman audience or the Christian congregation would traditionally have been found. This is

not a misunderstanding of his sources but an acknowledgment of the difference between an autocratic assembly and a democratic one. In the
Supreme Court chamber, the judges sit in the place where they can best
hear, not in the place from which they can best be heard. It is the voice
of the litigants that is amplified by the space. In the House and Senate,
it is the voices of legislators, not those of the speaker of the House or the
vice president, that the spaces strengthen.

Only two chief justices presided over the Court during the sixty years
it met in the Senate basement. John Marshall, who remains the longest
serving chief justice, took the oath of office in January 1801, during the
last months of Adams's presidency. At the time, he was secretary of
state, an office he continued to hold even after administering the presidential oath of office to Thomas Jefferson a few months later. Despite
their cordial relations, the two men held contrasting views of the powers
of the national government. Their disagreement came to a head over last-
minute judicial appointments by outgoing President Adams that were
interpreted as an effort to defy Congress and the new president and
ensure the legacy of strong federalism in the courts.

The controversy led to the first test of the Court's status as a wing of
government on a par with the Legislative and Executive branches. In the
landmark case *Marbury v. Madison,* the principals were William Marbury—granted a commission by President Adams—and James Madison,
Jefferson's second secretary of state, who had refused to ratify the commission. Marshall ruled that Marbury had a right to the commission but
that the Supreme Court had no right to intervene on his behalf, because
the 1789 law that had granted jurisdiction to the Supreme Court in this
case contradicted its powers under the Constitution. In his ruling, Mar-

shall spelled out the Court's unique authority: "It is emphatically the province and duty of the judicial department to say what the law is," not to make the law or enforce it.

When Marshall died in 1835, his place was filled by Roger Brooke Taney of Maryland. The Senate had already refused to ratify Taney's earlier appointment to the Court, and it delayed three months in confirming him as chief justice. The divisive issue that occupied the Court during Taney's long tenure was the extension of slavery to the territories of the growing United States. The future justice was raised on a Maryland tobacco plantation worked by slaves, whom he eventually freed. Despite this act of manumission, Taney was not an abolitionist but a colonizationist who favored the return of emancipated slaves to Africa. A short-lived and contradictory movement before the Civil War, colonization could be characterized as a blessing or a curse to African Americans. Both slaveowners and abolitionists advocated it, though for very different reasons. Many black leaders denounced it as an attempt to exile the nation's tiny free black population.

Chief Justice Taney ruled consistently in favor of controversial laws that required every citizen to assist in the capture and return of fugitive slaves. These laws were the prime targets of abolitionists, and their enforcement caused riots throughout the Northeast. Taney's most notorious contribution to United States history was his opinion in the Dred Scott case. Dred Scott was a slave who, with his wife Harriett and two daughters, was taken by his owner at various times out of the slave state of Missouri, where he lived, into both the state of Illinois and the Wisconsin territory. The congressional act admitting Missouri to the union in 1820 established a line of demarcation between slave and free territories. Under the terms of what became known as the Missouri Compromise, Dred Scott and his family had been moved from a slave state to both a free state and a free territory. In 1846 Scott and his family sued for their freedom. The suit was turned down, but on appeal in 1850 the original ruling was reversed and the Scotts were declared free. Suits and countersuits continued for seven more years until the case reached the Supreme Court.

The case was complex, and even though seven of nine justices reached the same decision, eight wrote differing opinions. In his ambitious and ill-fated judgment, Taney made an effort to settle once and for all every issue that the case raised regarding slavery. First, he ruled that as a slave Dred Scott was not a person under the law but property, and so he had no standing to sue in federal court. Taney went further, however, and argued that not just slaves but emancipated blacks, even if they were free citizens of individual states, could not be citizens of the United States. He argued that "there are two clauses in the Constitution which point directly and specifically to the negro race as a separate class of persons, and show clearly that they were not regarded as a portion of the people or citizens of the government then formed." With this ruling, Taney changed the debate about slavery from an argument over the civil rights of slaves to an argument over the civil rights of blacks. Race, not slavery, became the critical factor.

Taney also found room in his decision to reconsider and invalidate the Missouri Compromise. The federal government could not legally restrict slavery, he declared, because it had no right to interfere with how citizens of individual states disposed of their property. He declared the compromise legislation, which had allowed expansion while maintaining an equilibrium between free and slave states, invalid. This part of Taney's decision did away with the middle ground of negotiation and equivocation that had kept the pro- and anti-slavery factions from each other's throats. Two years after its fateful Dred Scott decision, the Court moved to new quarters in the old Senate chamber.

The small Senate Rotunda was originally designed as a stairwell linking the two floors of the north wing. Latrobe redesigned it as a combination light shaft and superimposed vestibules. (14) The vestibule on the upper floor served the Senate, while the one below served the Supreme Court. An oculus in the domed and coffered roof illuminated the top floor directly and, through a well in its center, shed light on the bottom floor. The oculus is now enclosed, and a chandelier lights the space.

Aside from its wonderful proportions, the room's best known and most cherished features are the capitals Latrobe designed for the columns sur-

rounding his light well. These are variations on Corinthian columns, which are traditionally decorated with leaves of the acanthus plant. To Americanize the Corinthian order, Latrobe substituted tobacco leaves and flowers. The leaves were gilded and the flowers painted in the same bright colors used in the coffering of the small dome. (15) For the vestibule of the old Senate chamber, Latrobe had designed columns with shafts like bundles of cornstalks and capitals like corncobs, and he was especially pleased that these much admired objects had survived the fire of 1814.

14

Other than these columns, only the semidomed brick roof of the old Senate wing had remained intact after the British torched it. Latrobe was

still satisfied with the original design of the room, and
he was reluctant to sacrifice a roof that had proven its
durability. But he recognized that the expansion of the
United States meant that the Senate would soon out-
grow its old meeting room. Even during the difficult
years of the War of 1812, the number of states had
grown to eighteen. Several more territories were close
to achieving statehood, and by 1821 forty-eight senators would have to be accommodated by the Senate

15

chamber. In redesigning the room, Latrobe simply stretched his compass
a bit wider to trace out a semicircle seventy-five feet in diameter, about
twenty-five percent larger than the Senate's original dimensions. He
found the space he needed by cannibalizing a stairwell and a cluster of
water closets at the edge of the old room.

Latrobe's plan called for a colonnade across the flat end of the room.
Despairing of finding suitable material at reasonable cost, he suggested
using sandstone, but at the urging of the Senate committee in charge of
renovations, he explored marble outcroppings near Baltimore and others
along the Potomac River and its tributaries. He settled on a beautiful
pebbled marble from land near the banks of the Potomac. The stone was
native, which reduced cost. Most important, its location meant that column shafts could be floated on rafts down the river to Washington during
the spring flood.

After Latrobe was fired, Bulfinch completed the room according to his
predecessor's design, and in 1820 the Senate met there for the first
time. The defining feature of the room is a great proscenium arch that
springs from heavy piers at each side and supports the apex of the half-

16

dome while it frames a marble colonnade and a visitors' gallery along the flat wall. (16) This long arch, spanning the width of the chamber, is a more adventurous and dramatic treatment of the end wall than the arcade in the courtroom below. The half-dome that butts against the arch has four rows of gilded coffers in its lowest part, topped by an ornamental frieze and a wide band where circular lights alternate with organic reliefs. There is a semicircular window at the height of the dome. Latrobe designed a unique double canopy over these openings, which were originally unglazed so that they could ventilate as well as light the room. The canopy both protected the openings from the weather and illuminated the room indirectly.

A double row of gilt coffers mark the underside of his great archway. Latrobe's Maryland marble column shafts and piers, fitted with Ionic capitals and bases that were quarried and finished in Italy, support an undecorated entablature. Pilasters of the same materials are set into the outside wall of the chamber under an iron-railed gallery that was added in 1828.

The Senate's presiding officer is the vice president of the United States, whose chair and desk are centered at the flat end of the room under the great arch. A wooden frame above his chair supports a tentlike canopy of fringed velvet drapes. This curious installation makes the vice president's seat suspiciously thronelike, though the canopy actually serves to insulate the presiding officer from noise and distracting movement in the open colonnade behind him. At the front edge of the canopy frame, a gilded American eagle holding a shield soars above the assembly. The eagle's history is unclear. No one knows who carved it or exactly when it was placed in the Senate. It is mentioned for the first time in 1838, and it appears in engravings of the Senate chamber from the 1840s.

The most important art object in the room is Rembrandt Peale's portrait *George Washington (Patriae Pater)*—father of his country. (17) The painting is displayed on the back wall of the gallery directly above and behind the vice president's chair. It was first placed there in 1832, the centennial year of Washington's birth, when the Senate bought it from the painter. It moved with the Senate to its new location in the north wing and was returned to its original place in the bicentennial year.

In 1795, when the artist was seventeen, he and his father, Charles Willson Peale, both painted Washington from life. In creating what he hoped would become the standard image of Washington a quarter century after the first president's death, Rembrandt Peale reviewed these sketches, along with portraits by Gilbert Stuart and John Trumbull and a portrait bust by the French sculptor Jean-Antoine Houdon. In this unusual approach, Peale was following the dictates of classical writers, who urged a painter aiming to represent the ideal to draw his inspiration from multiple models. In so doing, Peale visualized Washington less as a historical figure than as the object of pious and devoted public memory.

17

Dressed in ceremonial black, Washington is starkly silhouetted against a glowing golden sky. His head and shoulders are seen through a fictive oval frame of carved stone which is surrounded by a wreath of oak leaves, surmounted by a figured keystone, and underscored by a carved inscription in Roman capitals that reads *Patriae Pater.* Peale believed that he was imitating a Roman tradition of funerary painting, but his curious frame soon earned the picture its nickname "the porthole portrait."

The other details of the painting are inspired by Roman traditions as well. While the title "father of his country" has long been associated with Washington in American lore, the Roman Senate first voted to use it for one of its most famous members, Marcus Tullius Cicero, to honor his success in overcoming the conspiracy of the would-be dictator Catiline. Soon afterward the title was given by a more obsequious Senate to Julius Caesar when he assumed dictatorship. After it was awarded to Caesar's successor, Augustus Caesar, the title became part of a collection of honorifics routinely awarded to Roman emperors.

The wreath of oak that surrounds the portrait is also a Roman symbol. Called the *corona civica* (civic crown), it was at first awarded to a Roman citizen who had saved the life of a comrade in battle. Its significance soon expanded. A senator proposed that it be offered to Cicero along with the title *Pater Patriae,* and eventually the wreath too became a formulaic imperial honor. According to Peale, the mask at the top of the frame represents Jupiter, or Zeus as he was carved by the fabled Greek sculptor Phidias. Phidias crafted a figure of the god for Zeus' temple at Olympia. The father of the gods was seated on a throne, holding an image of victory in his right hand and a scepter in his left. Peale was not the only artist to see Washington as an American Zeus. Horatio Greenough created a seated figure of the first president based on the same ideal.

Like the Senate chamber, Peale's portrait of Washington was an articulate and well-understood imitation of the art and iconography of the

Romans. Peale's classicism, like that of Jefferson, Latrobe, and Bulfinch, was thoughtful and well researched. His understanding of Roman objects and contexts, like theirs, was deep and certain. These men were not, however, slavish imitators of the past. Each of them was able to extemporize on classical themes in imaginative and innovative ways.

The first half of the nineteenth century has been described as the Golden Age of the Senate. Presidents came and went, but the most prominent senators served for twenty or thirty years. Before ratification of the Seventeenth Amendment to the Constitution, senators were elected by the legislatures of each state rather than by direct popular vote. Indirect election made their seats relatively secure, and their extensive terms gave them the luxury to take a longer view than other members of the government could afford. The major issues that the most prominent and durable senators grappled with were the uncertain relationship between state and federal powers and the terrible problem of slavery.

Senator John C. Calhoun of South Carolina, who served in the Senate from 1832 until 1850, was slavery's most powerful and outspoken advocate. In a speech delivered in February 1837, he declared: "We of the South will not, cannot, surrender our institutions. To maintain the existing relations between the two races, inhabiting that section of the Union, is indispensable to the peace and happiness of both . . . But let me not be understood as admitting, even by implication, that the existing relations between the two races in the slaveholding States is an evil—far otherwise; I hold it to be a good, as it has thus far proved itself to be to both, and will continue to prove so if not disturbed by the fell spirit of abolition. I appeal to facts. Never before has the black race of Central

Africa, from the dawn of history to the present day, attained a condition so civilized and so improved, not only physically, but morally and intellectually."

In Calhoun's mind, and in the minds of many southerners, the survival of slavery was clearly linked to the survival of the federal union. Daniel Webster, an opponent of slavery from Massachusetts who served from 1827 until 1850, was the strongest advocate of federalism. In a famous speech in 1830, he upheld the sovereignty of the federal government against proponents of states' autonomy. And in a crucial speech on March 7, 1850, he rose to protect the union at the expense of his own beliefs about slavery, and at fatal risk to his political career. Defending the various fugitive slave acts as the law of the land, he addressed the divisive issue of slavery this way:

"In the excited times in which we live, there is found to exist a state of crimination and recrimination between the North and South. There are lists of grievances produced by each; and those grievances, real or supposed, alienate the minds of one portion of the country from the other, exasperate the feelings, and subdue the sense of fraternal affection, patriotic love, and mutual regard. I shall bestow a little attention, Sir, upon these various grievances existing on the one side and on the other. I begin with complaints of the South . . . and especially to one which has in my opinion just foundation; and that is, that there has been found at the North, among individuals and among legislators, a disinclination to perform fully their constitutional duties in regard to the return of persons bound to service who have escaped into the free States. In that respect, the South, in my judgment, is right, and the North is wrong."

Abolitionists like Emerson and Thoreau crucified Webster in their writings. The Massachusetts Legislature followed suit and rejected Webster's bid to return to the Senate. Calhoun, whom Webster's speech was designed to conciliate, died less than a month later. Clay, architect of the Missouri Compromise, died in 1852, and Senator Thomas Hart Benton, who opposed it, was defeated in his reelection bid in the same year that the bill was passed. Of the five portraits chosen to hang in the Senate lobby and represent the most significant members of that august body, three of the five—Clay, Webster, and Calhoun—served before 1850.

The north wing could accommodate not only the Senate but the Supreme Court and the Library of Congress. But the much larger House of Representatives required all the space the south wing offered. Thornton had designed an elliptical meeting room for the congressmen, but immediately after the fire Latrobe began to imagine a new shape for this chamber, one that would make it a larger version of the semidomed theaters he preferred. Though the influence of the plan approved by Washington had diminished, Thornton himself was still active, and he opposed Latrobe's revision. The greatest obstacle to a redesign was the state of the room itself. The British soldiers who set fire to the north wing had been diligent and well supplied with fuel, but the sudden flaring up of fire in the south wing had chased them from the building before their work was done. In the old House chamber, a file of columns brought from Italy at great expense, and the heavy entablature they supported, remained undamaged.

To reshape this space, Latrobe needed to dismantle this colonnade. If a column fell during the course of the work, not only would a costly and irreplaceable object be destroyed, but the column's weight as it crashed to the floor would crush the vaults below. Latrobe ordered a temporary roof to be placed over the House wing, and his crew began the careful dismantling and salvaging of the colonnade. He also ordered additional capitals from Italy and began the search for a sculptor to replace artworks damaged in the fire.

While the Supreme Court and Senate chamber had their flat sides against the east wall of the Capitol and received little direct light, the redesigned House chamber was set against the south wall. Light coming from that side illuminated the chamber directly. The old House chamber had been lit by skylights, but most of them were curtained to reduce glare. Many of them leaked, and others were jammed shut, providing no ventilation for the room. Latrobe solved all these problems, as he had done in the Senate, by placing a lantern on the roof of the chamber that shielded the windows in its ceiling from direct sunlight and weather while allowing hot air to escape.

The House chamber Latrobe designed is a magnified variation on the forms he worked out in the Senate. It is a half-domed room with colonnades on both its flat and semicircular edges. A proscenium arch completely detached from the colonnade and its flat entablature supports the height of the coffered half-dome, which is lit by a round skylight off-center near its peak. (18) The hall is enclosed at floor level but opens half way up the colonnade to a visitors' gallery. Representatives sat in desks of different sizes arranged in widening semicircular rows around the room.

There were 185 representatives in 1817. By the time the House moved to an even newer wing in 1857 (two years before the new Senate quarters were complete), there were 237 congressmen. In 1864, when the number of representatives was reduced by secession to its 1817

level, the old House chamber was designated as National Statuary Hall. Each state
remaining in the union was invited to con-
tribute two sculptures of prominent citizens for permanent exhibit there. Though
the location was new, the idea was not;
L'Enfant's plan had called for the creation
of state exhibits at the intersections of his

18

grand avenues. He imagined that these would include commemorative
columns and obelisks as well as statues, to perpetuate the memory of
important counselors, military leaders, and those whose achievements in
other fields "rendered them worthy of general imitation."

Statuary Hall appealed to the states, which, Noah-like, began to con-
tribute images of their heroes two by two. In 1933, as statues stood
three-deep against the walls, Congress revised the 1864 law to assert
more control over the room and reduce the state contributions to one
apiece. In the bicentennial year, the number of statues in the room was
again reduced—this time to thirty-eight—and most of the dispossessed
sculptures were reassigned to spots along the building's endless corridors. Statues from the thirteen original colonies were placed in a new
area created by the extension of the east porch. Nathanael Greene of
Rhode Island and Ethan Allen of Vermont are the longest standing figures
among those still in Statuary Hall.

While the national collection of statues was a late addition, three
sculptures decorated the original room that Latrobe redesigned. Enrico
Causici's *Liberty and the Eagle* stood in a niche centered between the
great arch and the entablature over the speaker's platform. A massive fig-

ure of Liberty, cast like the rest of the group in plaster, balances stiffly on one foot with her knee slightly upraised. She extends her right hand in a gesture of command above an eagle with outspread wings. Rolled up in her hand, like a field marshal's baton, is a copy of the Constitution. The right side of the image suggests power and the rule of law together.

Liberty's left arm is hidden under the folds of her flowing robes. At her left, a serpent twined around what appears to be a bundle of rods appears ready to strike. The serpent is a conventional symbol of wisdom, but here it looks like a fasces. In Roman times, a fasces was a cylindrical bundle of rods tied tightly together, symbolizing authority. In American history, a bundle of rods has often been used to represent the power of union. The mace of the House, the symbol of its authority, is shaped like a fasces, and two fasces, wreathed with oak, frame the flag displayed behind the speaker's desk in the modern House of Representatives.

Beneath the giant figure of Liberty, another eagle in low relief, carved by Giuseppe Valaperta in sandstone, decorates the entablature. But the most famous and most successful sculpture in the old House chamber is named the *Car of History.* A chariot with great feathered wings balances improbably on one wheel, which in turn rests on a sphere circled by the belt of the zodiac. **(19)** The chariot's wheel is marked with the hours of the day, and a working clock mechanism is inside. The car appears to represent "Time's winged chariot." On its front, the image in low relief of an infant (putto) with a long horn suggests Fame. History, veiled in the complex folds of a Hellenistic gown, with a short cape thrown back over her shoulder, steps on the rim of the car. She writes in a book held on her upraised knee.

While most of the early nineteenth-century sculptures in the Capitol

are much less adept than the architecture that surrounds them, this work by Carlo Franzoni, though
curious and unconventional, is both intelligent and
well-executed. Making the chariot appear to hover
magically on a two-dimensional wheel that barely
touches the sphere beneath it is visually interesting
and intellectually satisfying. Time is a fleeting and
precarious thing. The contrast between the solid figure of Clio and the unstable vehicle in which she
stands emphasizes the stability of history. The won-

19

derful wings and the beautiful, skillfully carved drapery of the figure are
evidence of an artistry that neither Causici nor Persico could measure up
to. A curious feature of the sculpture is the clock mechanism in the
wheel. Fusions between the plastic and mechanical arts were popular at
the turn of the nineteenth century, but most works of this kind were
small. French clocks of that period often combined classical ornament,
small figures, and sophisticated works. Franzoni's sculpture is unusual in
its scale more than its concept.

Unlike the Senate, where a careful calculus of territorial admissions
preserved a balance between spokesmen for slavery and emancipation,
the House of Representatives mirrored the disproportion in the population
of the North and South. Even though slaves counted as three-fifths of a
person in determining representation, antislavery voices predominated in
the House. But southern representatives were more strident and occasionally even given to violence. In one notorious incident in 1856, Preston Brooks, a representative from South Carolina, went to the Senate
chamber and with his cane beat senseless the senator from Massachu-

setts, Charles Sumner. In a speech called "The Crime against Kansas," Sumner had attacked Senators Stephen Douglas of Illinois and Andrew Butler of South Carolina.

Though Brooks's behavior was extreme, he expressed something of what the framers had in mind for the House. It was popularly elected, subject to biannual recall, and so more likely to represent the passions of the moment than the deeper currents of history. While the vice president always presides over the Senate, the House elects its own speaker. The Constitution gives representatives primary power over revenues and budget, and responsibility for impeachment.

As the House grew in the early nineteenth century, it evolved from a deliberative body in which every issue was openly debated to a more closely controlled organization. Political parties, which became influential in the first half of the century, grouped House members around key issues and narrowed the range of debate. By mid-century, standing committees, headed by representatives with secure districts and partisan support, dominated the legislative process, and floor debate diminished. With the increased power of committees, the right to appoint members, which the speaker of the House retained, became increasingly important. Parties vied to gain a majority, elect the speaker, and control committee appointments, just as they do today.

Before becoming a senator, Henry Clay served twelve years as speaker of the House, and he used that power to further his own views and the platforms of the various parties he served. Clay's unrelenting politicization of the office established a model for those who succeeded him. All of them were men until Nancy Pelosi of California became speaker in 2007—two centuries after the House of Representatives first occupied the chamber Benjamin Latrobe designed.

Chapter Three

TEMPLE OF FREEDOM

After Benjamin Latrobe was fired as Capitol architect, his replacement, Charles Bulfinch, faithfully looked after the completion of Latrobe's plans for the House and Senate wings. But Bulfinch alone was responsible for the design and building of the central pavilion that would at last link the two increasingly independent legislative bodies. Expansion of its membership made the House especially greedy for more office space. Many members considered the central part of the building either a frivolous project or unclaimed territory where more committee rooms could be carved out. In redesigning the center of the Capitol, Bulfinch responded to these pressures in a way that allowed him to both amplify the useful space in the building and leave room for the dome and Rotunda that had been projected by every architect since Thornton.

Jefferson had envisaged a Hall of the People at the center of the Capitol, based on the Roman Pantheon. Bulfinch shared Jefferson's belief that the Pantheon was the ideal architectural model, but he had a different sense of what that central drum should symbolize. On the first floor, Bulfinch created a wonderful circular room that he intended as an underpinning for the Rotunda. (Map 2) Heavy piers bearing up its walls are drawn into a circle. Inside this ring, Bulfinch created a smaller circle of Tuscan columns yoked

20

in pairs by sturdy entablatures. To join the outer piers with the inner colonnade, he created a ring-shaped vaulted roof that is intersected by groined cross vaults between each set of columns. A dome transected by other groined cross vaults and supported on a ring of single columns fills the center space. **(20)** The heavy piers and columns support the Rotunda and the massive dome above it, while the multiple openings among the piers and columns allow easy passage between the House and Senate wings.

The source of Bulfinch's design is not known, but the architect might have seen one of several circular buildings on the edges of Rome when he visited that city in 1788. Among them are two with similar structures. Though damaged in the eleventh century and remodeled in the Renaissance, the church of San Stefano Rotondo on the Celian Hill has a single inner core supported on pillars and encircled by a drum. A closer link to Bulfinch's design is found in the church of Santa Costanza outside the city walls. Built in the fourth century AD to hold the tomb of the daughter of Constantine, the building has a domed inner circle surrounded by a ring-shaped vaulted outer space.

Like the designer of Santa Costanza, Bulfinch was creating a burial shrine. Soon after George Washington's death in 1799, Congress passed a resolution that would have provided a tomb for the first president. As Bulfinch's plans for the Rotunda neared completion, the request that both the first president and Martha Washington be reinterred there was renewed. Washington, however, had included explicit instructions for burial in his will, and his heir rejected the congressional proposal. Had he agreed, Washington's remains would have gained the prominence that St. Peter's Basilica in the Vatican gave to those of the venerated apostle. The grave of Saint Peter is in a crypt immediately beneath the high altar of the church, and the great dome of the cathedral is centered above them. If Bulfinch's plan had succeeded, the Capitol dome would have served as an amplified gravestone marking the final resting place of the father of his country in the basement of the Capitol.

Even though George Washington was not to be buried in the Capitol, the idea of his presence helped transform the Rotunda into a memorial honoring the founders of the republic and their ideals. The circular space that finally came into being in the 1820s—Bulfinch called it a rotundo—was a stripped-down version of the Roman Pantheon. Its broad circular floor was unbroken by columns or obstructions of any kind. Its curving walls were marked off in sections by pilasters. Narrower sections outlined each doorway. Panels of various shapes with friezes of twining vegetation filled the top of each section of the wall. Above the pilasters was an entablature decorated with wreaths of oak. The original ceiling of the room was a coffered dome with an opening at its center that very closely duplicated the Pantheon ceiling.

Four massive paintings in oil by John Trumbull were the first memorials in the Rotunda. An admirer of Copley, a student of Benjamin West, and onetime roommate of Gilbert Stuart, Trumbull spent years researching and painting small versions of scenes from the Revolutionary era. In the aftermath of the war, the painter, who had served briefly as an aide to Washington, traveled to England and Europe to draw the already far-flung participants in the events surrounding the birth of the nation. He sketched Adams in London and Jefferson in Paris in 1786 while both were American ambassadors. During his time in Paris he also sketched French officers who had returned home after serving with the Revolutionary army. In 1816 President Madison chose four scenes from Trumbull's gallery of paintings—*The Declaration of Independence, The Surrender of General Burgoyne, The Surrender of Lord Cornwallis,* and *General George Washington Resigning his Commission*—for the Rotunda. Trumbull began the work of enlarging the selected images to fit their new site.

Trumbull's first picture, painted in 1819, is his best known. (21) The scene is the room in Philadelphia's Federal Hall, where on June 28, 1776, the committee to draft the Declaration of Independence presented

its final document to the assembled colonial delegates. During Trumbull's Paris visit, Jefferson had offered him a sketch of the room where the signing took place.

In Trumbull's painting, scarlet curtains cover the windows and a trophy of crossed

21

banners, a drum, and bugles decorate the back wall. These emblems of warfare look forward to a long campaign to win the independence that had already been declared. The door frames are surrounded by classical moldings, and a very fine entablature with brackets supports its projecting cornice; a frieze of triglyphs with dentils beneath them runs around the back and side walls. The room in which the signing actually took

place has neoclassical features, but they do not correspond to the lavish

details in this picture. As a symbol rather than a fact, the neoclassical

ornament points to the great
Greek and Roman tradition of
debate, democracy, and resistance to tyranny.

22

The committee who drew
up the Declaration included
Thomas Jefferson, John
Adams, Benjamin Franklin,
Roger Sherman of Connecticut,

and Robert R. Livingston of New York. These five men stand in front of

John Hancock's desk and present their report, while the rest of the dele-

gates look on. In a letter to Jefferson, Trumbull wrote that "the picture

will contain Portraits of at least forty seven members: for the faithful

resemblance of at least thirty six, I am responsible, as they were done by

myself from the Life, being all who survived in the year 1791. Of the

remainder, nine are from pictures done by others."

On October 17, 1777, near Saratoga, New York, the British general

John Burgoyne presented his sword to the American general Horatio

Gates. The seven thousand British troops commanded by Burgoyne had

been defeated in two battles by a force of American regulars and local

militiamen. Trumbull's second painting illustrates two phases of the sur-

render. (22) The turning over of the defeated general's sword is repre-

sented in the foreground, counterpointed in the background by a long file

23

of British and German soldiers, closely guarded by American troops, who are depositing their arms in a meadow.

General Gates, dressed in a blue frock coat with gold epaulettes and yellow breeches and vest, stands in the center. Burgoyne and his adjutant, wearing red coats, stand to the left. On the right side of the picture, framed between a cannon in the foreground and the American flag in the upper corner, are members of Gates's staff. Colonel Daniel Morgan of the Virginia Riflemen is the prominent figure dressed in white in the foreground. In 1780 Congress promoted him to the rank of brigadier general and gave him command of the southern theater of war. In the decisive Battle of Cowpens in January 1781 Morgan's troops defeated a superior British force.

Burgoyne's surrender to Continental troops not only secured the northern frontier against further British advances, it also proved that American troops could defeat British regulars. Despite France's sympathy for the American cause and long-standing opposition to the British presence in North America, the French government had refused to ally itself with the colonists. Four months after Burgoyne's defeat, France signed a treaty with the United States. The French alliance brought money, materiel, and trained personnel. In Trumbull's third painting, French officers grouped under the white banner of the House of Bourbon sit on horseback to the left. (23) American officers under the Stars and Stripes are on the right. Led by Washington's mounted emissary, Benjamin Lincoln, British soldiers march on foot between the two groups. Washington sits on his horse between Lincoln and the American flag. General Lafayette wears a red cockade in his hat. His special link to the American cause prompted the painter to include him among the American rather than the French officers.

Trumbull's fourth painting, like his first, is set in a assembly hall rather than a battlefield. (24) It depicts the events of December 23, 1783, the day when Washington resigned his commission as military commander. The scene is a room in the Maryland statehouse in Annapolis, where the Continental Congress met for six months before moving on to Trenton, New Jersey, and then to New York City. A triangle of light and a break in the wall and pediment draw the

24

eye to the central figure of Washington. But they also accentuate the difference between the wall in Federal Hall, hung with the emblems of war, and this one, where trophies are no longer appropriate.

Washington extends his commission to the seated members of Congress. The retiring general has just risen from a thronelike chair, which is draped with his scarlet-lined cloak. Visitors crowd the floor behind him, and Martha Washington watches from a gallery at the back of the room. Like the meeting room in Philadelphia where the Continental Congress signed the Declaration of Independence, the Senate Hall of the Maryland State House is here richly ornamented in a neoclassical style. A plain entablature with bracketed cornice runs around the room. A niche framed by Ionic columns and a small pediment stands behind the delegates. The gallery at the far end of the room is supported by a similar structure.

The neoclassical architecture in the painting is the only clue to suggest the Roman tradition that lies behind this scene. The story of the Roman dictator Cincinnatus, who surrendered his power to the Roman Senate and went back to his farm at the end of his successful campaign, was well known in the eighteenth century. The French sculptor Jean-Antoine Houdon, whose life-size statue of Washington was installed at the Virginia Statehouse in the late 1780s, made explicit reference to the story. This standing figure, with a walking stick in his right hand and a plow at his left side, is the image of a man who renounced absolute power and returned to civilian life. Washington himself was well aware of the connection and very proud to associate himself with it. He was a founder and long-term president of the Society of the Cincinnati, an organization of retired officers of the Continental Army.

Trumbull's most fortunate decision is visible only when his works are compared to others in the Rotunda. He did not turn his scenes into allegories but rather presented them as symbolic histories. His figures are dressed in contemporary clothes rather than the Greek and Roman garments often used in eighteenth-century painting. Benjamin West was one of the first American artists to defy this tradition, and this innovation was imitated by his pupil Trumbull.

Trumbull's stiff figures and overly symmetrical compositions are less skillful than they might be, and their historical inaccuracy has often been pointed out. The scene depicting the signing of the Declaration of Independence is criticized by historians because it represents no particular event but rather a conflation of the drafting committee's presentation of the document, its signing, and its publication, all of which occurred on different days. Horatio Gates looks more like a befuddled host making introductions at a woodland fête than a victorious general. Martha Washington was not present when her husband resigned—she was waiting for him back home, at Mount Vernon. The figure represented as Benjamin Lincoln in the Yorktown surrender is actually a portrait of Cornwallis; Trumbull changed the uniform and labeling without changing the face. Yet these shortcomings pale in comparison with the paintings' ability to preserve portraits of vast numbers of key figures of the period, to identify critical moments in the Revolution, and to give them a clear and compelling, if imagined, form.

Though the fight for independence was already under way, Trumbull makes the political act of signing the Declaration—not the battles of Bunker Hill or Lexington—the crucial event that started the Revolution. The victory at Saratoga stands for the entire military campaign in the North; Yorktown represents victory in the South, while recognizing the contribution of the French allies. Washington resigning his commission closes the story not on the battlefield but in the halls of Congress, where it began. In Trumbull's paintings, the work of nation-building begins and ends in meeting rooms. The hero of the battlefield is at his most glorious when he submits himself to the authority of elected representatives. Even Trumbull's method—his assembly of hundreds of historical likenesses—

emphasizes collaboration among many rather than the contributions of a few. His architectural framing of the council scenes underscores the message of neoclassical architecture in the Capitol itself: the Greek and Roman tradition of democratic action and free debate gave form to America's own political ideals.

In 1834 the House of Representatives appointed a select committee to commission four additional paintings for the remaining bays of the Rotunda. While these history paintings are superficially like Trumbull's, they represent events of an entirely different kind. They appeal to a different set of values, and their imagery comes from different sources. Trumbull, like many of the founders, was a secularist. These men believed in God and attended church, but they resisted any replication of the close link between the English monarchy and the Anglican Church. In keeping with this tradition, Trumbull excluded religious objects and symbols from his work, in favor of classical references and architecture.

In the four paintings commissioned by the House and hung in the 1840s, classicism is absent, and history is represented through Christian events and Christian symbolism. The so-called historical scenes are all works of imagination recreated in studios with the use of models. Their sources are to be found in the political and social issues of the 1830s and 1840s rather than in the past events that the paintings profess to chronicle. John Gadsby Chapman unveiled his *Baptism of Pocahontas* in 1840. (25) According to the account of Captain John Smith of Jamestown (though most historians today dispute it), the favorite daughter of the powerful chief Powhatan, Pocahontas, intervened in 1608 to save Smith's life. She also befriended the colonists, whom she seemed to find fascinating. During the first Powhatan War, which began in 1609, Captain Samuel Argall kidnapped Pocahontas and brought her to Jamestown. Confident that the young woman would be well treated by her English friends, Powhatan refused to bargain for her release.

25

While she was in custody, Pocahontas lived in the home of the Reverend Alexander Whitaker, where she began to attend Christian services. Competent in spoken English but unable to read or write, she memorized the Apostles' Creed, the Lord's Prayer, the Ten Command-ments, and canonical responses to the questions in the short catechism. In the spring of 1614 she was baptized by Whitaker and received the baptismal name of Rebecca. The Biblical Rebecca—wife of Isaac and mother of the twin brothers Jacob and Esau—is, after Abraham's wife, Sarah, the most important matriarch of the Old Testament. Through Jacob's twelve sons, who founded the legendary twelve tribes of Israel, Rebecca became the mother of the Jewish nation, into which Jesus was born. The choice of this baptismal name for Pocahontas suggests that Whitaker believed her conversion would lead to the Christianization of all Indians.

But Pocahontas never returned to her people. She was courted by the Englishman John Rolfe, and in April 1614 the couple married. She soon gave birth to a son, named Thomas. In 1616 the family and a group of Powhatan Indians sailed to Britain, where Pocahontas met Rolfe's family; she was received at court and lionized throughout London. The rigors of the trip and the strange climate affected her health, however, and she died suddenly at Gravesend in the spring of 1617.

Chapman's 1840 painting is a highly fanciful representation of the baptism, which borrows details from the wedding of Pocahontas and John Rolfe. The Reverend Whitaker, in a white robe, stands at a baptismal fount framed between two massive columns. He looks toward the viewer and extends his left hand toward Pocahontas, who wears a white dress and kneels at his feet with one of the columns behind her. The rest of the scene is jammed with onlookers. Colonists sit in the choir stalls above and behind Pocahontas. Men in armor with a white banner fill the left foreground and cluster near the second column.

While many of Pocahontas's relatives attended her wedding, which they and her father approved, none were present at the baptism. In Chapman's scene, five Indians appear among the crowd on the right. A mother and child look on from the floor; a man draped in red gazes intently from the right corner. Another man sits on the floor and stares sullenly toward the viewer. The fifth resolutely turns his back on the scene. The diverse reactions of these Indians have no part in history; they reinforce the painting's theme of the importance and difficulty of converting the Indians.

The architecture of the church is equally fanciful and equally symbolic, especially the two columns. The one that Whitaker gestures toward and Pocahontas kneels in front of probably represents faith. In a pamphlet about the painting, Chapman described Pocahontas as standing "foremost in the train of those wandering children of the forest who have at different times—few, indeed, and far between—been snatched from

the fangs of a barbarous idolatry, to become lambs in the fold of the
Divine Shepherd. She therefore appeals to our religious as well as our
patriotic sympathies and is equally associated with the rise and progress
of the Christian Church as with the political destinies of the United
States." The second column, surrounded by armed men holding a banner, probably represents the more pragmatic arm of American political
destiny, military force.

   The 1830s, when this work was commissioned, was a turbulent and
contradictory period in relations between Indian tribes and the United
States government. The Indian Removal Act, which President Andrew
Jackson signed into law at the beginning of the decade, authorized U.S.
agents to make treaties with Indian tribes that traded their traditional
homelands east of the Mississippi for land west of the river. Tribes north
of the Ohio River that were resettled under its terms included the
Shawnee, Ottawa, Potawatomi, Sauk, and Fox. In the South, a series of
separate treaties led to the removal of more than fifty thousand Choctaw,
Creek, Chickasaw, and Seminole Indians.

   In 1838, under the Treaty of New Echota, the most vicious and notorious of all the Indian removals was forced upon the Cherokees. Protests
against this manipulative agreement were widespread. The Cherokee
leader, John Ross, who opposed the treaty and condemned the removal,
summed up the Indians' situation in a message to the Senecas sent on
April 14, 1834: "Ever since [the whites came] we have been made to
drink of the bitter cup of humiliation; treated like dogs . . . our country
and the graves of our Fathers torn from us . . . through a period of
upwards of 200 years, rolled back, nation upon nation [until] we find our-

selves fugitives, vagrants and strangers in our own country." General John Wool, originally assigned to oversee the removal, resigned his commission in protest.

Soldiers commanded by General Winfield Scott began the eviction of the Cherokee nation in May 1838. Twenty thousand men, women, and children were forced to march. The suffering and loss of life were enormous and egregious. Despite his opposition to the treaty, Chief John Ross asked to be allowed to lead his people in small groups through the wilderness, where they could forage for food, which limited mortality somewhat. At least twenty percent of those who started from Georgia in May—some four thousand people—died on the way to Oklahoma. The cross-country march became known as the Trail of Tears.

At the same time that Indian tribes were being forcibly removed from the East, they were being romanticized in the immensely popular novels of James Fenimore Cooper. In the *Last of the Mohicans,* published in 1826, Cooper described his principal Indian character, Uncas, as "an upright, flexible figure that is graceful and unrestrained in the attitudes and movements of nature." Though he was dressed like "the white man, there was no concealment to his dark, glancing, fearful eye, alike terrible and calm; the bold outline of his high haughty features, pure in their native red; or to the dignified elevation of his receding forehead, together with all the finest proportions of a noble head, bared to the generous scalping tuft." Native Americans are present in two of the remaining three pictures commissioned by Congress and hung in the Rotunda. As individuals, they share the healthy bodies and noble bearing of Cooper's idealized Indians. As a group, however, they are passive spectators of the alien history that unfolds around them.

In *The Landing of Columbus* by John Vanderlyn, Indians hide behind trees and watch with trepidation as the Italian explorer lays claim to their island. But the work that sums up all the major themes of the rest is William H. Powell's *Discovery of the Mississippi,* which was not hung until 1855. (26) Hernando de Soto leads his Spanish troops past a small cluster of Indians toward the banks of the Mississippi. The Indians include some nearly nude women and a handful of feather-bedecked men who gaze passively at the flamboyantly dressed explorer. Objects in the foreground tell a more complex story. On the left, partially hidden in

shadow, is a cannon recently used in a skirmish with the Indians. On the right, a group of friars and soldiers erect a crucifix. The cross and the sword are the instruments of conquest and assimilation that Chapman put at the center of his Poc-

26

ahontas picture, but here they are far more than veiled symbols.

Charles Bulfinch resigned as Capitol architect in 1829, and for two decades the building as he completed it remained the meeting place of Congress and the symbol of American democracy. By the late 1840s, territorial growth and the multiplication of offices and committees again strained its limits. A Philadelphia architect, Thomas U. Walter, won a competition to expand the structure. Walter's proposal included a choice of three different ways to increase usable space.

One design called for an eastward extension of the building that would transform its ground plan from a rectangle to a square. In this plan, the principal façade created by Thornton, Jefferson, Latrobe, and Bulfinch would be eliminated. The other two proposals called for extending the building on the north and south ends, by either adding new blocks directly to the old Senate and House wings or linking new blocks to the old building with corridors. Daniel Webster argued for the corridors, because he thought that more distant wings would entail less construction noise and confusion as legislators went about their business in the old Capitol. The Senate Committee on Public Buildings, which was responsible for the renovation, agreed.

Walter drew the buildings and the connecting corridors. At the suggestion of Captain Montgomery C. Meigs of the Army Corps of Engineers, who became the overseer of the project in 1853, he placed the meeting chambers in the center of each wing. Through the collaboration of Walter and Meigs, the Capitol was transformed from a building of modest proportions to a massive structure more than seven hundred feet wide topped by a dome that soared nearly three hundred feet above Jenkins Hill.

An engineer by training and profession—he was the principal designer of the city's water supply—Meigs believed, with the founders, that neoclassicism was the proper architectural style for the American Capitol. Under his supervision, the most up-to-date materials of nineteenth-century construction—cast iron and glass—were bent to the shapes prescribed by a severe and often unimaginative classical decorum. In one of the great ironies of American history, the man to whom Meigs reported, and who took a great personal interest in the expansion of the Capitol,

was Jefferson Davis,
future president of the
southern Confederacy.
As secretary of war
under President
Franklin Pierce, Davis,
who had served on the
Senate Committee on
Public Buildings, man-

27

aged to shift control of the Capitol expansion from the Interior Department to his own War Department. An early photograph shows Davis
watching from the porch of the Senate as a marble column is hoisted
into place.

The vast Senate and House additions threatened to pull the Capitol
apart. Unlike the old congressional wings, the additions featured pediments and stairs on the eastern side. These innovations, which Meigs
supported and Walter wisely but ineffectively opposed, created separate
grand entrances for each chamber. The rich decoration of the pediments, also opposed by Walter, overshadowed the figures huddled
together in the central pediment. Bulfinch's modest dome was much too
small to maintain the central weighting on which the Capitol's symbolism
depended. As the nation itself fragmented into sectional strife, plans for
the Capitol additions threatened to tear apart the one building that signi-
fied union.

The feature that restored visual unity to this vast structure was a new
dome on an unprecedented scale. (27) In Walter's design, the four flat

28

sides of a pedestal look toward each of the outside walls of the building; on top of the pedestal, a circular base supports a giant peristyle—a circular span of columns—that creates a fictional walkway around the dome. (28) Inside this colonnade, pilasters alternate with steep round-topped windows. Above the colonnade, an entablature holds up a balcony. Stepped back from the balcony's edge, a second series of pilasters frame a file of smaller windows shaped like those in the peristyle below. A cornice above these windows supports a row of outsized brackets that anchor the rim of an elongated dome. Vertical ribs separated at their bases by lozenge-shaped windows divide the dome into sections. Horizontal striations suggest enormous tiles.

A small balcony tops the dome and anchors a pedestal from which a high lantern in the form of a round colonnaded shrine—a tholos—rises. The tholos repeats the features of the peristyle at the base of the drum. Standing on a tapering plinth, the figure of Liberty surmounts the structure. (29) Cast in bronze by the American sculptor Thomas Crawford in his Roman studio, the figure represents freedom triumphant. She holds a sword in one hand while the other hand, which rests on a shield, holds a wreath. In Crawford's original design, the figure wore a Phrygian cap— a Roman symbol of liberty. Roman citizens regarded their freedom as a birthright; those who had gained their liberty through manumission rather than birth wore a Phrygian cap. At Jefferson Davis's insistence,

Crawford substituted a helmet with eagle head and feathers for this symbol of slavery's end.

In designing the dome, Walter took account of several European
precedents. He had traveled to London, Paris, and Rome in the late
1830s and knew a number of majestic domed buildings first hand. The
three models that seemed most useful to him were
Michelangelo's sixteenth-century dome above St. Peter's
Basilica in Rome, Christopher Wren's seventeenth-century dome of St. Paul's in London, and the mid-eighteenth-century Panthéon in Paris. Each of these domes
was elongated rather than hemispherical, and its height
was increased by a supporting drum. Bramante's diminutive Tempietto, designed in the early sixteenth century as
a rough draft for a new Renaissance St. Peter's, stood in
the background of all these projects. Like the Tempietto,
both St. Paul's and the French Panthéon featured peri-

29

styles around their drums. Michelangelo's dome for St. Peter's included
paired columns between windows in the same position. Profiting from the
example of these designs, Walter's most innovative feature was the addition of a second colonnade above the peristyle.

The nine million pounds of metal that form the dome appear to rest
on the roof of the Capitol, but they do not. The ample foundations of
Bulfinch's Crypt, deeply rooted in the bedrock of Jenkins Hill, support the
superstructure. Once Bulfinch's old wooden dome had been dismantled,
work on the new dome began with the creation of a high circular brick
wall reinforced with iron braces and set firmly on Bulfinch's piers. While

30

the back of the peristyle rests directly on this circular wall, the colonnade is supported on hidden brackets cantilevered out from it. The square pedestal that appears to carry the weight of the whole dome actually hangs from the brick ring like a curtain and blocks it from view.

Meigs had hoped to build a foundry on the site to forge the components of the dome near where they were to be set in place. But castings from an established ironworks in Baltimore could be delivered to Washington at lower cost. Columns were cast in pieces, and workers bolted or riveted shafts, bases, and capitals together before lifting them into position. Floral ornaments were delivered separately and bolted to the column capitals to complete their classical design. Neither Meigs nor Walter had any clear idea how long the project would take to complete. Their first estimate was an astounding one year, and many congressmen returned to Washington in the fall of 1855 expecting to see the new dome towering above the Capitol.

While the soaring dome restored a sense of proportion to the outside of the expanded building, it threatened to overwhelm the Rotunda below. Bulfinch's room was wide to begin with, but it could not grow any wider even as its roof suddenly exploded to an apex now almost two hundred feet from the Rotunda floor. The iron and plaster work of Walter's addition begins above Bulfinch's stone entablature. Two cornices—one inset very improbably with coffers—circle the structure below a wide frieze. (30) Originally intended to be filled with narrative sculptures in low relief, this band was eventually painted in a technique called grisaille, which imitates sculpted stone. A balcony with coffers set into square pedestals supports a row of pilasters between high windows. These are the windows that are closed in on their outside by the peristyle. An entablature completes the vertical thrust; above it, a coffered dome bends inward. An oculus in this dome opens to reveal a painting on the surface of a second dome. (31) This feature, based on the French Panthéon, reduces the height of the interior dome and helps to reconcile it somewhat to the proportions of the Rotunda floor.

31

In 1878 Constantine Brumidi began to paint a series of narratives from American history in the frieze beneath the first row of windows. An Italian fresco painter, Brumidi had been raised in Rome under the oppressive rule of a succession of conservative popes. He came to America in 1852 because he longed for the liberty and equality that were denied him in his native city. He learned the democratic principles then in vogue from the politicians he worked among.

Superficially, the figures of his frieze are like those in the Panathenaic Processional removed from the Parthenon in Athens early in the nineteenth century and installed in the British Museum. Brumidi never saw this ancient Greek frieze, but he knew Roman examples well. The multitude of little figures, the variety of postures, and especially the incorpora-

32

tion of tools makes his frieze look more like a version of the narrative sculptures that spiral up the Column of Trajan and the Column of Marcus Aurelius. In hundreds of scenes, each of these columns narrates events of Roman military campaigns led by the two emperors.

Against a dark background—more like printer's ink than stone—Brumidi's stark white figures appear three-dimensional. Individual scenes are marked off by columns or trees and, in one case, a tuft of river grass. Because the breaks are so muted and the figures so bright, they seem to march in continual procession around the room. The frieze gives the sense that American history is a single-minded unimpeded march from the past to the present.

The frieze begins in an allegorical assembly. Liberty with an eagle at her feet, unabashedly wearing her Phrygian cap and holding a barred shield, introduces the story. She is flanked by Clio, the muse of history, who is also represented on the old House chamber clock. From behind a book on Clio's knee a plank angles toward the ground. Christopher Columbus walks down it from his tiny crowded ship and sets American history in motion. Columbus is watched by bare-breasted native women clutching their babies, and by a feathered chief striking a noble pose. Beside him, Cortés enters the throne room of Montezuma in a scene that resolutely fails to show the greedy slaughter that followed. **(32)**

Pizarro conquers Peru; De Soto is buried in the Mississippi. As in the

paintings of Indians on the walls below, these scenes of Spanish conquest have been adopted as an integral part of the North American narrative. Pocahontas reappears, this time in the legendary scene where she
rescues Captain John Smith. The Pilgrims land; Penn makes his treaty
with the Indians. The trees of New England are leveled by men with axes,
and Oglethorpe establishes peace with the Indians in Georgia—a peace
that will be shattered many times before being extinguished completely
by the removals of the 1830s.

In contrast to Trumbull, Brumidi begins his Revolutionary War cycle
on the battlefield at Lexington, not in Congress. In the next scene, the
Declaration of Independence is proclaimed rather than debated. Cornwallis surrenders, but Washington does not resign his commission. The great
Indian leader Tecumseh is killed at the Battle of Thames in 1813—
though Brumidi declines to show the flaying and mutilation of his body
by Kentucky militiamen. Winfield Scott enters Mexico City in 1847; Gold
is discovered in California; and the Civil War ends in a handshake. Two
scenes, added much later, represent the Spanish-American War of 1898
and the Wright Brothers' first successful flight in 1903. Leonardo da
Vinci stands with a model of his ornithopter behind the brothers, and an
American eagle with outstretched wings inaugurates a new century.

For Brumidi, as for most American politicians of the late nineteenth
century, the American story was a tale of unflinching conquest. Europeans subdued native peoples from Peru to Ohio through force more
often than persuasion or religious conversion. America's might and influence ranged from one shore of the continent to the other, and their shadows hovered over South America. But as Trumbull alone of the Capitol

artists appears to have understood, democracy is the work of citizens in free debate as well as soldiers in armor; it cannot be reduced to the imposition of America's will.

Behind the oculus of the Rotunda's dome, on a second umbrella-like ceiling hanging from the building's iron frame, Brumidi painted his most ambitious and most improbable work. Soaring one hundred and eighty

feet above the floor, the scene, painted in 1865, represents the *Apotheosis of Washington.* The rulers of the Roman world were worshipped as living gods by their non-Roman subjects; after death they were typically deified in Rome and worshipped as patron gods of the state. Rembrandt Peale's portrait of Washington in the Senate assigns him Roman honors and implies that he

33

has passed triumphantly through the portal that separates this life from that beyond. In the mask above the picture's fictive frame, he draws a link between Washington and Olympian Zeus. Brumidi's fresco in the Rotunda dome does away with innuendo and simply places Washington, still dressed in his blue frock coat, on the throne of Zeus, holding the hilt of a sword in his upraised arm. (33)

A curious wreath of cloud separates the central figures of Washington and his circle of goddesses from other scenes centered on the gods as personifications. Freedom in arms—a tame version of Delacroix's rampant

Liberty Guiding the People—presides over a cluster of men in armor and an old man with a cannon. Ceres, goddess of agriculture, sits on a hay cart (though critics of the day thought a McCormick reaper would have been more appropriate). Vulcan stands with his foot on a cannon. A prudently draped Mercury, with his winged hat and Persian sword, offers a bag of gold to Robert Morris, the entrepreneur who financed much of the Revolutionary War and afterward worked for the foundation of the national bank. Mercury here appears to be the god of commerce.

Surrounded by nymphs and tritons, Neptune and Aphrodite drive their chariot across a tiny sea. The scene, which is loosely based on Raphael's *Triumph of Galatea* in the Villa Farnesina in Rome, represents the laying of the transatlantic telegraph cable. The unruly cable twists around the figures like the serpents strangling Laocoön and his sons in the Hellenistic sculptural group displayed in the Vatican's Belvedere Palace. In the final scene, Minerva, the Roman Athena and goddess of wisdom, converses with American inventors and men of science—Benjamin Franklin, Samuel F. B. Morse, who in 1843 erected the first telegraph line between Washington and Baltimore, and Robert Fulton, who built the first steam-powered ship. The kneeling figure with an open compass on the left of the painting is modeled on Raphael's famous *School of Athens* in the Vatican Palace.

From 1841 to 1843 the center of the Rotunda was occupied by a statue of Washington as Olympian Zeus carved by the expatriate American sculptor Horatio Greenough in his studio in Rome. Commissioned by Congress in 1832, the centennial of Washington's birth, the seated figure is bare to the waist, with a muscular torso and powerful arms; the face is a younger and more determined version of the Houdon head. Washington's right arm, draped with the trailing edge of a toga, is uplifted and his index finger is raised. In his extended left arm he holds a sheathed sword with its hilt forward. Feet in Roman sandals project from beneath his drapery.

Everyone hated the sculpture, and after only two years it was removed. Greenough's portrayal of Washington as a pagan god raised some hackles, but the reason for the hasty removal was the embarrassing seminudity of the first president. After its eviction, Greenough's figure was placed outdoors, at no benefit to the marble, for sixty-five years before it was given shelter in the Smithsonian. In 1964 the statue was relocated to the National Museum of American History on the Mall, where it sat ingloriously at the base of an escalator in the building's east wing.

Peale's porthole portrait and Brumidi's painted figure in the *Apotheosis* remain the only vestiges in the Capitol of a plan to memorialize the first president and make him the focus of the nation's central building. Had all the parts of that plan come together, the Capitol Crypt would have enshrined the president's remains, a monumental sculptural representation of him would have been the centerpiece of the Rotunda, and an image of his divinized form in the heavens above would have been its culmination. Washington's presence in three manifestations would have made him a virtual Trinity, and the Capitol would have found a cohesive image for itself in its hypostasized first president. That did not happen, and painters have instead transformed the Rotunda into a hall that celebrates America's providential guidance, not that of its great leader.

Brumidi's first commission for the Capitol was to supervise the
painted ornamentation of hundreds of feet of vaulted corridors in the
enlarged Senate wing. Directing a multinational crew of assistants working in a variety of media that included fresco and tempera, Brumidi oversaw a lavish decorative scheme based on small-scale scenes set into
complex floral and architectural frames. Raphael's work in Rome was the
model for these compositions. But rather than turning to the painter's
masterworks in the Vatican Stanze or the Farnesina, Brumidi based his
design on Raphael's decoration of a long vaulted corridor partly exposed
to the weather—a loggia—on the second floor of the Vatican Palace. The
loggia represented the fruit of Raphael's exploration of the Golden House
of Nero—a vast palace that was constructed in the first century AD, preserved underground, and first visited by architects and artists in the early
sixteenth century.

The walls and vaulted ceilings of the Golden House were adorned with
fantasies of vines and tendrils, fictive busts and three-dimensional
medallions, tiny genre scenes and historic frescoes in a variety of scales
and qualities that ranged from wallpaper art to masterpiece. Raphael imitated these decorative fantasies, which came to be called "grotesques"
because Nero's long-buried house was, at first, thought to be a cave or
grotto. Under Raphael's influence over the centuries, ornamentation in
the grotesque style embellished many sections of the Vatican corridors.
Brumidi, who worked for awhile in the Vatican, probably painted some of
them himself. But Brumidi's work in the Capitol reflects more knowledge
of ancient painting than even Raphael possessed. Other styles of Roman
wall decoration were uncovered when excavations began at Pompeii in

the late eighteenth century, and Brumidi's Corridors, as these halls are called today, reflect the strong blacks and reds of Pompeian fresco instead of the light backgrounds Nero preferred. Brumidi's decorative scheme, like Raphael's, includes larger commemorative or allegorical compositions. (34)

Brumidi began making designs for the corridors in 1856, while construction of the new wings was under way. The bulk of the decoration was

accomplished between 1857 and 1859, but he continued to paint the lunettes and add other details until his death in 1880. While some overlap with the themes of the Rotunda is evident, the arts of peace and the democratic process play a larger role in Brumidi's scenes for the Senate corridors. Historical moments of deliberation include the *Cession of Louisiana* and *The Signing of the First Treaty of Peace with Great Britain,* both painted in the last decade of his life. Portraits of scientists and inventors like Franklin and Fulton appear here, as they did in the Rotunda. A lunette depicting *Columbus*

34

and the Indian Maiden (1875) is an obvious if distasteful allegory of discovery. (35) The explorer, with a dagger in his belt and a leer on his face, lifts the veil from a seated and, for once, fully dressed Indian woman. She seems none too pleased.

A surprising contrast to this image is offered in Brumidi's portrait of Bartolomé de las Casas, painted one year later. The Spanish priest, who knew Columbus, was an early traveler to the New World and a witness to

the slaughter and enslave-
ment of native peoples. He
protested against these outrages to the Spanish authori-
ties and to the pope, with
some success. Emperor
Charles V attempted to
enforce more moderate policies toward the Indians, which

35

the colonists strongly resisted. In a papal bull entitled *Sublimis Deus,*
Pope Paul III in 1537 declared that Indians were rational beings with
souls capable of receiving Christian truth but entitled to life and property
even in its absence. The language of the pope's decree was not supported by sanctions like excommunication, and it had little concrete
effect.

An unselfconscious program can be discerned in the multiple scenes
that proliferate throughout the Brumidi Corridors. And despite the great
geographical and historical barriers that separate these walls from the
winding galleries of Nero's Golden House or the buried dining rooms and
bedrooms of Pompeii, there is an underlying similarity between the
worldview of the Romans and that of the nineteenth-century Americans
who took such pleasure in imitating Roman decoration. The Romans were
pragmatic, worldly people who were intensely curious and likely to have
satisfied that curiosity in odd corners of the Mediterranean world. The
decoration they chose for their houses, though it varied in style over time,
was always eclectic and far-ranging. Mosaics of fish or birds, exotic and

domestic, fill atrium floors. In other rooms, a life-size group of doves or a lakeside villa is depicted from an imagined bird's-eye perspective. A bust of Hercules stands next to a three-dimensional architectural fantasy or a still-life of domestic chickens. A dog barks near the door, while a frieze of pygmies and crocodiles borders the ceiling.

Roman art is a little like the doodling of a talented and obsessive person who is easily bored but interested, in a vague way, in nearly everything. The preoccupations of a scribbler are certainly easy to overread, but the range of Roman and American decoration suggests a universal and omnivorous appetite for life experience. Brumidi's frescoes hint that America, like Rome, is about *everything*—that it imagines itself as a country without limits, that it sees no reason whatsoever to rein in its imagination. The Capitol, as Brumidi's illustrations define it, is a center-point from which to consider the whole world. As the functions of the Capitol come to be dispersed into a variety of second-generation build-ings and institutions in the late nineteenth century, this curiosity about all the undertakings of people and all the richness of nature would find expression in the Library of Congress and the many museums of the Smithsonian Institution.

Fortunately for the Capitol complex, Meigs and Walter's Senate and House wings reflected the neoclassical style of the rest of the building. A Gothic addition, like the nearly contemporary Smithsonian Castle on the Mall, is all too easy to imagine. But the neoclassicism of Walter and Meigs was timid, and the main meeting rooms of their Capitol additions followed classical precedents that were banal. The curved walls, soaring arches, and coffered domes of the old Capitol gave way to rectilinear

walls punctuated by modest pilasters and shallow niches. In the new rectangular chambers framed by raked galleries, where the House and Senate still meet today, an architecture of planes replaced an architecture of
volumes. Rooms with the acoustics of a concert hall were replaced with
chambers where the voices in debate were lost in dead air under the skylights and above the galleries. By the 1940s the new rooms were deemed
unusable, and redesign of their ceilings, walls, and galleries was carried
out over the next decade. With electric lighting and microphones, along
with modern air conditioning, heating, and ventilation, the rooms finally
became comfortable
and effective. Nothing,
however, could remedy
their unfortunate form.
   Except for continu-
ing repair and mainte-
nance, and interven-
tions prompted by
security demands or

36

political urgencies, the Capitol is poised to retain its present shape for-
ever. (36) The ideals the Capitol represents have settled into place without
ever being settled, or even settled upon. More capable of resisting what it
did not like than deciding on what it did, the Capitol evolved by rejecting
ideas it could not or would not live with. Jefferson would have nothing to
do with Washington's conference room, and so it quietly disappeared
from the plans. Bulfinch resisted incredible pressure from fierce and
irreconcilable patrons to cede the space for his Rotunda to more immedi-

ate needs. Washington's family refused to make the building his tomb. Public taste rejected the half-naked image of the founding father as its centerpiece. When stubbornness kept the building from becoming a presidential mausoleum, commissioned art turned the echoing space of the Rotunda into a celebration of Manifest Destiny—a belief in the United States' divine right to become a transcontinental nation.

Abraham Lincoln's death in 1865, following a tragic and bloody Civil War, altered the Rotunda's meaning in yet another way, this time transforming it into something like the national church that L'Enfant had envisaged. On November 6, 1860, the presidential candidate of the seven-year-old Republican Party won a plurality of the popular vote and a majority of the Electoral College vote. Lincoln had characterized slavery as immoral but pledged not to challenge it in the states where it was already established. Nevertheless, radicals throughout the Deep South treated his election as a provocation.

On December 20 the legislature of South Carolina passed "an ordinance to dissolve the union between the State of South Carolina and other States united with her under the compact entitled 'The Constitution of the United States of America.'" The law annulled the state's eighteenth-century ratification of the Constitution and declared that "the union now subsisting between South Carolina and other States, under the name of the 'United States of America,' is hereby dissolved." By the time of Lincoln's inauguration on March 4, 1861, six more states had seceded from the union and formed the Confederate States of America, with former senator and army secretary Jefferson Davis as president.

Lincoln took the oath of office on the east porch of the Capitol on

March 4, 1861. The drum of the incomplete dome loomed over the crowd; a wooden scaffold sticking out of its open top supported the arm of a giant crane. Lincoln had planned to end his speech on that day with a direct question to the people of the seceding states, "Shall it be peace or the sword?" At the last minute, he redrafted the conclusion of his First Inaugural to express his hope that war might be averted. "The mystic chords of memory, stretching from every battle-field, and patriot grave, to every living heart and hearthstone, all over this broad land, will yet swell the chorus of the Union, when again touched, as surely they will be, by the better angels of our nature."

On his first full day in office, Lincoln received word that the federal garrison at Fort Sumter, which guarded the harbor of Charleston, South Carolina, had only six weeks of supplies in its storerooms. He informed South Carolina Governor Pickens of his plan to reprovision the fort. The Confederate government decided to attack the fort preemptively on April 12, and at midday on the thirteenth the garrison surrendered. On April 15 Lincoln declared that the southern states were in revolt and called for seventy-five thousand volunteer militiamen to restore them to the union. Within the next two months, Virginia, Arkansas, North Carolina, and Tennessee joined the Confederacy, bringing its total membership to eleven states.

One of the most articulate interpreters of these events was the poet Walt Whitman: "Even after the bombardment of Sumter, however, the gravity of the revolt, and the power and will of the slave States for a strong and continued military resistance to national authority, were not at all realized at the North, except by a few. Nine-tenths of the people of the free States looked upon the rebellion . . . with a feeling one-half of contempt, and the other half composed of anger and incredulity. It was not thought it would be join'd in by Virginia, North Carolina, or Georgia. A great and cautious national official predicted that it would blow over 'in sixty days,' and folks generally believ'd the prediction" (*Specimen Days*).

The event that changed the picture and prepared the people of both North and South for a prolonged and bloody struggle was the First Battle of Manassas. Volunteers had flocked to both armies after Lincoln's mid-April call. Union Brigadier General Irvin McDowell commanded a force of nearly forty thousand, the largest army ever assembled on the American continent. On July 18 he marched his troops toward Manassas, Virginia, the meeting point of railroads that led to the Confederate capital, recently relocated from Mobile, Alabama, to Richmond, less than a hundred miles south of Washington. A Confederate force about half the size of McDowell's, commanded by Brigadier General P. G. T. Beauregard of Louisiana—ex-superintendent of West Point and leader of the attack against Fort Sumter—was stationed along the far side of a meandering creek called Bull Run.

A spy for the Confederacy, Rose O'Neal Greenhow, had informed Richmond of McDowell's force and plan of march. Additional Confederate troops commanded by General Joseph E. Johnston eluded Union forces and joined Beauregard's troops. Fighting began in earnest on July 21 and continued into the next day. Because the weather was hot and clear and the battlefield no distance from Washington, carriage parties from the capital streamed into Virginia to enjoy a picnic and a view of what most expected to be a bloodless rout. Instead, the poorly trained and disorganized troops fought desperately, and both sides suffered heavy losses. The Union forces bolted and ran, leaving Washington unprotected. Many historians believe that capture of the city was within Beauregard's grasp.

"The defeated troops commenced pouring into Washington over the Long Bridge at daylight on Monday, 22d—a day drizzling all through with rain . . . returning to Washington baffled, humiliated, panic-struck . . . The sun rises, but shines not. The men appear, at first sparsely and shame-faced enough, then thicker, in the streets of Washington . . . They come along in disorderly mobs, some in squads, stragglers, companies. Occasionally, a rare regiment, in perfect order, with its officers (some gaps, dead, the true braves) marching in silence, with lowering faces, stern, weary to sinking, all black and dirty, but every man with his musket, and stepping alive; but these are the exceptions. Sidewalks of Pennsylvania avenue, Fourteenth street, crowded, jammed with citizens, clerks, everybody, lookers-on; women in the windows, curious expressions from faces, as those swarms of dirt-covered returned soldiers there (will they never end?) move by; but nothing said, no comments; (half our lookers-on—*secesh* of the most venomous kind—they say nothing; but the devil snickers in their faces) . . .

"Good people (but not over-many of them either) hurry up something for their grub. They put wash-kettles on the fire, for soup, for coffee. They set tables on the side-walks, wagonloads of bread are purchased, swiftly cut in stout chunks. Here are two aged ladies, beautiful, the first in the city for culture and charm, they stand with store of eating and drink at an improvised table of rough plank, and give food, and have the store replenished from their house every half-hour all that day; and there in the rain they stand, active, silent, white-haired, and give food, though the tears stream down their cheeks, almost without intermission, the whole time" (Whitman, *Specimen Days*).

The Battle of Manassas brought the horror and grinding bitterness of war home to a city used to governing from afar. In the eighteenth century, the capital's location on the border between North and South had linked together the long chain of states strung out along the seacoast. That same geographical fact now placed Washington on the frontier between warring regions. Indeed, in most ways the city was beyond the front lines and deep within enemy territory. Southern Maryland, to the north, was tobacco plantation country just like Virginia, and slavery was essential to its economy. The commercial interests of Baltimore were tied to the South, and the sentiments of its people were also southern. On his way to his inauguration, Lincoln, fearful of assassination, traveled through Baltimore without stopping. Troops sent to secure the capital after Bull Run were attacked by Baltimore mobs; some were killed and many wounded before they could reach Washington.

The embattled capital was quickly defended by a ring of fortifications. Northern Virginia, occupied by Union forces immediately after secession, was included in the defensive circle, which also shielded the city against invaders from Maryland. Washington DC became a garrison. Hundreds of acres of unused land were covered with tents and parade grounds. When Lee began his invasion of the north in 1863, casualties poured into makeshift hospitals throughout the city. Government buildings were crammed with beds for the sick and wounded. The Capitol building, with its vaulted corridors and committee rooms, become a battlefield infir-

mary. Massive ovens constructed in its basement produced the daily
bread ration for thousands of troops, both under arms and wounded.

Because it lay on the frontier of Confederate territory, Washington was
a mecca for thousands of escaped slaves. The first small groups of fugitives were housed in the old Brick Capitol across from the new Senate
wing, and then were moved to housing further east on Capitol Hill. Barracks were opened to them and new ones created. By 1862 when slavery
was abolished in the District, thirteen thousand African American
refugees were already living in the city. In that same year, Lincoln authorized black enlistment. Two regiments were formed, and some three thousand African Americans from Washington joined in the course of the war.
Many other refugees served the Union army as drovers, road builders,
cooks, and laundry workers.

The Emancipation Proclamation of 1863, which further embittered
the South and provoked riots and lynchings as far north as New York,
increased the flow of African Americans to the capital. Philanthropic
organizations created housing tenements in various parts of the city, but
the surge of refugees overwhelmed them. Predominately black settlements sprung up overnight. All had curious names, some sinister. Foggy
Bottom, Vinegar Hill, and Murder Bay ringed the White House. Bloodfield
lay just south of the Capitol. Swampoodle, just north of the commercial
center, became home to two great African American institutions of postwar Washington, Howard University and the Freedmen's Hospital. In the
twentieth century this area, renamed Shaw, would become the center of
black life and culture.

When the statue of Liberty on top of the Capitol was unveiled in

1863, Lincoln was too sick to attend the ceremonies. With Lee's defeat at Gettysburg, the Confederacy began to lose ground, and the war news after 1863 was steadily brighter for the Union. On April 3, 1865, Grant's troops took Richmond. Six days later, Lee surrendered to Grant under dignified and humane conditions at Appomattox Courthouse. Five days after that, too late to do any good for the Confederacy to which he had devoted the last year of his life, John Wilkes Booth shot Lincoln at Ford's Theatre. The president was carried across Tenth Street, where he died early on the morning of the Saturday before Easter, April 15.

His body lay in state in the East Room of the White House until his first funeral on April 19. A massive procession then carried the bier down Pennsylvania Avenue. The journalist George Alfred Townsend was an eloquent eyewitness: "The cortege passed to the left side of the Capitol, and entering the great gates, passed to the grand stairway, opposite the splendid dome, where the coffin was disengaged and carried up the ascent. It was posted under the bright concave, now streaked with mournful trappings, and left in state, watched by guards of officers with drawn swords . . .

"The storied paintings representing eras in [the republic's] history were draped in sable, through which they seemed to cast reverential glances upon the lamented bier. The thrilling scenes depicted by Trumbull, the commemorative canvases of Leutze, the wilderness vegetation of Powell, glared from their separate pedestals upon the central spot where lay the fallen majesty of the country. Here the prayers and addresses of the noon were rehearsed and the solemn burial service read. At night the jets of gas concealed in the spring of the dome were lighted up, so that their bright reflection shone masses of burning light, like marvelous haloes, upon the little box where so much that we love and honor rested on its way to the grave. And so through the starry night, in the temple of the great Union he had strengthened and recovered, the body of Abraham Lincoln, zealously guarded, is now reposing."

During the closing months of the Civil War, Congress passed the Thirteenth Amendment abolishing slavery and permitting involuntary servitude only as a punishment for crime; in December of that year the amendment was ratified by the states. Though unable to rejoin the union until new state constitutions could be written and approved, the former Confederate states reacted in legal and extra-legal means to the new federal policies. Most southern states enacted so-called black codes, which, masquerading as paternalism, designated underage blacks as wards of their former masters. Vagrancy laws allowed sheriffs to fine and imprison unemployed men and women, then hire them out to employers who would pay their fines, thus circumventing the Thirteenth Amendment.

Most former slaves were skilled in agriculture but lacked urban work experience. During the war, many found jobs in and around the army camps, but hundreds, eventually thousands, found no work at all. Congress created the Freedmen's Bureau at the close of the war to provide and regulate employment, administer justice, and organize education. Through its efforts and those of community and philanthropic organizations, Washington established schools at all levels for African Americans. While segregation was the nineteenth-century norm, integration of public schools was debated (and defeated) in 1871. African Americans served on the District police force and fire companies. Washington also had its share of black doctors and lawyers. For a brief period before the abandonment of Reconstruction and the emergence of Jim Crow legislation in the former Confederacy, the city hosted black representatives and senators.

Job opportunities for the average black Washingtonian increased over time, up to a point. Low- and middle-level occupations were open to blacks, but the most secure and lucrative positions higher up in the federal bureaucracy were generally closed to them. Limited to working as laborers and messengers, few were accepted in even the bottom ranks of the burgeoning Civil Service. By 1874 the population of Washington was one fourth African American. By no coincidence, in that same year Congress revoked the city charter and put control in the hands of federal commissioners.

Former Confederate officers in Tennessee—the first secessionist state readmitted to the Union—founded the Ku Klux Klan in 1866. This long-enduring secret organization, famous for its white-hooded riders, cross burnings, and night raids, was more open about its activities in its founding years. During congressional hearings, a witness described their audacity:

"Last Sunday night the rowdies actually shot a Negro man about a mile out from town. After disturbing the people on their return from church, they proceeded to the Camden ferry and called for the boat. The man came, and while crossing the narrow river, was asked: 'Is that William Kinney?' He replied in the affirmative. Pop went a pistol. Some dozen or fifteen shots were fired, and one ball passed through the body near the kidneys. Not much is said about it, and I have not learned whether it is likely to prove fatal or not. What surprises me most is to witness the indifference on the part of the citizens generally. They take no more notice apparently of these outrages and murders than if so many dogs had been bruised and shot at. The persons who commit these acts are seen the next day mingling with the people on the streets and in the shops as though nothing unusual had happened."

The Fourteenth Amendment to the Constitution, passed in 1866, bolstered the Thirteenth. Responding to Taney's Dred Scott decision, it declared all native-born and naturalized Americans, except Indians, to be citizens of the United States and entitled to equal protection under its laws. The refusal of southern states to ratify this amendment, along with the spread of black codes and interracial violence, was met by an escalating series of congressional acts that strengthened the mechanisms of integration. In 1867 the official reorganization of the former Confederacy—Reconstruction—was placed under direct military authority.

President Andrew Johnson continued to veto punitive legislation targeting the South. But in 1868, when Johnson fired the leader of military Reconstruction, Secretary of War Edwin Stanton, the House immediately voted to impeach the president. By a single vote, the Senate refused to convict, and Johnson served out the remaining months of his term. Within the next ten years Congress passed the Fifteenth Amendment, which enfranchised all male citizens without regard to race or previous condition of servitude. African Americans began to vote, and in the next few decades a total of twenty-two representatives were elected to Congress.

As quickly as it was put together, Reconstruction began to collapse.

The Freedmen's Bureau was abolished in 1872; the Supreme Court over-turned a vital piece of Reconstruction legislation, the Civil Rights Act of 1875. Wade Hampton, a former major general in the Confederate Army, was elected governor of South Carolina in 1876. After the withdrawal of U.S. troops from the state in the following year, former slaves were left to fend for themselves without federal protection. Having circumvented the Thirteenth and Fourteenth amendments successfully, southern states had little difficulty in depriving African Americans of their Fifteenth Amend-ment right to vote. Poll taxes, literacy tests, and grandfather clauses were quickly put in place throughout the South and remained unchallenged by the federal government until the civil rights movement of the 1950s and 1960s provoked reform, a century after the Dred Scott decision was handed up from the basement of the Capitol.

Chapter Four

THE HILL AND BEYOND

Thomas Jefferson's finished drawing of a federal government with its Legislative and Judicial branches enclosed in a single circular building was partially transformed by water damage. The fate of the drawing foretold the fate of Jefferson's compact government. Over the centuries the functions of the Congress and the Court have oozed outside the lines of their original settings and spread themselves across the Washington landscape. Yet even in their wanderings, most buildings have not strayed far from their source.

In the early nineteenth century, Congress appointed temporary committees to address particular problems, and it settled most questions by open debate among all legislators. By the end of the century, standing committees were the norm, and each one had its permanent meeting room in the new wings of the Capitol. The proliferation of congressional offices and growth of congressional business put increasing strains on a building that, even with the enormous expansions of the 1850s, had reached its physical limit. The only practical option was to find new homes for the Library of Congress, the Supreme Court, the major committees, and the offices of individual legislators.

Facing the Capitol's east side, directly across First Street from the House wing, stands the earliest of three Capitol Hill buildings that now hold the collections of the Library of Congress. The original library was located in the Senate wing of Latrobe's Capitol. In August 1814, British marines threw books and manuscripts from its shelves onto the pyre of Senate desks. Sprinkled with gunpowder and set ablaze, the books fueled the destruction of the Capitol's north wing. All three thousand volumes that then made up the national library were destroyed.

During the Capitol's reconstruction, Latrobe designed a new fireproof library, and in 1815 Jefferson, whose private collection of books was the largest in the nation, sold more than six thousand volumes to Congress. But Jefferson did more than simply provide books. Narrowly conceived, the Congress's library might have been merely a storehouse of legislation and legal precedents—little more than a national law library. The extraordinary breadth of Jefferson's books set the pattern for a collection that has continued to range over every subject a legislator might conceivably want to explore.

In 1851 a fire burst out in a chimney next to the fireproof Capitol library. Though twenty thousand books were saved, four thousand volumes from Jefferson's collection, and more than thirty thousand others, were destroyed by fire and water. Congress appropriated funds to replace the lost and damaged books, and by the end of the Civil War the Library of Congress included more than eighty thousand volumes.

Ainsworth Rand Spofford, who was appointed librarian of Congress in 1864, lobbied for passage of a copyright act. In 1870 the legislation was signed into law. Anyone seeking copyright protection for any published item—book, pamphlet, engraving, photograph, or sheet of music—had to

submit two copies of the work to the library. The sudden influx of copyright materials meant that every odd space and unused room in the Capitol was viewed as a potential book depository. The basement was heaped
with boxes, and librarians were measuring every vacant niche for book-
shelves. By 1873, when Spofford argued for the creation of a separate
library building, Congress was eager to oblige.

   Even though a new building for the library was in everyone's best
interest, the process of choosing a location and a design dragged on for
thirteen years. In 1886 the local architects John L. Smithmeyer and Paul
J. Pelz submitted the winning proposal. General Thomas Casey, head of
the Army Corps of Engineers, supervised construction, which began in
1888. In 1892 Casey gave his son Edward responsibility for the extraordinarily rich decoration of the interior. By 1897 the transfer of books
from the Capitol to the new building was complete. Fittingly, the original
Library of Congress building was renamed the Jefferson Building in
1980. Two additional buildings behind and beside it are named for
Adams and Madison.

   Stylistically, the Library of Congress did not travel any farther from the
Capitol than it had
traveled geographi-
cally. (37) The archi-
tecture of the oldest
Library of Congress
building is typically
described as Ital-
ianate, though the

37

style was refined by nineteenth-century French neoclassicism. But the building is also a response, in a slightly different key, to the Capitol building itself. The library's west façade, facing the Capitol, is a five-part structure with an enormous central block, two extended wings that step back from the central mass, and diminutive but still prominent blocks at each end. Colonnades distinguish the center and corner structures; a large dome and cupola stand behind and above the main façade. Lacking pediments atop the colonnades to tie the building closely to the east front of the Capitol, the library reflects more directly the western elevation. This seems historically appropriate, since the western projection of Bulfinch's central pavilion was the last Capitol home of the congressional library.

Like the west façade of the Capitol, the Jefferson Building has two rusticated stories. Stairs in multiple flights lead to arched doorways flanked by columns on the second level. At their center is a two-story colonnaded portico, with a heavy entablature and balustrade. The pavilions at each corner of the building are reduced-scale versions of the central block. The connecting wings are divided into four apparent stories by entablatures; classical window embrasures provide the only other ornament. The copper-covered dome of the building is considerably smaller than the colossal Capitol dome, though its profile is changed by a small lantern and a gilded torch. This modest dome is more in tune with the low Capitol dome proposed by Thornton but never built.

These similarities in style disguise great structural differences between the two buildings. The Capitol, which grew outward from both ends, is wide in proportion to its depth. The Library of Congress building is almost as deep as it is wide, and though its exterior walls define it as a solid block, it is actually pierced, as many Washington buildings are, by interior courtyards. In plan, oddly enough, the library resembles both a castle and a prison. Its four corner pavilions are like watchtowers, and the long corridors that link them, though they are broken by windows, are much like the walls of a fortress. The dome is actually the top of a free-standing octagonal structure linked to the outer walls by an extension of the central block in front and by corridors at the side and back. Prisons enclosed by high walls overlooked by corner towers, with cellblocks that radiate from a center building, were very common in the nineteenth century.

In his *Précis des leçons d'architecture,* the French neoclassical architect Jean-Nicolas-Louis Durand described the plan of an ideal library. An illustration accompanying his description shows a square building with corner pavilions surrounding an independent central structure shaped like a wheel, with the reading room at its hub and books stored in the projecting spokes. The Library of Congress is a simplified and improved version of this plan. "A library," Durand wrote, "may be considered on the one hand, as a public treasury enshrining the . . . knowledge of mankind, and on the other as a temple consecrated to study. Such a building must be organized to ensure the greatest security and tranquility. An enclosure, at the corners of which are placed the librarian's lodgings, the guard-rooms, and all those other parts where fires may be required, isolates the library proper from all other buildings. The construction which is entirely in stone, completes its defense against the danger of fire . . . The specific arrangement of its reading rooms, all converging upon the position

38

of the librarians at the center, would assure order and facilitate internal surveillance."

Durand's reference to surveillance ties the library design and the prison together. Nineteenth-century prisons reflected an ideal structure invented by the pragmatist British philosopher Jeremy Bentham. The twentieth-century French philosopher and social critic Michel Foucault made Bentham's concept a cornerstone of his analysis of punishment in industrial society. Called the panopticon, Bentham's ideal prison arranged the cells around a central core reserved for guards, who keep constant watch on the inmates. In Durand's plan, the circular reading room, with the library staff at its midpoint, serves the same purpose. Since the reader shares the central space with the librarians, however, it is also possible to see the library panopticon in a more benign way. Seated at the core of the treasure house of knowledge, the reader is poised to survey all of culture.

Ceremonial entrances at the top of the exterior stairway of the Library of Congress were intended to lead visitors into the building, but these grandiose doorways are rarely used. Reclining figures in the spandrels of their arches and masks at their summits surround cast bronze doors representing Tradition, Writing, and Printing. Access to the library is through the basement entrance under the stairway. On the main floor, just inside the bronze doors, a magnificent vestibule with gilded coffers in its stuccoed ceiling and marble facing on its arched openings leads to the Great Hall. (38) Statues of Minerva—the Roman equivalent of the Greek

Athena—stand in pairs
between each arch. Carved by
Herbert Adams, these figures
represent the goddess as a
symbol of knowledge in both
war and peace.

39

The soaring Great Hall was
designed as a magnificent
overture to the library, an ideal
as well as a pragmatic lobby
through which visitors move to the various offices and reading rooms. It
is a two-story space with stairways on each side. (39) Its form derives
from the elegant and impressive entry courtyards of Late Renaissance
and Baroque palaces. The brightly painted, multicolored ceiling is
recessed behind an ornate cornice. (40) Stained glass skylights with
images of peacock feathers are held up by griffins at each of its corners.
Standing directly opposite the entrances from the vestibule is an
enlarged arch with pairs of engaged columns on pedestals, an entabla-

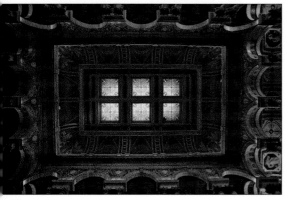

ture, and an attic. It is
modeled on a Roman
triumphal arch, and
inscriptions above it
identify the library and
memorialize the archi-
tects and engineers
who designed and built
it. (41)

40

41

If the exterior of the Jefferson Building recalls the west façade of the Capitol, the interior is clearly indebted to Brumidi's Corridors in the Senate wing. **(42)** The themes of the frescoes on the second-floor ceiling are eclectic and embrace—as the library's collection itself embraces—the spectrum of human activity. The American historical and philosophical prospect in the nineteenth century was universal. Frescoes in the North Corridor by Boston painter Charles Sprague Pearce illustrate Family, Recreation, Study, Labor **(43)**, Religion, and Rest. American poets, including Poe and Longfellow, and international poets, from the Greek Theocritus to the German Romantic Heinrich Heine, are represented somewhat surprisingly as seraphs or children in frescoes in the South Corridor. America was an ideal gateway through which the patrimony of European culture drove westward into a new continent.

The centerpiece of the library, both physically and philosophically, is the towering domed Main Reading Room. Earning admission to the great research libraries of the

42

world—the Bibliothèque Nationale in Paris, the Apostolic Vatican Library in Rome, or the British Library in London—is generally difficult. Potential readers and researchers are carefully screened, and only those with

scholarly credentials and significant research projects are welcome. The
Library of Congress is a democratic institution, and despite the current
climate of suspicion that pervades Washington, its collections and reading rooms remain open to anyone above high school age with valid identification.

As conceived in the nineteenth century, democratic citizenship was a
passport to the intellectual and artistic riches of the whole world—no
additional social status was required.
Individual readers may be feckless and
downtrodden, but the library receives
them into a structure of unrivaled
grandeur. In our era, which has become
accustomed to the linking of wealth with
privilege, the Library of Congress is an
almost shocking reminder of how craven

43

that association appeared to our forebears. Their democracy was imperfect in many ways, but they understood that public resources were for
public use, and that every citizen was entitled to that bounty. Against the
tide of exclusion and privatization, the contemporary Library of Congress
maintains that democratic tradition.

The Main Reading Room reflects many ideals. Durand's library plan is
evidently at the heart of it, but other structures also contributed to its
design and meaning. In the mid-nineteenth century, circular reading
rooms, which earlier had been an unrealized ideal of visionary French
architects, came into vogue. The old British Library's Reading Room was
an immense circular structure with a soaring iron dome pierced by huge

44

Romanesque windows. Ten years after the British Library was completed, Henri Labrouste designed a circular reading room for the Bibliothèque Nationale. Decades earlier and much closer to home, Jefferson designed a circular library for the University of Virginia. Based on the Pantheon and set at the end of a group of college buildings he called the Academical Village, Jefferson's library was the focal point of the campus. Of course the Capitol Rotunda as well as the Capitol exterior also served as a model for the Reading Room. Within a functional democratic institution, the Reading Room rotunda was a version not of Bulfinch's shrine to Washington but of Jefferson's original Hall of the People.

The interior of the Main Reading Room bears a clear relationship to the Capitol Rotunda in its coffered dome, lantern, and ornament. The most striking differences are in the proportions between cylindrical drum and hemispherical dome and in the structure of the lower levels of the room. A colossal arcade supported on massive piers of red Egyptian marble with gilded capitals encloses the octagonal space. (44) Demilune windows at the top of each arch flood the room with light. In a detail borrowed from imperial Roman architecture, smaller superimposed arcades link each pier. At ground level, each arcade has three openings; seven smaller arches above enclose the first balcony. Balustrades edge the second balcony at the level of the pier capitals. Statues representing abstractions, such as Art, and writers, including Homer and Shakespeare, top the balconies. Stucco figures on each capital represent Religion, Philosophy, Law, and Science.

In the fresco surrounding the oculus, allegorical figures stand between labeled plaques. (45) Its theme, the Progress of Civilization, was very dear to nineteenth-century sensibilities. Twelve figures represent the sequence of nations and artistic movements that propelled mankind from barbarism to enlightenment. The same conception that makes Cortés or Pizarro a part of North American history conspires here to enlist ancient Athens and the Italian Renaissance in the building of American culture. A second fresco inside the lantern represents human understanding. Its central figure is an image of Truth, who lifts her veil to reveal her face. She is flanked by putti. The signs of the Zodiac scroll along the edge of the dome below. Despite the pervasive religiosity of the nineteenth century and its universalizing of Christian revelation—well represented in the Rotunda paintings—it is noteworthy that any reference to a truth that transcends human understanding is absent here.

45

Seen from the Visitors' Gallery on the second floor, the main floor of the Reading Room centers on a counter reserved, as in Durand's plan, for the library staff. Readers' slant-topped desks in concentric rings fill the rest of the floor space. The arcades at each side open to a catalog and a reference collection of some seventy thousand volumes that readers are free to consult. Books from the closed stacks are ordered and delivered at the center desk. A gorgeously decorated Congressional Reading Room, off limits to visitors, occupies the pavilion at the southwest corner of the building, but legislators wishing to borrow books have never needed to actually go to the library. Orders can be placed from their offices, and books are delivered through underground tunnels.

After the Library of Congress left the Capitol, the congressional meeting rooms and offices were not far behind. The Capitol was once large enough to provide office space for every member of Congress, but by 1890 legislators were being housed wherever space was available. Some senators had offices in the Maltby building, a former hotel across the street from the Capitol grounds that was condemned within the decade. Responding to this real estate crisis in 1901, the Senate District Committee, headed by James McMillan of Michigan, appointed a Park Improvement Commission that included the architects Daniel Burnham and Charles Follen McKim, the landscape architect Frederick Law Olmsted Jr., and the prominent sculptor Augustus Saint-Gaudens. Burnham and Olmsted had worked together to create a master plan for the World's Columbian Exposition in Chicago, held in 1893. McKim, who trained at the École des Beaux Arts in Paris, was a leading advocate of neoclassical architecture. Within ten months, this select committee produced a remarkable document.

The McMillan Commission Report did not limit itself to the park system but took on the whole issue of development in the District of Columbia. The committee's recommendations revived the L'Enfant plan, both in concrete physical terms and in spirit. The members recognized that this

plan was not just an organization of space but was also
a grouping of functional
buildings that exemplified
and clarified the structure of
government. (Map 3) Deviations from this original
vision over more than a century had led to a muddled

46

mix of government and private structures in the center of the city. The
committee's first task was to restore clarity and order by regrouping government offices and reinstating the neoclassical style that had once distinguished them.

For the Capitol, they recommended the creation of a separate
Supreme Court building and the removal of some legislative offices. But
rather than scatter these government functions throughout the city, their
recommendations called for a cluster of buildings in the immediate
shadow of the Capitol itself. In 1909 the first of these outbuildings, an
external Senate office building in the French Beaux Arts neoclassical
style, was opened near the northeast corner of the Capitol grounds. (Map 4)
The stately building, with its rusticated lower story and colonnaded upper
levels, is, like the Capitol, an offshoot of the High Renaissance palazzo
style of Bramante and Raphael. Set on an irregular plot, its main entry is
in an oblique corner to the northeast of the Capitol. (46) And like the
Library of Congress, its Italianate origins were filtered through French
neoclassicism. In 1972 the building was renamed in honor of Senator

Richard Russell of Georgia. The nearby Dirksen (1958) and Hart (1982) buildings have since extended the office space available to senators.

Typical of the sibling rivalry between the two legislative chambers, the Senate and House have an equal number of office buildings, even though the House has more than four times as many incumbents as the Senate. The Cannon Building is identical to the Russell Building, and its site opposite the southeast corner of the Capitol mirrors that of its Senate counterpart. When a sweeping redistricting in 1910 increased the number of representatives, a second building, later named Longworth, was begun, though it was not completed until 1933. The Rayburn Building, completed in 1965, is the most recent. These three buildings line up along Independence Avenue, and their names, voted long after construction, commemorate notable speakers of the House.

The standing committees of the House and Senate, which carry on most of the work of each chamber, have also migrated from the Capitol to new quarters in these buildings. The Senate Caucus Room in the Russell Building is large enough to hold party meetings. It has also been the scene of some of the most notorious and significant Senate hearings. Special committees met here to investigate the sinking of the *Titanic* in 1912 and the Teapot Dome scandal that shattered Harding's administration. Senator Joseph McCarthy conducted his infamous hearings there in 1954, and the Senate Watergate Committee held the room in 1973.

When the Senate moved into its new wing in the Capitol just before the outbreak of the Civil War, the Supreme Court moved upstairs from its basement grotto into the luxurious quarters of the old Senate chamber. If the Court had required nothing more than a glorious room in which to hear oral arguments, it might never have moved again. But justices, like legislators, needed offices for themselves and their growing staffs, conference rooms where they could discuss and vote on cases, a law library they could access easily, and storage rooms for archives. In 1929, almost three decades after the McMillan Commission Report, the chief justice and former president William Howard Taft convinced Congress that the Court required its own home.

Architect Cass Gilbert, who had designed the Woolworth Building in New York City, at one time the world's tallest, and who had consulted on the design of the George Washington Bridge, was commissioned. Gilbert's architectural style combined modern technology with period styles. His Woolworth tower is Gothic in inspiration but soars eight hundred feet in the air. Its steel frame allows it to reach three or four times the height of any true Gothic structure. In many of the public buildings he designed for states and cities throughout the country, Gilbert worked in the neo-classical style.

In 1929 the site opposite the north wing of the Capitol where the Court would be built was still occupied by the old Brick Capitol. Erected in haste after the invasion of 1814, the building that was once the temporary home of the federal government had served as a barracks for refugee slaves during the early months of the Civil War. Southern spies and prisoners of war were held there also. In the last decades before its destruction, the building served as the headquarters of the National Woman's Party.

While the Library of Congress takes its form from the west façade of the Capitol, the design of the Supreme Court building, next door to the

Jefferson Building, is based most directly on Meigs and Walter's design for the Capitol's extensions. The building's main feature is a classical porch with multiple columns and a pediment set at the top of a sweeping staircase. (47) Sustained by an interior steel frame, this temple front is four stories tall. The central section of the building stretches behind it at the same height. Two lower, unornamented wings project on either side. An elliptical piazza with a flagpole and round fountain at each end stands in front of the building. Its marble pavement is marked by a white grid that encloses squares of dark marble. Inside each alternate patch is an inset circle or square. This pattern, based on the floor of the Pantheon, gives this exterior space the suggestion of a rotunda—a feature that was hard to leave out in any imitation of the Capitol.

Like the façades of the Library of Congress and the Capitol, the outside of the Supreme Court is thronged with allegorical sculptures. Two large marble candelabra set the scene. Their bases hold relief sculptures of Justice and the Three Fates. Massive seated figures on both sides of the main steps represent the two faces of jurisprudence. On the left, a female figure stands for the Contemplation of Justice. The male figure on the right represents a more active guardianship of the Authority of Law.

The equally programmatic pediment figures embody other aspects and benefits of the law. The center figure of Liberty is surrounded by personifications of Order, Authority, Council, and Research. The sculptures are portraits of actual people, including Taft as a young man and the architect Gilbert. Like the Capitol and Library of Congress, the Supreme Court has its own figured bronze doors that depict a wide-ranging history. A judgment scene from the *Iliad* and a scene representing Roman law

occupy spaces alongside
such lawgivers as Moses and
the Greek Solon. Here, for
the first time, a non-Western
philosopher, Confucius, is
included in what is otherwise the typical American
survey of world culture.

47

Though skillfully done,
these figures share a com-
mon failure. As abstractions in human form, they belong to a long tradition of representation, but as individual icons they have no history that
fixes their form and attributes, and so in practical terms they have no
identity. The visitor to the Supreme Court—or to the Capitol, for that
matter—is likely to be impressed by the sculptures but unlikely to learn
anything from them. They are pure architectural ornament, the neoclassical equivalent of gargoyles.

   Long before pictorial realism died in the third or fourth decade of the
twentieth century, pictorial symbolism had become extinct. Traditions of
iconography, especially well developed in religious painting, had made it
possible for an experienced viewer to easily recognize an Annunciation or
a Deposition and to distinguish an image of Saint Barbara from Saint
Catherine, John the Baptist from Saint Sebastian. As if anticipating a crisis of skepticism, religious painting in the nineteenth century lost all the
dynamism evinced in the works of Michelangelo or Caravaggio and sank
to the level of stereotyped and uninspired decoration.

The tradition of nonreligious allegorical painting lived on in nineteenth-century history painting, but it relied increasingly on detailed, specific programs. By the mid-nineteenth century, neither painters nor sculptors shared a reliable vocabulary of visual symbols with their audiences. Brumidi was trained in the last decades in which allegorical painting was still possible. The sculptors who decorated the Supreme Court building nearly a century later were fighting against the main thrust of contemporary art, which not only had abandoned allegory but despised it, and to an increasing extent shunned verisimilitude and the human figure altogether.

The Supreme Court's early history of confinement in the Capitol basement was not just a matter of finding space but a reflection of the Court's marginal status in the government. It is the most fluid and the least defined of the three branches. The Constitution's framers were careful to spell out how many senators and representatives there might be, and to provide for a chief justice. But they were silent on the number of associate justices. In 1789 Congress set the number of associates at five. In 1807 a sixth was added. In the middle of the Civil War the number was upped to nine. In the aftermath of the war the number was reduced to six—a total that was to be achieved by waiting for three justices to retire. Before they did, however, the numbers were changed once again. From 1869 to the present the Supreme Court has consisted of eight associate justices and a chief justice.

Pressures to increase or reduce the number have always been driven by politics. Southern justices on the Civil War Court were countered by new Republican appointees. Congress reduced the number of justices

after the war ended so that President Johnson could make no appointments to the Court. Under Grant, who was considered safer than Johnson, Congress reinstated the traditional number. Dismayed at the Court's
repeated striking down of New Deal legislation, Franklin Roosevelt threatened to pack the court with additional justices, but he never did.

The nine justices hear arguments in a lofty rectangular chamber. The
considerable dignity the room projects reflects their reputations and the
solemnity of the proceedings. The space itself is as lifeless and unimaginative as a high school auditorium. The judges' curved bench is backed
by four Ionic columns screened with red velvet curtains. Ionic colonnades
along both sides of the room open onto long aisles with high windows. A
double row of wooden benches for spectators fills the center space.
Desks for opposing counsel sit at the front of the benches.

Friezes in low relief decorate the upper walls between the entablature
and the coffered ceiling. The friezes on the side walls of the room show a
long procession of lawgivers, starting with Menes of Egypt and Ham-
murabi of Babylon and passing through the familiar Greeks, Bible figures,
Confucius, and the Roman Octavian. The cycle continues through Late
Antiquity, where Justinian and Muhammad are shown, then through the
Middle Ages and on to the eighteenth century, where the parade ends
with the English commentator on the law, Sir William Blackstone, the
Emperor Napoleon, and Chief Justice John Marshall. The two narrow
walls include figures representing Wisdom, the Majesty of the Law, and a
chorus of figures meant to illustrate the Defense of Human Rights and
the Protection of Innocence. Like the allegorical figures outside, these
personifications are impossible to decode without an authoritative guide.

48

The Sewall-Belmont House across Constitution Avenue from the Court is one of the earliest surviving structures on Capitol Hill. **(48)** Built about 1800 on a lot drawn in L'Enfant's plan, the brick Federal style house with its dormers and hipped roof was one of very few nongovernment buildings set afire by the British in 1814. Damage to the house was minimal, and it remained in the Sewall family until the 1920s. In 1929, when the old Brick Capitol was destroyed to make way for the Supreme Court Building, the National Woman's Party needed a new home. They bought the Sewall-Belmont House, which they still occupy.

Exhibits inside document the history of the organization that was founded by Alice Paul in 1917 and its often troubled relations with the National American Woman Suffrage Association. The goal of both groups was passage of an amendment to the Constitution permitting women to vote. Originally proposed in 1878 by Susan B. Anthony, the amendment finally passed the House and Senate in 1919. In 1920 it was ratified as the Nineteenth Amendment. Once the voting rights amendment was passed, Paul and her organization began to lobby for passage of a second amendment that would grant equal rights to women. More than fifty years later, Congress passed the ERA guaranteeing that "equality of rights under the law shall not be denied or abridged by the United States or by any state on account of sex." The amendment failed when it was ratified by only thirty-five states. It has been reintroduced in each successive Congress since 1972.

Diagonally across East Capitol Street from the Supreme Court and directly behind the Library of Congress stands a privately funded research library with an unrivaled special collection. The Folger Shakespeare Library is nearly contemporary with the Court building. Designed by Paul Philippe Cret in a style meant to harmonize with the buildings around it, the Folger avoids direct use of the neoclassical vocabulary of columns and entablatures. A marble-faced block with a file of steep windows along its sides, the building appears to be a rectilinear reworking of the Senate and House office buildings. The fluted slabs of wall between the Folger's windows are like the columns on those buildings; the blank wall above, separated from the windows by a thin cornice, is the equivalent of an entablature. Cret intended to place decorative friezes illustrating scenes from Shakespeare's plays in this upper space, but the Folger family asked that the scenes be placed below the windows so they could be seen more readily. The doors and windows are shielded by aluminum grilles in Art Deco style.

Henry Clay Folger, long-term president of Standard Oil of New Jersey, and his wife, Emily Jordan Folger, were collectors of Shakespeare publications. In 1879, while he was a student at Amherst College, Folger heard Ralph Waldo Emerson lecture on the playwright. The talk inspired a lifetime of serious and adventurous acquisition. When the Folgers decided to build a library for their collection, they chose Washington and spent many years buying bits and pieces of property on Capitol Hill. According to Emily Folger, the library was dedicated to a poet who "is one of our best sources, one of the wells from which we Americans draw our national thought, our faith and our hope." In addition to an unmatched collection of books and manuscripts related to Shakespeare and his era, the library houses a reproduction of a typical Elizabethan theater, where plays are regularly performed.

Union Station, just north of the Capitol, is one of Washington's most magnificent buildings. (49) The structure was a crucial piece of the McMillan Commission's plan, and it was also one of the few projects they recommended that was immediately carried out in the form they advised. At the end of the nineteenth century, each of the railroads serving Washington had its own train station, and one of them stood right on the Mall at Fourth Street. Its tracks crossed the Mall and ran at grade level along downtown streets and avenues. The removal of this terminal and its tracks was essential to the commission's goal of restoring the Mall to L'Enfant's original conception and revitalizing Pennsylvania Avenue.

Commission member Daniel Burnham designed the massive new train station in the first decade of the twentieth century. As one of the principal architects of the Chicago Exposition, he had created exotic pavilions and engaging vistas; but one of the greatest strengths of the fair's design had been crowd management,

49

both within the site and between the site and the city. This success made Burnham an excellent choice to envisage a station that would serve

as a gateway to Washington for thousands of visitors. Its location was but a short walk to Capitol
Hill and the Mall, and accessible to the downtown shopping district as well as the White
House. Massachusetts Avenue, which passed
directly in front, and North Capitol Street, along
the station's western side, led to residential
areas throughout the District.

Covering more than twenty-five acres, Burnham's enormous building was based on the
largest and most magnificent of Roman struc-

50

tures, the imperial baths. These opulent, multi-acre complexes featured a
suite of central vaulted rooms of dizzying length and height. The buildings both sheltered great crowds and accommodated their movement
from one room to another as they followed the set itinerary of the baths.
At the edges of the complex, aqueducts led off through the city toward
the hills, where water was fresh and abundant. Burnham, along with
many other neoclassical architects of the late nineteenth century, realized
that the Roman imperial baths could serve as an excellent model for a
train station.

Waiting rooms, ticket offices, even tracks could be sheltered under
enormous vaults. **(50)** Iron and glass could be substituted for the heavy
Roman masonry, but the columns, piers, and entablatures that they used
as supports could be retained. The rich decoration of the baths, an
emblem of imperial generosity, could be recreated as a symbol of the
grandeur of the city itself. And even the aqueducts could be reconceived

as viaducts carrying tracks above street level in and out of the city. The adaptation of Roman bath architecture to the demands of the railroad, with its reputation for dynamic modernism, was one of the last great successes of the Neoclassical movement.

Rail lines running to every section of the country served Union Station. Millions of passengers passed through it, and at the height of its success during World War II nearly a quarter of a million people arrived or departed from the building every day. But by the late 1950s a steep decline in passengers, caused by expansion of the highway system and the growing acceptance of air travel, led the railroads to pull back, and Union Station was all but abandoned. It was reconfigured at great expense as a National Visitor Center in 1968 but was seldom visited. In 1978 it closed. But Congress, to its great credit, passed the Union Station Redevelopment Act in 1981, which called for the secretary of commerce to establish a workable plan for an adaptive reuse that would make the building self-sufficient. A public-private partnership rearranged and refurbished the structure to house a mall of more than a hundred shops and restaurants. Office spaces in the building became the headquarters of Amtrak. Since its opening in 1988, this beautiful station with its frequent exhibitions and interesting, well-placed shops has been a commercial and aesthetic success. It draws more visitors than any other Washington site.

To the southeast of Union Station, Massachusetts Avenue meets five other avenues—and East Capitol Street—at Lincoln Park. This intersection was highly significant within the symbolic geometry of L'Enfant's design. Major transportation arteries radiated outward from this hub; and

through intermediate squares, the park served as a symbolic counter-
weight to the Capitol. Long before the Lincoln Memorial was planned to
meet this need at the west end of the central axis, Lincoln Park stood in
a similar position to the east. During the Civil War, the square was occupied by a temporary hospital named for President Lincoln. After his
assassination, Congress named the square in his honor. Despite its
prominence on L'Enfant's plan, at the time of its dedication in 1867 the
square sat at the outer edge of settlement. Fields marked by a few scattered houses stretched in every direction toward the Anacostia River. The
undeveloped landscape looked much as it had in 1790.

After Lincoln's assassination, Charlotte Scott, an ex-slave from Virginia, donated the first wages she earned as a free woman to the project
for a Freedmen's Memorial Monument near the center of Lincoln Park.
Funded by contributions Scott raised from other former slaves, the new
monument was unveiled in 1876, on the eleventh anniversary of Lincoln's assassination and the centennial of the Declaration of Independence. In the bronze group sculpted by Thomas Ball, Lincoln stands with
his arm outstretched over a kneeling slave. The figure is Archer Alexander, the last slave captured and returned to bondage under the terms of
the Fugitive Slave Act. Lincoln's right hand grasps a copy of the Emancipation Proclamation. The document rests on top of a column-shaped
Roman altar. Fasces decorate each edge of the altar; two of them frame a
portrait bust of Washington in low relief.

In 1974 a sculptural group representing Mary McLeod Bethune and
two young children was dedicated at the eastern end of the park.
Bethune, a pioneer in education and women's clubs, founder of the

51

National Council of Negro Women, and vice president of the NAACP, was the first woman and only the second African American to be memorialized by a public monument in Washington.

The Capitol neighborhood spreads beyond the tight enclave of official buildings on Jenkins Hill. The homogeneous solid ground on the threshold of the piedmont spreads to the Anacostia River on the east and south, and this area became the home of many public markets that once fed the District. The Eastern Market, stretching along Seventh Street SE for nearly a block at C Street, is one of only two survivors. Designed by Adolph Cluss and built in 1873, the South Hall, with its extension and open cast-iron pavilion, is made of brick and decorated with granite. An entryway at its center is divided into three bays and topped with a cornice and central pediment supported on brackets. In the long wings to either side, alternating wide and narrow bays, their summits decorated with pensile arches, frame windows and doors topped by porthole-shaped oculi. Vendors' trucks are parked outside; inside, two long aisles of permanent booths sell local meats, poultry, seafood, produce, and baked goods to neighborhood shoppers. (51)

In 1775 the Continental Congress authorized the raising of "two battalions of marines," and in 1798 the U.S. Congress passed a bill creating the United States Marine Corps. Two years later, when the federal government moved from Philadelphia to Washington, the Marine Corps also relocated. Eighteenth-century marines were amphibious foot soldiers assigned to naval vessels but trained to fight on land. The site of their

new barracks, midway between the new Navy Yard on the Anacostia River
and the Capitol, suggests that Congress had both these capabilities in
mind. The original barracks were two-story brick dormitories laid out
around three sides of an open parade ground. The commandant's house,
built in 1806, was placed on the fourth side. The barracks were also the
headquarters of the Marine Band. Between 1880 and 1892, John Philip
Sousa was its director. During his tenure he wrote "Semper Fidelis" and
the "Washington Post March." In 1939 a bridge crossing the Anacostia
River at Pennsylvania Avenue was named in his honor.

The Washington Navy Yard was established in 1799 on land along the
Anacostia River reserved for federal use in L'Enfant's plan. Its boundary,
marked out a year later, is still traced by a brick wall laid in 1806. The
yard quickly became the navy's main producer of warships and served as
a harbor where even large vessels like the USS *Constitution* could dock
for repair and refitting. When British troops broke through American lines
at Bladensburg in 1814, the yard was burned to keep it from falling into
enemy hands. In the early nineteenth century, silting of the Anacostia
River and the increasing size and draught of warships ended the Navy
Yard's shipbuilding career. After the middle of the nineteenth century, its
specialty shifted to weapons manufacture.

While the Navy Yard's importance grew during the Civil War, space
was still available and many refugee slaves were housed there. At the end
of the war, six of the Lincoln assassination conspirators were imprisoned
on ironclad ships anchored off the yard. Today, one of the shops of the
former Gun Factory houses the Navy Museum, which illustrates the history of the navy from the Revolution to the present. Its exhibits include

model ships, uniforms, guns, paintings, and photographs as well as larger artifacts. The Navy Art Museum is especially rich in paintings and photographs from World War II to the present.

The Navy Yard was soon surrounded by tracts of working-class housing, some of which still survive. The demand for nearby housing led to the construction of the first bridge across the Anacostia River in 1804 and the development of small communities on the far side. In 1862—one of the darkest years of the Civil War—the Washington and Georgetown Railroad Company began running horse-drawn trolleys along standard-gauge track laid down the middle of Pennsylvania Avenue. The first line ran from Georgetown in the northwest, past the White House and Capitol, to the Navy Yard in the southeast. Horse cars were a common form of urban transit in many U.S. cities in this period. In most of them, African Americans, whether free or slave, were barred from riding with whites and had to wait for the infrequent Jim Crow cars.

Sojourner Truth, a former slave who became a champion of emancipation and liberation, refused to comply. "Unwilling to submit to this state of things, she complained to the president of the street railroad, who ordered the Jim Crow car to be taken off. A law was now passed giving the colored people equal car privileges with the white. Not long after this, Sojourner, having occasion to ride, signaled the car, but neither conductor nor driver noticed her. Soon another followed, and she raised her hand again, but they also turned away. She then gave three tremendous yelps, 'I want to ride! I want to ride!! I WANT TO RIDE!!!' Consternation seized the passing crowd—people, carriages, go-carts of every description stood still. The car was effectually blocked up, and before it could move

on, Sojourner had jumped aboard . . . The angry conductor told her to go
forward where the horses were, or he would put her out. Quietly seating
herself, she informed him that she was a passenger. 'Go forward where
the horses are, or I will throw you out,' said he in a menacing voice. She
told him that she was neither a Marylander nor a Virginian to fear his
threats; but was from the Empire State of New York and knew the laws as
well as he did" (*Narrative of Sojourner Truth*).

The Congressional Cemetery, some thirty acres in extent near the Anacostia River just north of Pennsylvania Avenue SE, was organized in
1807 by a group of Capitol Hill residents. In 1812 land along the river
was deeded to Christ Episcopal Church, and soon after part of it was set
aside for burial of members of Congress. The relationship with the federal
government was never clear, congressional attention was wayward as ever,
and over the years only a few congressmen have actually been buried in
the cemetery. Every one of the hundreds who died while serving in Congress between 1807 and 1877, however, was honored by a peculiar and
forbidding cenotaph designed by Capitol architect Benjamin Latrobe. A
sandstone cube, inset with an inscribed marble panel honoring the
deceased, sits on a rectangular base. Atop each cube is a circular cap
with a conical tip that looks a little like
the stub of a sharpened pencil. These
strange monuments combine the cube,
cylinder, and triangle in a way that recalls
the pure geometry of eighteenth-century
French visionary architecture. **(52)**

In 1835 Congress appropriated funds

52

to build a Public Vault where bodies could be sheltered until permanent burial was arranged. John Quincy Adams, William Henry Harrison, and Zachary Taylor were its most notable temporary occupants. William Thornton, the first designer of the Capitol, is buried in the cemetery, along with John Philip Sousa and Mathew Brady, the photographer famous for his images of the Civil War.

Obelisks are prominent among the cemetery's monuments, along with statues of all kinds. A vertical cannon resting improbably on four cannon balls honors Navy Lieutenant John T. McLaughlin. A late Victorian monument dedicated to Marion Ooletia Kahlert features a life-sized statue of the ten-year-old. The Arsenal Monument remembers victims of a June 17, 1864, explosion and fire at the Washington arsenal at Fort McNair on the south shore of the Anacostia. Rocket shells carelessly stored exploded and tore through a long shed where one hundred and eight women were at work making cartridges. Twenty-one were killed and many more wounded. Lincoln and Stanton attended the mass funeral and rode in a procession of more than a hundred carriages to the graveside commemoration in Congressional Cemetery. The tall spire of the Arsenal Monument is topped by a brooding angel carved by Lot Flannery.

After years of neglect, the cemetery was rescued by a group of volunteers organized as the Association for the Preservation of Historic Congressional Cemetery. Under their care, the monuments and grounds have been restored. Though thick with gravestones, the cemetery gives a sense of the landscape of Washington in its earliest years—the wide fields of the floodplain, edged with trees, open to low wooded hills that mark the beginning of the piedmont.

Chapter Five

THE PRESIDENT'S HOUSE

L'Enfant set aside eighty acres for the President's Grounds and projected an executive mansion that rivaled the Louvre. In March 1792, after the contentious Frenchman had been fired, Congress announced a competition to design a smaller house. While the Capitol design competition, which was held at the same time, had clear guidelines, the ground rules for the President's House competition were few and general. It was assumed that the building would be built where L'Enfant had placed it, near the edge of solid ground just north of Tiber Creek.

Contestants were urged to study the contours of the site, but the "Number, Size and Distribution" of the rooms in the house were left to the designer's sense of what was appropriate. The clearest guideline was one that seemed to look back wistfully at L'Enfant's grand scheme: "It will be a recommendation of any Plan, if the central Part of it may be detached and erected for the present, with the Appearance of a complete whole, and be capable of admitting the additional Parts, in future, if they shall be wanting." This would have been an excellent proviso for the Capitol, which continued to grow beyond the limits of Thornton's design until the Civil War. One of the most striking features of the history of the White House is the resolute preservation of the building in its eighteenth-century form.

The seven entries received by the July 15 deadline included one that Jefferson submitted anonymously. His design called for a domed, centrally planned house that was based on Andrea Palladio's Villa Rotunda near Vicenza. James Diamond's scheme also adapted the work of this great sixteenth-century Italian architect. Andrew Carshore's proposal featured a multistory center block like the college buildings at Harvard that could be extended in time by the addition of wings. Jacob Small, a Baltimore builder, submitted a series of plans based on similar models. An eighth entry that arrived on July 16—one day late—was refused.

On July 17, President Washington and the District commissioners chose the winner—a drawing of a three-story mansion in the popular Georgian style submitted by the Irish architect James Hoban. Hoban had attended architectural lectures at the Drawing School of the Dublin Society for Promoting Husbandry and Other Useful Arts, before emigrating to the United States in the late eighteenth century. He designed the now largely forgotten first State House in Columbia, South Carolina, which burned during the Civil War.

Hoban's winning entry was in part inspired by a plate in James Gibbs's 1728 *Book of Architecture.* The proposed elevation and some details of the floor plan were also very close to those of Leinster House in Dublin. This building had an areaway (a sunken space that allows light and air to the basement), a ground floor with a rusticated central bay, and a doorway approached by a flight of stairs. The rustication supported an applied portico on the face of the three-story upper façade. Hoban's original submission had only two stories, but at Washington's suggestion he added a third floor. Both Washington and the commissioners found this revised submission appealing but too expensive.

Hoban lowered the building once again, by removing the first story. This did away with most of the visible rustication on the principal (north) façade and brought the portico down to ground level, where it absorbed the entryway. An elaborate cornice and pediment marked by dentils remained unchanged. Hoban added a balustrade at the roofline that Leinster House lacked. **(53)** The windows in the areaway were surrounded by alternating rough and ribbed blocks, a pattern that in English architecture was

53

known as Gibbs rustication. The sills of the first floor windows were supported on brackets and had alternating peaked and curved lintels.

The south side was identical to the principal façade along Pennsylvania Avenue, with two exceptions. The applied temple front was replaced by a cylindrical bulge (apse), and, according to one of his few surviving drawings, Hoban intended to place a portico along the entire south face of the building that would trace its irregular outline. Sweeping stairs led from the portico down to ground level. The basement area that was hidden by the height of land on the north side was exposed in the back. The elevations of the shorter east and west sides were compatible but slightly different from the main faces of the building. Pilasters on short pedestals stretched from the first floor to the entablature at the top of the third story, dividing the façades into five bays. Four of these contained vertical pairs of windows identical to those on the front, while the wider center bay framed a Palladian window on the main floor and a demilune window on the floor above.

The entire structure was built of bricks made on the site and of tawny aquia sandstone from Virginia. The porous stone was sealed with a protective coating of lime that gave it a snowy sheen. The white-washed house was still unfinished when President John Adams and his family moved in during the last months of 1800, at the very end of his term. Adams lived in the house for only four months before Thomas Jefferson succeeded him. Benjamin Latrobe sketched a floor plan of the house in 1803 and made notes on the way the various rooms were used during the two administrations. (54) A wooden platform spanned the areaway on the north side of the house, like a drawbridge over a moat, and led to an entrance hall outlined by engaged columns and a pediment. Instead of Hoban's portico, a wooden deck surrounded the southern projection, and wooden stairs led down to the ground.

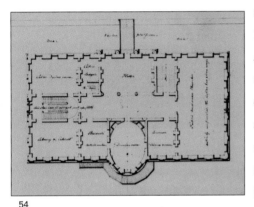

54

Adams used this improvised south-facing entry as the principal door to the building. The oval room partly outlined by the central bulge was the vestibule where the president greeted guests. Standing under Gilbert Stuart's portrait of Washington and dressed in an identical black velvet suit, Adams received visitors with a formality that gave antifederalists the willies. The east end of the building held a single room that ran the full depth of the house. Called the East Room, it has been the main reception room throughout the history of the White House. In Latrobe's sketch, this room was called the Public Audience Chamber. Latrobe described it as "entirely unfinished, the ceiling has given way." Abigail Adams is said to have used the unlovely and drafty space to hang the presidential laundry.

Jefferson immediately moved the primary entrance of the house around to the more formal north side. To access the doorway, Latrobe later designed and supervised construction of an arched stone bridge across the areaway. Inside the front door, visitors stepped into a rectangular atrium, separated by a colonnade from a wide transverse hall, now called the Cross Hall. This central corridor channeled visitors to the left, in the direction of the East Room, or to the right, toward what Jefferson called the Public Dining Room on the northwest corner of the building. Stairs at the end of the hall next to this dining room led to the second floor residence. The door to the elliptical room Adams had made his vestibule was at the center of the corridor. Jefferson used it as the Drawing Room. Like so many features of the White House, this oval room (which is now the Blue Room) was based on similarly shaped salons in a handful of Irish great houses of the eighteenth century.

Jefferson's Common Dining Room, intended for everyday use, was between the East Room and the Drawing Room on the south. Jefferson's office, labeled Library or Cabinet on Latrobe's sketch, was in the southwest corner. It could be reached directly from the base of the stairs to the residence or indirectly from a small antechamber that opened onto both the Cross Hall and the oval room. Jefferson's office suite began with the Drawing Room and led through the antechamber into his corner sanctum. Since Jefferson conducted most official business in the two outer rooms, this inner chamber was a place that few outsiders entered. Margaret Bayard Smith, a frequent visitor, described a long table in the center, books on high shelves, and maps, globes, and charts around the walls. Evidently several desks and writing tables were positioned around the room, and potted plants, which Jefferson himself tended, sat on the window ledges. The president kept a mockingbird in a cage, which he occasionally let free to fly around the room.

All other offices of the Executive Branch of government were outside the President's House. To the east and west, where the Treasury and the Executive Office buildings now stand, were structures housing the War Department and the Treasury. Jefferson wanted to link these offices to the President's House in a convenient way that was also unobtrusive. He drew designs for long one-story service corridors that reached out from both sides of the central building. On their ground floors these buildings would make room for many of the functions that an eighteenth-century country house required, while flat terraces on the tops would provide direct access from Jefferson's office on the west and from the East Room.

Many of the houses that Palladio illustrated in his well-known *Four Books of Architecture* had service corridors of this type. Single-level, sometimes arcaded wings that connected main houses with pavilions to either side, these were the descendents of the ubiquitous porticoes in ancient Roman towns that created sheltered passages within villas, around the edges of piazzas, and along the sides of some important streets. Jefferson designed corridors like this at Monticello, which he called dependencies. Those he designed for the President's House included an insulated ice house, a coal cellar, rooms for servants, and a hen house.

Latrobe, who was generally respectful of his patron and comfortable with Jefferson's neoclassical tastes, was imprudently sarcastic about these dependencies. On May 3, 1805, in a nasty letter sent to John Lenthall that was misdirected and actually opened by Jefferson, Latrobe complained, "I am sorry I am cramped in this design by [Jefferson's] prejudices in favor of the old French books, out of which he fishes everything—but it is a small sacrifice to my personal attachment to him to humour him, and the less so, because the style of the colonnade he proposes is exactly consistent with Hoban's pile—a litter of pigs worthy of the great sow it surrounds, and of the wild Irish boar, the father of her." Despite Latrobe's disdain, Jefferson's unobtrusive dependencies were built and, in one form or another, have remained a part of the President's House to this day.

Latrobe was making plans for further renovations when the British raid of August 1814 caught President James Madison and his household by surprise. While British troops overwhelmed American forces a few miles north on the Bladensburg Road, Dolley Madison hurriedly gathered the president's papers and those of his cabinet and loaded them into her carriage, along with some books, silver, and the velvet curtains from the oval room. In a letter to her sister, the first lady described her most important job:

"Our kind friend, Mr. Carroll, has come to hasten my departure, and is in a very bad humor with me, because I insist on waiting until the large

picture of General Washington is secured, and it requires to be
unscrewed from the wall. This process was found too tedious for these
perilous moments; I have ordered the frame to be broken, and the canvas
taken out. It is done! and the precious portrait placed in the hands of
two gentlemen of New York, for safe keeping. And now, dear sister, I
must leave this house, or the retreating army will make me a prisoner in
it by filling up the road I am directed to take. When I shall again write to
you, or where I shall be to-morrow, I cannot tell!" The stretched canvas
was hidden in a farmhouse somewhere on the outskirts of Georgetown.

After setting fire to the Capitol, British marines marched in silent
close order down Pennsylvania Avenue to the President's House. The surprising events that followed were graphically described in 1821 by
George Robert Gleig, a young divinity student from Oxford who fought for
the British: "When the detachment sent out to destroy Mr. Madison's
house, entered his dining parlor, they found a dinner-table spread, and
covers laid for forty guests . . . They sat down to it, therefore, not indeed
in the most orderly manner, but with countenances which would not have
disgraced a party of aldermen at a civic feast; and having satisfied their
appetites with fewer complaints than would have probably escaped their
rival gourmands, and partaken pretty freely of the wines, they finished by
setting fire to the house which had so liberally entertained them . . .

"This was a night of dismay to the inhabitants of Washington. They
were taken completely by surprise; nor could the arrival of the flood be
more unexpected to the natives of the antediluvian world, than the arrival
of the British army to them. The first impulse of course tempted them to
fly, and the streets were in consequence crowded with soldiers and sena-

tors, men, women, and children, horses, carriages, and carts loaded with household furniture, all hastening toward a wooden bridge which crosses the Potomac. The confusion thus occasioned was terrible, and the crowd upon the bridge was such as to endanger its giving way. But Mr. Madison, having escaped among the first, was no sooner safe on the opposite bank of the river than he gave orders that the bridge should be broken down; which being obeyed, the rest were obliged to return, and to trust to the clemency of the victors."

The torching of the house was systematic. Windows were broken out all around to increase ventilation; the president's books and papers, furniture, paintings, and draperies were piled in the center of the oval room. Fifty marines took up positions outside the house, each carrying a long pole with a basketball-sized mass of oil-soaked rags at its end. Once the house had been cleared of British personnel, live coals brought from a nearby tavern were used to ignite the long-handled torches. On command, the marines hurled the flaming poles through the broken windows like javelins. Dr. Thornton's wife described the result as "instantaneous conflagration . . . The whole building was wrapt in flames and smoke: The spectators stood in awful silence, the city was light and the heavens reddened with the blaze."

The fire burned out within a few hours. But the prodigious rainfall that preserved a portion of the Capitol saved only the stone shell of the President's House. (55) Madison was severely criticized for deserting his post, and even Dolley Madison, who remained in the city until the last moment and secured what little was saved from the house, became a target of abuse.

55

The devastation of the city and its evident vulnerability to attack renewed arguments for moving the nation's capital inland. Much had changed in the quarter century since Washington picked the site. The fact that the father of his country had chosen this place mattered less than it once did, and westward expansion made the coastal city less central. A site on the Ohio River near Cincinnati was discussed; it would be both secure from foreign invasion and nearer the geographic midpoint of the expanding country. In the larger political framework of the War of 1812, however, the Washington raid was equivocal. Despite the self-control of the troops and their sparing of lives and private property, the raid was not a public relations success in London. Rather than bolster the victors, it seems to have caused them embarrassment.

American spirits were lifted and a momentous political career was launched in 1815, when General Andrew Jackson led his troops to victory over British forces attempting to invade and capture New Orleans. Based in Jamaica, the British forces included two West Indian Regiments made up of free blacks. Some American slaves escaped from their masters and joined these regiments, which promised them emancipation. African Americans also fought on the American side. The First and Second Battalions of Free Men of Color commanded by the first African American officers commissioned in the United States were among the city's defenders. Soldiers from the Choctaw Indian tribe also served.

Though the battle occurred after the peace treaty had already been
signed, the decisive victory gave a great boost to American morale. Jackson became a national hero and the leading candidate for the presidency,
which he won for the first time in 1828. In the wake of the New Orleans
victory, the city of Washington ceased to be a symbol of defeat. It
became instead an innocent victim, a sacrifice that paved the road to victory. A renewed desire to rebuild the capital where it was and (at least in
outward appearance) as it was reflected that change of attitude.

In the last months of 1814, while the Madisons were still in disgrace
and the displacement of the capital was an open question, George Hadfield was commissioned to survey the damage to the President's House.
Hadfield had served briefly as Capitol architect and was in private practice in Washington. He would soon become the designer of Arlington
House, the Custis-Lee mansion just across the Potomac. With his career
rooted in the threatened capital, Hadfield had every reason to underesti-
mate the damage to the executive mansion, and that is what he did.
While he acknowledged the complete destruction of the principal floors of
the interior, he asserted that a great portion of the exterior "remains
uninjured, as also the greater part of the Basement Story." On the
strength of his report and in the giddy aftermath of Jackson's victory,
Congress appropriated half a million dollars to rebuild the President's
House, along with the Treasury and War buildings. The two office blocks
were finished first.

Madison emphasized to all involved that the work was a "rebuilding"
and that in no particular were the new structures to deviate from those
the British had destroyed. In keeping with this policy, and also to free
Latrobe to restore the Capitol, James Hoban was called back into service

as the project's reanimator. Work began in the spring with a careful cleaning of the site and a detailed inspection of the outer walls, block by block. What the inspectors discovered was that much of the damage had been caused by the soaking rain that quenched the fire. The sandstone cracked as it expanded in the heat; then it cracked again as it cooled and contracted in the drenching rain. In 1816, after Congress adjourned, Hoban and his crew took down every part of the north wall except the middle third. Even in that relatively well-preserved section, both the pediment and capitals of the engaged columns required replacement.

The corners on the east were sound, but the midsection of the eastern wall, with its columns, Palladian doorway, and arched window, had to be dismantled. No portion of the west wall remained stable enough to stand. The damage extended around the corner to the south wall. The area around the great bulge was the least damaged of all. From that curve eastward and around the corner, the original wall stood firm. Hadfield had been indeed optimistic—or calculating. In the end, less than half of the outer fabric was worthy of preservation.

Stonecutters, many hired in New York, were at work on the site for a year before the cracked walls were pulled down. As soon as demolition was complete in one section, masons began setting new blocks, and the rebuilt walls rose rapidly. They were liberally covered with a milky paint composed of lime and linseed oil. Many people believe that this innovation was intended to cover blocks blackened by smoke, and they date the name White House to this era. But in fact the house had been covered with whitewash to seal the block since the building's completion in the 1790s, and the name White House was in use informally as early as the Jefferson administration. The new coating was more durable than white-

wash, however. And more impor-
tantly, it disguised the joining of
old and new block and made the
extent of the repair to the house
impossible to assess.

56

After the walls were sealed
and the house was roofed, carpenters began working on the interior.
Hoban's original house had brick and stone partitions and subfloors. In
the rebuilt house, he substituted wood for most of the interior structure.
This speeded up the work, but it made for a weaker and less durable
building. Between 1948 and 1952, during Harry Truman's second term,
the house was gutted and every bit of the interior structure Hoban's carpenters had built in the aftermath of the fire was replaced with steel and
concrete.

In 1807 Latrobe had drawn an east elevation that showed important
changes to Hoban's original design, but the house had been torched

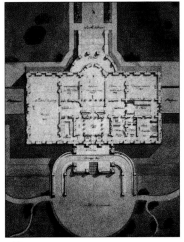

before the plans could be executed. (56)
On the north face, Latrobe had called
for the conversion of the pedimented
centerpiece into a three-dimensional
extension. On the south side, a portico
around the projecting apse replaced
Hoban's original colonnade running
across the entire façade. (57)

After the fire, both Hoban and
Latrobe drew new designs for this structure. Latrobe's scheme featured a cen-

57

tral stairway. Hoban's drawing showed smaller stairs at each side, follow-ing the curve of the apse in the basement section—a design that recalled the wooden stairway Jefferson removed from the apse when he reoriented the interior of the house toward its doorway on the north. Though archi-tectural historians are divided over whom to credit for the final design of the colonnade around the apse, they all acknowledge that Hoban directed

its construction. In 1824 the two-story Ionic colonnade with its simple entablature was com-pleted. Hoban's off-center stair-cases connect its terraced floor to the grounds. (58)

The house was still unfin-ished when James Monroe, the

58

last of the founders to serve as president, was inaugurated on March 4, 1817. A student at William and Mary and an early volunteer in the Revo-lutionary War, Monroe was wounded in the Battle of Trenton. After resign-ing his commission, he read law with Jefferson, who was fifteen years his senior. In 1788 Monroe served on the Virginia body debating ratification of the Constitution. Because it did not provide for direct election of sena-tors or the president, and because it did not include a Bill of Rights, Monroe voted against it.

Despite his "no" vote, Monroe served as United States senator from Virginia. He was ambassador to France under Washington and Jefferson and secretary of state under Madison. With his wife, Elizabeth Kortright Monroe, the new president moved into an unfinished house in October. To cure the still-damp plaster, fires burned continually in fireplaces with-

out mantles. Floors and doors remained unvarnished, walls unpainted
and unpapered. For the next year, reception rooms were put in order
whenever protocol demanded that the house be opened to guests, and
then stripped of furnishings and turned over to the construction crews
after the guests departed.

Monroe's main contribution to American government was the doctrine
of foreign policy that bears his name. In his annual message to Congress
of December 2, 1823, Monroe stated that "we owe it . . . to candor and
to the amicable relations existing between the United States and [the
European powers] to declare that we should consider any attempt on
their part to extend their system to any portion of this hemisphere as
dangerous to our peace and safety." President John F. Kennedy would
invoke the Monroe Doctrine during the Cuban Missile Crisis of 1962, one

of the most dangerous moments
in the decades-long Cold War
with the Soviet Union.

By the time the hero of New
Orleans took office in 1829, the
White House was essentially
complete. On the north side of
the building, Latrobe's projecting
pedimented porch, designed as a

59

porte-cochere (a shelter that coaches can drive under to receive or discharge passengers), was at the center of a circular drive. At the front of
the porch, four Ionic columns supported on a continuous foundation and
pedestals carried an entablature and pediment decorated only with dentils. (59) Two columns at the sides of the porch were grouped between the

areaway and the drive. A balcony stood on top of the entablature and formed a second flat roofline behind the pediment.

New versions of Jefferson's wings were also in place. On the north side, they were hidden by the slope of the land, but their colonnaded fronts were visible across the treeless south lawn. A later drawing from the south, perhaps made by Thornton, shows a line of regularly spaced poplars in front of the wings that partially screened them from view. Jefferson's plan to extend these wings all the way to the executive offices on either side of the house was not carried out, however. Chickens, ice, beer, and apples were kept here, as they had been in Jefferson's day. Some of the slaves Andrew Jackson brought from his Nashville mansion lived in rooms along these corridors. When the breeze was favorable, guests at state dinners were forcefully reminded of the presence of stables at the end of the western projection.

Since Washington's administration, the Executive Branch of government had included five cabinet offices: attorney general and secretaries of state, treasury, war, and navy. During the 1816 rebuilding and expansion of the executive offices next to the President's House, the two buildings that had existed before the fire had grown into four. The State Department joined Treasury on the east side, and the Navy Department joined the War Department on the west. The four buildings housing these cabinet offices were of a piece. Each was a two- or three-story multi-windowed structure wider than deep, with a peaked roof, several chimneys, and a center bay topped with a pediment. The State and War buildings had applied columns under their pediments. Each structure was an easily recognizable version of the executive mansion. Just as the much later

Library of Congress and Supreme Court Buildings declared their connections to the Capitol by imitating its architecture, these buildings asserted
their links to the Executive Branch of government.

The attorney general was the lone cabinet officer without a building.
This anomaly reflected his peculiar status as the only member of the
president's cabinet who did not head a government department and had
no budget beyond his own modest salary. Madison tried to improve the
situation, but Congress refused to vote funds. Monroe managed to per-
suade the legislature to appropriate some two thousand dollars to hire a
clerk and rent and equip an office. In 1822 the attorney general was
assigned one room on the second floor of the War Department building.
In 1839 his staff was expanded, and new quarters were found in a brick
building three blocks west of the White House. Finally, in 1870 an act of
Congress established the Department of Justice, with the attorney general
at its head.

The president himself no longer used the southwest corner room on
the White House's main floor for his office. That room had become the
State Dining Room, and the president's office was now located on the
second floor of the house. In Hoban's rebuilding, the entire main floor
was given over to ceremonial use, but only minor changes were made in
the layout of its rooms. The large Entrance Hall was rebuilt as before,
and a file of double columns again separated it from the Cross Hall. On
the east end of that hall was a single large room running the full depth of
the house. Even though Hoban believed that the more intense fire on the
west end of the house was fed by air rushing up the stairwell, he still
recreated it. He placed the State Dining Room in the southwest corner,

where Jefferson's office had been, and the private dining room moved to the northwest corner. On the south side of the Cross Hall, the two small rectangles and the elliptical center space were recreated.

Despite periodic remodeling and the complete gutting of the interior during Truman's second term, Hoban's plan for the State Floor of the White House remains in place today, with only one major change. During Theodore Roosevelt's administration, the stairway at the west end of the Cross Hall was removed and the State Dining Room expanded. An enclosed stairway on the east side of the Entrance Hall was created to provide ceremonial entry for the first family from their second-floor residence.

Jefferson had filled the White House with furniture from Monticello. When his second term was over, the furniture went back to Virginia with the retiring president. The British invaders had used the Madison family's furnishings for fuel when they burned the building. Though some objects were retrieved after the fire, Monroe was forced to refurnish from scratch. Like Jefferson, he was deeply impressed by the way of life in Paris, and he imported several boatloads of furniture, ornamental pieces, and dinnerware from France; many items are still in the White House collection. The task was complicated by the unfinished state of the house during much of Monroe's first term, and also by Congress's reluctance to spend good money on French furniture.

During his one term, the frugal sixth president, John Quincy Adams, added little to the decoration of the executive mansion. Despite the reputation of Adams's successor (and nemesis) as a populist and a rabble rouser, Andrew Jackson shared Monroe's taste for the finer things and continued to fill the mansion with furnishings in the French style. This time around, Congress was lavish in funding his projects. Each succeeding president made a contribution of one kind or another to the interior. Lincoln preferred to spend the summer months in a cottage on the grounds of the Soldier's Home, and he felt that federal money was better spent maintaining the troops than outfitting the White House. Mrs. Lincoln disagreed. While the president opened the East Room to Union soldiers, she spent enormous sums on furnishings without his knowledge or consent. **(60)**

Lincoln's opening of the house and grounds to the army was an extreme example of the hard use that democratic ideals imposed on the presidential residence. Part of the reason Jackson needed such a big budget to furnish the newly rebuilt house was that his supporters virtually sacked it on the day of his inauguration, March 4, 1829. Previous presidents had opened the house to the public on New Years Day and other holidays, but a prevailing sense of decorum, along with light-handed but

effective crowd control, had limited access and minimized damage. While the debacle of Jackson's first inaugural was not repeated, the house continued to suffer from its openness. Not just curious citizens but office seekers thronged it, hoping to

60

receive some patronage appointment from the president. Twenty thousand jobs had to be filled in the Jackson administration. By the end of the Civil War, that number had grown to over fifty thousand.

For a brief period after the election of James Garfield in 1880, Charles Guiteau was one of the thousands begging for work from the new president. A rabid Garfield supporter and self-styled lawyer, theologian, and politician with a history of mental illness, Guiteau pressed Garfield and his secretary of state for a position. When his application was refused, Guiteau abruptly turned against his idol and made plans to assassinate him. On July 2, 1881, as Garfield prepared to board a train, Guiteau shot him first in the arm, then the back. The president lived for an astonishing and agonizing eighty days after the shooting, while doctors and other experts, including Alexander Graham Bell, tortured him in the name of advanced medicine.

Doctors testified to Guiteau's instability during his trial, but the press and the public persisted in framing the assassination as a calculated act of vengeance by a disappointed office seeker. In the popular imagination, the assassination was an outrage provoked by the evil spoils system of political patronage. This reaction led to passage of the Pendleton Act in 1883, which established the Civil Service Commission. The commission was to oversee "competitive examinations for testing the fitness of applicants for the public service now classified or to be classified hereunder. Such examinations shall be practical in their character, and so far as may be shall relate to those matters which will fairly test the relative capacity and fitness of the persons examined to discharge the duties of the service into which they seek to be appointed. Second, that all the offices, places, and employments so arranged or to be arranged in classes shall be filled by selections according to grade from among those graded highest as the results of such competitive examinations." Since not all federal positions fell under Civil Service classification, patronage remained a problem, but the number of exam-based jobs increased steadily.

After Garfield's death, Guiteau sent a letter to the former vice president, Chester A. Arthur. "My inspiration is a godsend to you . . . It raised you from a political cypher to the president of the United States." Arthur was a widower with expensive tastes. In his former job as customs collector for the port of New York, his salary was four times that of the president. After Garfield's death, Arthur refused to move into the White House until significant improvements were made. The house by then was furnished with an ill assortment of objects damaged by decades of abuse. Twenty-four wagon loads of furniture and household paraphernalia of every kind were gathered up and auctioned off on the White House lawn. Some five thousand people attended.

Then Arthur hired a fledgling New York company offering an entirely new service to its few wealthy clients—interior decoration. The firm was Louis C. Tiffany and Associated Artists. Under the company's supervision, the White House was redecorated with an eye to harmonizing the interior throughout. Wall treatments, ceiling decoration, curtains, rugs, and other furnishings were chosen to create an atmosphere of opulent good taste in the style of the Aesthetic Movement. The ceiling of the oval room was decorated in overlapping and interlocking circles, and its walls were adorned with snowflakes or buttercups in kaleidoscopic colors. A patterned carpet covered the floor, and camel-back Victorian sofas were arranged along the walls. An enormous gas chandelier hung above a gilded circular sofa. But Tiffany's most striking innovation was a stained-glass screen that divided the Cross Hall from the Entrance Hall. Charles McKim, who oversaw the redecoration of the house during Theodore Roosevelt's administration, took it down. In fact, all of the Tiffany decorations were removed by later presidents.

Arthur's wife had died soon before he took office, and the president lived in the White House alone. He probably felt at sea in such a big residence, but presidents with families found the building extraordinarily cramped. Most of the changes carried out after the Jackson administration were intended to provide more living space on the second floor. Teddy Roosevelt, the first president to use "The White House" as his official address, was only forty-two when William McKinley's assassination at the hands of a professed anarchist made him the chief executive. He had one daughter with his first wife, Alice Lee, who died suddenly in 1884. Two years later he married Edith Kermit Carow, a close childhood friend. The couple had five more children. When the Roosevelts entered the White House in 1901, their oldest child was seventeen, the youngest five.

Roosevelt was an eccentric, hyper-energetic, and exceedingly paradoxical man. Raised in privilege, he worked hard to win the respect of ward politicians and western ranch hands. Because of his stand against the great trusts, he was regarded by many as a traitor to his class. Roosevelt was fiercely competitive and proud of his endurance. He sometimes played ninety games of tennis in a day; he lost sight in his left eye after boxing with the world heavyweight champion John L. Sullivan. His high-speed hikes through the woodlands around Washington were notorious. After a walk with the president, the naturalist John Burroughs was asked what they had seen. "We didn't see any birds," Burroughs quipped. "They could not keep up."

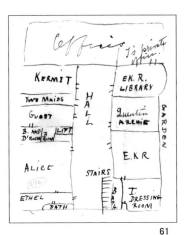

61

As a parent, Roosevelt encouraged the same level of activity from his children. At the time he took office, living space in the White House was limited to the western half of the upstairs floor. Two large adjoining bedrooms and a dressing room on the south side were used by the president and Mrs. Roosevelt. The children and servants shared rooms across the hall. In a sketch she drew as part of a letter, Edith Roosevelt inaccurately showed two baths—wishful thinking, perhaps. (61) Everyone had to take turns in the residence's one bathroom. The lack of indoor play space led to roller-skating in the halls and sledding on the stairs. On the rare occasions when it snowed, snowballs were lobbed onto Pennsylvania Avenue from the White House roof. Once when Archie was sick, his pony, Algonquin, was smuggled into the elevator and brought to his room.

The eastern half of the second floor was the presidential office suite. Because of the location of the stairwell on the west side, official visitors had to pass through the residence to reach the White House office. They were met in a reception area at the top of the stairs. From there they walked past the family bedrooms down a center hall corresponding to the one on the main floor. At its eastern end was a clerk's office and waiting room. The president's secretary occupied a large office on the north side, and the president's office was to the south. Crammed into the southeast corner of the building was a small office for the White House telegrapher. The Cabinet Room adjoined the president's office. Mrs. Roosevelt used the upstairs oval room as her library.

Following recommendations made by the McMillan Commission, Congress passed legislation in June 1902 providing funds for an extensive remodeling of the White House. The New York firm of Charles McKim, who had served on the commission, was hired to plan and supervise the necessary changes. At Roosevelt's insistence, they were allowed a mere four months to carry out the renovations. Despite this severely constricted time frame, the remodeling program was ambitious. Not only would the State Floor be redecorated, but the staircases would be rearranged. On the second floor, the presidential offices would be removed, and the liberated space would be reorganized for the first family. On the ground floor, the kitchens would be modernized, and the oval room under the south porch—site of the White House furnace—would be transformed into a Diplomatic Reception Room.

Moving the president's office outside the White House was a sensitive matter. Both the domestic and official life of the American president had always been contained in the executive mansion, and while it was conceivable that the two functions could be separated, doing so would run against the grain of American history. The White House had become Washington's most tenacious symbol. Despite a century of hard use and repeated reworking, it still looked much as it had when Jefferson took office in 1801. Making it solely the official residence of the American president would have meant creating an office structure with equal symbolic authority somewhere else. This was certainly not a task to be accomplished in four months.

Recognizing the gravity of the problem, McKim proposed a compromise: "No location outside the White House grounds could be decided upon and secured in the short time available. To construct within those grounds a building sufficiently large and imposing to stand as permanent offices would be to detract from the White House itself so seriously as to be absolutely out of the question. The one possible solution, therefore, was to occupy the only available space with a temporary building, which should be comfortable within and inconspicuous in appearance."

On the east side of the house, the dependencies that Hoban had rebuilt on the traces of Jefferson's original portico were razed after the Civil War. Those on the west side survived, with greenhouses on top and at their end. McKim's plan was to tear down the greenhouse complex and replace it with a modest building to house the presidential offices. Congress voted an appropriation large enough to build a two-story structure, but McKim insisted on an inconspicuous one-story building.

In plan, his presidential office building was clearly a version of the White House itself. A rectangle wider than deep, it had a small-scale portico on the north and an apselike projection in the center of the long south wall. A deep lobby flanked by service rooms behind the northside entrance led directly back to a secretary's office, with an anteroom to one side and the telegraph room on the other. These three rooms corresponded to the oval room and its two smaller side rooms in the White House. The other rooms were organized in a mirror image of the White House first floor. A staff room filling the whole depth of the structure stood in for the East Room, though it was on the west side of the building. The President's Room and Cabinet Room filled the opposite end. In a sheltered position on the inside of the building, the president's West Wing office was the mirror image of the State Dining Room, which during Jefferson's administration had been the office of the president.

When Taft succeeded Roosevelt as president in 1909, the office suite in the West Wing was expanded, under the supervision of architect Nathan C. Wyeth. The one-story pavilion McKim had designed was extended southward and the building doubled in size. The remodeled office block still had a bulge on the southeast corner, but behind it now was a new office for the president. In a wonderful migration of symbols, the elliptical room that in Hoban's plan had served as a reception room and drawing room became—once it was transposed to the West Wing—the most common modern representation of the presidency itself. Any directive from "the Oval Office" is a directive from the president.

The West Wing was destroyed by fire in the 1920s and expanded again during Franklin Roosevelt's first term. A basement was dug and fitted with a swimming pool for the president. It was later converted to office space. The multiple, often tiny, offices are served by a maze of corridors. The Oval Office and the Roosevelt Room are the main ceremonial spaces. President Nixon named the Roosevelt Room in 1969 in commemoration of the two presidents who built and expanded the West Wing. Now used for conferences, the room was Theodore Roosevelt's corner office in the original McKim building. (Map 5)

Recognizing the damage to the house and the inconvenience to its occupants that the steady stream of tourists created, McKim designed a special entrance on the east side of the White House to accommodate them. Excavations recovered the foundations of Jefferson's dependency, and McKim built an enclosed corridor above these foundations. At its end he placed a Visitor Center, which freed the front entrance to the house for exclusive use by the family and state visitors.

On the State Floor of the White House, McKim made structural changes that both increased its usefulness and reinforced the separation between the president's ceremonial mansion and his private home. The State Dining Room had always been so cramped that dinners with large numbers of guests had to be served on long tables set up in the Cross Hall. McKim eliminated this awkward need by expanding the State Dining Room into the space Hoban's stairway had occupied. The smaller enclosed stairway he constructed on the east side of the Entrance Hall more effectively divided the public and private parts of the house.

Removing Hoban's grand stairway created a new room on the west end of the second floor, which is now a sitting room. It stands at the center of a suite that once included a bedroom, sitting room, dressing room, and bath on the south side of the house and two bedrooms on the north. These were replaced by a kitchen and dining room in the first year of John F. Kennedy's presidency. A two-bedroom suite occupies the north side above the portico. The old presidential offices were reorganized into a small sitting room at the eastern end of the central corridor, and the Queen's Bedroom and Sitting Room on the north. These names commemorate the visit of Queen Elizabeth II and Prince Philip during the Eisenhower administration.

The former presidential office on the south side is now the Lincoln

Bedroom, though the Lincolns never slept in this room and Lincoln thought the furnishings were an outrageous waste of money. Roosevelt's old telegraph room is now the Lincoln Sitting Room. The former Cabinet Room is now called the Treaty Room. The name commemorates President Kennedy's signing of the 1963 Nuclear Test Ban Treaty and recognizes the many similar accords signed in the White House in the past. The second floor's Yellow Oval Room serves as a formal drawing room in which presidential guests assemble with the family before being led downstairs for official functions. The windows of this room overlook the porch on the south side. During the Truman administration, a balcony was inserted halfway up the south colonnade. Doors in the Yellow Oval Room give the family access to this insufficiently private outdoor space.

Removal of the president's office suite from the second floor did not completely solve the problem of inadequate space in the residence. Early in Coolidge's administration, the Office of Public Parks and Buildings discovered that the roof was unsound. The president reportedly remarked that plenty of people would be willing to risk the roof falling in for the sake of living in the White House. Four years later, the danger had become acute, and the Coolidges moved into temporary quarters on Dupont Circle while the roof was repaired. The needed upgrades created an opportunity for further expansion. A new flat roof was substituted for Hoban's design, and an entire third story, virtually invisible from ground level, was installed. This innovation added eighteen new rooms to the first family's residence. Now the president could have an office in the main house, in addition to his official work place in the West Wing.

For many years, some of the remaining third floor space was taken up by offices for the first lady and her staff. Though not an elected official, the president's wife has always assumed many practical and ceremonial duties. Generally, these activities reflected on a public stage the expectations and limitations of women's roles in American society. Throughout the nineteenth century, the first lady acted as a hostess who received and entertained her husband's guests and her own. She managed the house and supervised the staff. Dolley Madison, an exceptionally skilled and much admired first lady, began serving as White House hostess during the widower Jefferson's presidency. Some early first ladies also expressed an interest in the maintenance and remodeling of the house. Edith Wilson and Grace Coolidge took the lead in expanding the third floor.

As women's roles broadened in the twentieth century, first ladies began to involve themselves in charitable and social causes. Wilson's first wife, Ellen, worked to improve housing conditions for African Americans in Washington. Edith, whom he married at the end of his first term after Ellen died, played a much larger and more controversial role. Wilson's failing health, aggravated by the bitter opposition to his beloved League of Nations, led to a stroke on October 2, 1919. His left side was paralyzed, he had only partial vision in his left eye, and his ability to speak was limited. Four days after the stroke, his physician was asked by the secretary of state to sign a certificate of disability, which he refused to do.

Medical bulletins in the following months continued to downplay the president's grave condition. Unable to sit up or work at a desk, and having a limited attention span, the president was prone to tears and angry outbursts, yet he remained in power. Edith Wilson was his only link to the outside world. She consulted him in his bed and returned with his orders or his scrawled signature. She described this period as her "steward- ship," but her detractors and Wilson's enemies mocked her as the first woman president. The Twenty-Fifth Amendment to the Constitution, adopted in 1967, set guidelines for relieving presidents of their duties when they are unable to carry them out. While President Ronald Reagan was undergoing surgery following an assassination attempt on March 30, 1981, the disability procedures were not invoked and confusion ensued. But on July 13, 1985, when Reagan underwent surgery for cancer, Vice President George H. W. Bush officially assumed the powers and duties of acting president for seven hours during and after the operation.

Eleanor Roosevelt was the most active first lady—less a hostess than a presidential ambassador. Because FDR's polio generally confined him to the White House, Eleanor stood in for her husband, making public appearances, holding press conferences, and traveling around the nation. In late 1935 she began writing a daily newspaper column entitled "My Day." Much of what the president knew about conditions in America dur- ing the worst days of the Depression came from Eleanor's visits to factory and mining towns, dustbowl farms, urban soup kitchens, and homeless shelters. The president's voice over the radio was a tonic to many, but Eleanor showed up in person to remind people that the federal govern- ment had a kindly face. She was widely admired and widely vilified. Crit- ics labeled her advocacy for the disadvantaged and disenfranchised as socialism or communism. Enforcers of public propriety called her strength and independence a shameful transgression of a woman's place.

Jacqueline Bouvier Kennedy was more traditional—or more canny—in her choice of roles. She confined her attentions to the White House and avoided commenting on public policy. The scope of her program for renewing the executive mansion and its decoration and for making the house a subject of wide public interest was unprecedented. On the advice of the National Park Service, Mrs. Kennedy organized and raised funds for the White House Historical Association. In 1962, a year after its founding, the association produced *The White House: An Historic Guide,* a book that has been published in more than twenty editions. The Kennedys were active promoters of the performing arts and often used the East Room to showcase outstanding performers. Nancy Reagan, herself a former actress, was also an active supporter of the performing arts and of White House restoration.

Claudia Taylor Johnson, known as Lady Bird, stepped outside the White House and turned her attention to the city around her. She established the First Lady's Committee for a More Beautiful Capital, one of the first organizations to address the sorry state of public spaces in Washington DC. The Johnsons were also the first presidential family to recognize that the nation's capital was a predominately black city. President Johnson's civil rights legislation, his war on poverty, and education initiatives such as Head Start had an enormous impact on residents of the District.

Betty Ford converted the role of first wife to first woman, by publicizing her battles with breast cancer and addiction. She was outspoken in her support of the failed Equal Rights Amendment to the Constitution. Rosalynn Carter took a more direct role in government, campaigning independently for her husband and often attending cabinet meetings after his election. She headed the President's Commission on Mental

Health and was actively involved in other social causes, including care for the elderly. In 1977 Rosalynn Carter formally established the Office of the First Lady and located it on the second floor of the East Wing. This wing also housed the White House social secretary, correspondence staff, and (on the ground floor) the family theater.

Barbara Bush emphasized volunteerism, as did Pat Nixon. During Bill Clinton's two terms in the White House, Hillary Rodham Clinton played an open role in policy formation. She headed the Task Force on National Health Care Reform and worked for passage of the Children's Health Insurance program and other health care initiatives. She was also an outspoken advocate for women's rights. Her active role in policy-making laid the foundation for her successful campaign to become senator from New York, but it drew intense criticism from political opponents. Laura Bush, a librarian by training and less controversial than her predecessor (or her embattled husband), initiated programs to address literacy, early cognitive development, and the education of girls and women throughout the world.

McKim's renovation of the White House during Teddy Roosevelt's term contrasted strongly with the approach Tiffany had taken. Though the two campaigns were separated by only twenty years, the designers' ideas of what the executive mansion should look like could not have been more different. Tiffany did everything possible to bring the interior of the house up to date. From the front hall to the oval parlor, the decoration and furniture expressed a uniform and rich taste. McKim believed that any restoration of the White House had to respect its historical character. The architect's first aim "was to discover the design and intention of the original builders, and to adhere strictly" to them. Viewed too narrowly, that ideal was an impossibility. Should the house be turned on its head, with its entrance to the south and the oval parlor used as a vestibule, as Adams had done? Should presidential laundry replace the chandeliers in the East Room?

What McKim in fact did was based on history, but in the end his work reflected two entirely different historical ideals. In the architecture of the house, he preserved most of Hoban's original plan on the first and second floors. In the decoration of the rooms, however, he recognized that individual presidents had always expressed their own taste. In redesigning the interior furnishings, McKim imagined what the White House would look like if each successive president had decorated a single room in the prevailing style of his time. With this ideal in mind, McKim decorated the rooms in styles representative of the span of time through which the house had lived. This led him to ornament the newly enlarged State Dining Room in a pastiche of English styles that had been popular in the mid-seventeenth to mid-eighteenth century. The room was paneled in dark oak; silver sconces extended from the walls; a silver candelabrum hung from the center of the elaborate ceiling. Rich tapestries decorated some of the walls and the chair backs.

The State Floor of the White House became an ideal suite that illustrated the history of the decorative arts in America more exactly than the history of the house itself. More representative than real, these rooms confirmed that the White House had become a historical museum, not an evolving building and certainly not just the residence of the current president. Many of McKim's specific choices were replaced during mid-cen-

62

tury renovations, but the principle behind his approach to interior design at the White House survived. Each room continues to represent a particular period style, and curators who have looked after the White House over the last century have tried to recover furniture and decorative objects with actual historical connections to the presidents who have lived there.

The Cross Hall in today's White House has the same footprint as Hoban's design, though McKim inexplicably substituted Doric columns and entablature for Hoban's original Ionic order. **(62)** The East Room also reflects the late eighteenth-century neoclassicism of McKim's restoration. Its walls are parceled into irregular bays by Corinthian pilasters. Three enormous chandeliers hang from a ceiling decorated with plaster medallions and rich moldings. Gilbert Stuart's portrait of Washington, rescued by Dolley Madison, hangs in this room, which is reserved for concerts and large gatherings.

Jefferson placed a green canvas rug on the floor of his informal dining room on the south side next door to the East Room. From this bit of unpretentious decoration, the small square room has become known as the Green Room. Today, opulent green watered silk covers the walls, and a reproduction of a nineteenth-century Hereke rug from Turkey graces the floor. **(63)** The marble mantle is one of a pair Monroe ordered from France after the fire; McKim removed it from the State Dining Room. Stone

posts (herms) with women's heads stand to each side of the opening and
support a shelf decorated with Attic motifs. A 1767 portrait of Benjamin
Franklin painted by David Martin in London hangs over the fireplace.

Franklin, in a blue velvet coat,
rests his chin on his right thumb
and holds a sheaf of printed
papers in his left hand. A bust of
Sir Isaac Newton looks on in evident approval. The furniture and
decorative objects combine
French imports with American
work in the Federal style that
became popular at the turn of

63

the nineteenth century. A secretary attributed to Duncan Phyfe stands
between the windows. Other pieces by this master furniture maker, or in
his style, are exhibited in the room.

In the central elliptical room on the south side of the house, blue vel-

vet curtains and a continuous valance as well as
blue upholstery establish
the identity of the Blue
Room. (64) Latrobe
designed furniture for the
room, but none survives.
Gilded chairs and a round
center table in Second

64

65

Empire style are the main furnishings. Monroe ordered the
furniture and many of the decorative objects from France. The
pink fabric on his gilded chairs
was changed to blue by President Van Buren. In the 1860s,
these pieces were removed, and
ornate Victorian furniture was

installed. McKim replaced these, in turn, with more subdued neoclassical
pieces.

Under Jacqueline Kennedy's supervision, the room was redecorated in
a style that fit Monroe's French Empire furnishings, and many were
recovered. A French chandelier hangs from the center of the ceiling.
Sofas, side chairs, and arm chairs by the French maker Pierre-Antoine
Bellange, along with some copies, have been restored to the room. A
gilded clock with a figure of the Carthaginian general Hannibal sits on
the mantle of a fireplace bracketed by herms. A portrait of Madison by
John Vanderlyn that was commissioned by Monroe hangs at the left of
the center window. It is paired with a portrait of Jefferson as vice president painted in 1800 by Rembrandt Peale.

The small Red Room to the west of the Blue Room is decorated in an
American Empire style that reflects the taste of the first third of the nine-
teenth century. (65) Furnishings include a mahogany sofa upholstered in
the same red silk as the walls, with an elaborate gold pattern woven in.
The Sphinx motifs that appear throughout the room are reminders of
Napoleon's conquest of Egypt. A marble bust of President Van Buren by

the American sculptor Hiram Powers rests on a bracket in the middle
of the south wall. The bust also appears in the background of a portrait of

the president's daughter-in-law
over the fireplace. A portrait of John
James Audubon, with a distant look
in his eye and a gun in his hand, by
the Scottish painter John Syme hangs
in the room, along with a well-known
painting of Dolley Madison by Gilbert
Stuart.

The State Dining Room has lost
its dark paneling and now looks more like the East Room than a musty

66

gentlemen's club. (66) The changes are more apparent than real, however.
Though the room was gutted during the mid-century renovation, McKim's
handiwork was carefully reproduced. In the Kennedy years, the oak was
painted white, the sconces and chandelier were gilded, and the windows

were draped with patterned cloth
accented in gold. A banquet table
acquired during the Truman renovation
occupies the center of the room; it is
ringed by high-backed side chairs
designed by McKim in Queen Anne
style.

A portrait of Lincoln painted by
G. P. A. Healy hangs over the mantle.
(67) In a paradoxical combination of
energy and absorption, a thin bearded

67

Lincoln seems both immobilized in thought and about to rise from his chair. Healy first used the image in a group portrait of Lincoln and his chief military advisors called *The Peacemakers*. That painting hangs in the Treaty Room on the second floor of the White House. Healy also made two other copies of the Lincoln portrait, one of which is exhibited in the National Portrait Gallery.

The small Family Dining Room in the northwest corner of the building has pale yellow walls and is decorated in the Federal style. A wonderful library bookcase in the room displays blue and gold china bought by Benjamin Harrison. The four large brass pulls on the cabinet's drawers are stamped with a commemorative bust of George Washington. A French mantle clock of the early nineteenth century has a small figure of Washington, an American eagle, and other symbols.

During most of the nineteenth century, the president's south lawn ended at Tiber Creek. This boggy, polluted channel advanced and receded with the rising and falling tide, and the smell was often overpowering. Most presidents found some place else to live during the summer months. Andrew Jackson Downing, one of the great American landscape architects of the nineteenth century, drew plans for improving the south lawn, but the outbreak of the Civil War prevented their completion. After the war, the Tiber was buried and the lawn was raised with fill excavated from the foundation of a vast new Executive Office Building just west of the White House. In the 1880s the Army Corps of Engineers graded the site, installed plantings, and created walkways that followed the general lines of Downing's plans.

On the south side of the White House, plantings were grouped to reveal the main structure of the residence while screening the corridors and outbuildings of the East and West wings from public view. Today, the tennis courts, putting greens, swimming pool, and private rambles that provide recreation for the first family are all hidden in the trees. Only Hoban's iconic south façade with its two-story porch is visible to the public from beyond a wrought iron fence. (68) But on the north side, the White House, sitting at grade, seems eerily near and surprisingly intimate. Walt Whitman, the poet who, better than most, understood the paradoxes and possibilities of the American project, described it this way in his journal, on one of the darkest days of the Civil War:

"February 24th. A spell of fine soft weather. I wander about a good deal, sometimes at night under the moon. To-night took a long look at the President's house. The white portico—the palace-like, tall, round columns, spotless as snow—the walls also—the tender and soft moonlight, flooding the pale marble, and making peculiar faint languishing shades, not shadows—everywhere a soft transparent hazy, thin, blue moon-lace, hanging in the air—the brilliant and extra-plentiful clusters of gaslight, on and around the facade, columns, portico—everything so white, so marbly pure and dazzling, yet soft—the White House of future poems, and of dreams and dramas, there in the soft and copious moon—the gor-

geous front, in the trees, under the lustrous flooding moon, full of reality, full of illusion—the forms of the trees, leafless, silent, in trunk and myriad-angles of branches, under the stars and sky—the White House of the land, and of beauty and night—sentries at the gates, and by the portico, silent, pacing there in blue overcoats—stopping you not at all, but eyeing you with sharp eyes, whichever way you move."

Chapter Six

BURGEONING BUREAUCRACY

The eighty acres L'Enfant set aside for the President's Grounds have been cut into over the centuries. Ellicott's 1792 map of the federal district carved two city blocks out of its northern end. The green space framed by these blocks was further separated from the White House when Pennsylvania Avenue was placed between them in the 1820s. The square was ceded to the city and named in honor of General Lafayette.

Throughout the nineteenth century, Lafayette Square was the most prestigious and the most political of Washington's neighborhoods. (Map 6) The sober but grand townhouses that ringed it belonged to wealthy families like the Maryland Blairs and Virginia Tayloes, or to political grandees like Henry Clay and Daniel Webster. Dolley Madison lived in a house on Lafayette Square until 1849. Henry Adams, a grandson and great-grandson of presidents, lived for decades in a house on the northwestern edge of the square, where he wrote his dark classic, *The Education of Henry Adams.* His house and that of his neighbor, John Hay, were replaced in 1927 by the Hay-Adams Hotel.

In 1902 the McMillan Commission recommended that the houses around Lafayette Square be razed and replaced with executive departments. Fortunately, the plan was never carried out, but the changing character of the surrounding area has transformed the square bit by bit. Government expansion, the commercialization of downtown, and the institutionalization of political lobbying have brought major innovations. An annex of the Treasury Department now stands on the southeastern margin of the square; it is linked to the old Treasury Building by a passageway under Pennsylvania Avenue. The Department of Veterans Affairs is on the north edge. The White House Historical Association is headquartered in a Lafayette Square house.

Benjamin Latrobe designed two buildings around the square that sur-

vive. St. John's Episcopal Church, completed in 1816, was meant as a worship center for the president and his family as well as the community around the square. Madison was the first president to attend the church. When the vestry offered him a pew in 1816, he chose number fifty-four, and that has been visited by every president since. (69)

Latrobe's original structure was designed in the shape of a Greek cross, with four equal vaulted arms raying out from a central space where the altar and pulpit stood. Like Jefferson, Latrobe was a rationalist who put more emphasis

69

on preaching than liturgy, and his structure was meant to group the congregation where they could hear the sermon. Latrobe's symmetrical plan met the fate of most such churches. During the nineteenth century, its western arm was extended, transforming the building into a Latin cross. An altar was built in the eastern arm and a balcony added above the

nave. A Greek revival pediment was
placed at the end of this extension and
a three-tiered steeple erected above it.
The house next to the church, which
once belonged to the British ambassador Lord Ashburton, is now the Parish
House.

70

In 1818 Latrobe also designed
Decatur House, named after the American celebrity Commodore Stephen
Decatur. Standing at the corner of Jackson Place and H Street, this plain
brick structure, with its semicircular fanlight above the front door, is one
of the oldest surviving homes in the city. (70) Decatur lived in the house
for only a year before he was killed in a duel. Politicians of various
stamps lived there for the next quarter century. In 1844 it was sold to
John Gadsby, a tavern owner and slave trader, who barred the windows of
a low outbuilding and used it as a holding pen. Slave auctions were held
in the garden behind the house, which is now open to visitors.

Around the corner at 1651 Pennsylvania Avenue stands Blair House.
This four-story stucco building, with its areaway and arched doorway
behind a square portico, was built for Dr. Joseph Lovell in 1824. Lovell
was surgeon general of the United States and founder of the Army Corps
of Engineers. His house was a short walk from the old War Department
office west of the White House. At Lovell's death in 1836, the house was
sold to Francis Preston Blair, editor of the Washington *Globe,* which was
the voice of Jackson's Democrats. Blair later became an antislavery advocate and one of the organizers of the Republican Party. His son, Montgomery Blair, a lawyer, represented Dred Scott in the Supreme Court

pleading and served as Lincoln's postmaster general. At the end of the Civil War, Blair split with the radical Republicans over Reconstruction and joined his father's old party.

In 1942 Blair House and its neighbor at 1653 Pennsylvania Avenue, which also belonged to the Blair family, became official residences for visiting dignitaries. The Truman family lived in the house between 1948 and 1952, while the White House was being gutted and rebuilt. On November 1, 1950, two gunmen who advocated Puerto Rican independence tried to assassinate the president. The intruders stormed Blair House, wounded two policemen, and killed a third before they were stopped.

Down the block from Blair House is a building now called the Renwick Gallery. A branch of the Smithsonian American Art Museum, it exhibits American crafts and decorative arts from the nineteenth century to the present. The gallery building takes its name from its architect, James Renwick, whose better-known Washington building is the Romanesque Revival structure on the Mall called the Smithsonian Castle. The Renwick Gallery was built in Second Empire style. In 1853 a French-trained Italian architect with the improbable name of Louis Tullius Joachim Visconti designed extensions to the Louvre in Paris. To make his additions harmonize with the rest of the structure, Visconti devised a formula based on the characteristics of French Baroque architecture. His style became the most popular pattern for French building during the explosive development of Paris in the reign of Napoleon III, who inaugurated the Second Empire.

The emergence of Paris as the paradigm of the modern city popularized Visconti's style far beyond the borders of France. His design combined long and low multi-storied blocks with upright pavilions. These pavilions, which projected beyond the line of the façade and were generally highly ornamented—typically with columns—marked entryways and gave focus and definition to meandering structures. Visconti favored the mansard roof, popularized by the French Baroque architect François Mansart. These roofs, which became a hallmark of the style in both France and the United States, stick almost straight up from the sides of buildings; they often frame architectural ornaments like pediments, and they are usually lit by dormer windows. Their height and openness makes them useful as additional stories.

Renwick adopted this style for a building that looks like a house but was always intended to be a gallery. (71) His client was William Wilson Corcoran, a Washington native who founded a bank in partnership with George W. Riggs. The partners took over the building diagonally across from Treasury that had once belonged to the Bank of the United States. Experts at marketing government debt, the partners raised fifteen

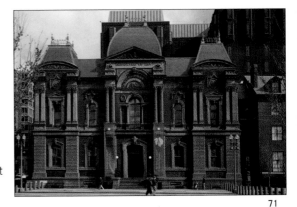

71

million dollars to support the Mexican War. Corcoran, who retired in 1854, was also interested in art. In 1855 he hired Renwick to design a gallery where his growing collection could be housed and exhibited free of charge to the public. While Corcoran, like many of his contemporaries,

72

began his collection with European paintings, he was atypical in his taste for American art. He bought Hiram Powers's sculpture *The Greek Slave,* and he collected works by Hudson River School painters like Thomas Cole and John Frederick Kensett.

During the Civil War, Corcoran left the country. Montgomery Meigs took over his gallery, which was directly across Pennsylvania Avenue from the War Department Building, and made it the headquarters of the Quarter-master Corps. After the war, Corcoran was accused of Confederate sympa-thies, and his property remained in government hands until 1869. Per-haps to prove his patriotism, the banker assembled a national portrait collection, which he added to his gallery. He also founded an art school based on life study and the copying of exemplary works. Corcoran died in 1888. In 1897 his collection was moved to a new, much larger gallery nearby on Seventeenth Street.

The new Corcoran Gallery was designed by Ernest Flagg in the French Beaux Arts neoclassical style, enriched with Hellenistic rather than Roman ornament. **(72)** Its closest Washington cousins are the oldest House and Senate office buildings on Capitol Hill. The gallery has a heavily rusticated basement story with an entablature above it that sup-ports a more finely rusticated first story. Rectangular windows rest on the top of the molding. Above a cornice, the second-story wall rises to an elaborate frieze of triglyphs and seemingly unworked disks. Small, closely

packed square windows high on the wall light the interior. Another entablature marks the roofline; its frieze contains the names of great artists of
the past. Above the cornice, ornamental tiles called acroteria edge the
roof. Sphinxes stand at each end of the roof beam. A projecting rounded
auditorium accommodates the building to the acute street angle at its
intersection with New York Avenue.

Diagonally across the street from the Corcoran, and also sited on an
irregular block, is Octagon House. Its original owner, John Tayloe, was
one of the very first people to purchase a building site in the newly laid
out federal city. By 1800 his completed house stood at the intersection
of New York Avenue and Eighteenth Street. The streets themselves were
incomplete, but there was already a scattering of houses in this area east
of the just-finished President's House. Until the Civil War, this neighborhood would remain as prestigious as Lafayette Square. Tayloe, a Virginia
planter who expected to do business with the new national government,
hired William Thornton to design his house. Evidently intrigued by the
site, Thornton shaped the building to fit its irregular geometry.

At the narrow front end is a three-
story towerlike apse that bulges from
the center of the main façade. (73) A
small square portico at the top of a
flight of marble steps marks the
entrance. The side walls flare out at an
oblique angle. At the back of the
house, end walls perpendicular to the
flaring sides are joined by a wall that

73

parallels the façade and makes the house, despite its name, an irregular hexagon, not an octagon.

The geometry of the interior rooms is a fascinating combination of circles, triangles, and rectangles. Behind the apse is a circular entrance hall. Two rectangular rooms aligned with the surrounding streets spread out from it. The large triangle framed by their inner walls contains a formal circular stairway, a hidden triangular servant's stair that runs the full height of the building, and a smaller triangular room Tayloe apparently used as an office. On the second and third floors the triangles next to the stairs were used for closets and storage space. The side blocks were divided in half for use as bedrooms.

The Tayloes raised fifteen children in the house. When the neighborhood began to decline after the Civil War as wealthy families moved away from the center of town, the building was subdivided into tenement apartments. At the urging of Charles McKim, the American Institute of Architects bought the house to serve as its national headquarters. In 1973 a much larger office building was opened in the backyard, and the house was renamed The Octagon Museum. Under the direction of the American Architectural Foundation, it hosts exhibits focused on architecture and design.

The Treasury Building to the east of the President's House was rebuilt after the British raid in 1814. It burned a second time in 1833. Congressional dithering over a site annoyed Andrew Jackson so much that he collared the architect, Robert Mills, stormed out of the White House, and stabbed his cane into the lawn. "Put the cornerstone here!" he reportedly yelled. "Put it right here!" In plan, the Treasury Building is a hollow rectangle with a center wing that separates its enclosed space into two square courtyards. The oldest part of the building, designed by Mills, was completed by 1842. It includes the short central wing and the mid-portion of the long eastern façade that now runs along Fifteenth Street for two blocks from Pennsylvania Avenue to G Street. The south wing was built in 1861, the west at the end of the Civil War. The building was complete by 1869. Thomas U. Walter, the architect of the Capitol expansion, designed the additions. Similar in style to Mills's original wing, the later additions replace stone and brick with structural ironwork.

Though it lacks a central focus, the eastern façade along Fifteenth Street, with its massive granite columns, is the grandest of the four. On the southern side, pilasters replace the columns, and an Ionic portico stands at the top of a stairway, overlooking a small piazza. This perspective, reproduced on the back of ten-dollar bills, features a statue of Washington's secretary of the treasury, Alexander Hamilton, who pressed for the creation of a national bank. The north façade is similar, except that a statue of Albert Gallatin, Jefferson's secretary of the treasury and Hamilton's rival, occupies the sunken plaza there.

Soon after the Treasury Building was completed, ground was broken on the opposite side of the President's House for one of Washington's most vilified structures. The Executive Office Building originally housed the departments of State, War, and the Navy. Today, the building (renamed the Dwight D. Eisenhower Executive Office Building, or EEOB) is home to various functions that have spilled over from the West Wing— offices for the vice president's staff, the Office of Management and Budget, and the National Security Council, to name just a few. The Executive Office Building has a footprint almost identical to Treasury's and mirrors that building's position on the White House grounds. In the eye of God or the lens of a satellite camera, the EEOB is the very image of Treasury. But from ground level, its design can be interpreted only as a repudiation of the Renaissance neoclassicism that harmonized the government buildings of pre–Civil War Washington.

Like Treasury, the Executive Office Building was completed in a series of campaigns. The south wing was begun in 1871, and four years later that area of the building was ready for occupancy by the State Department. Navy Department offices in the west wing were completed in 1879. The remaining areas of the building—an entire wing facing the White House, a north wing along Pennsylvania Avenue, and a central corridor—were turned over to the War Department in 1888. Alfred Mullett designed the structure in a scaled-up version of the Second Empire style of the Renwick Gallery, just across Pennsylvania Avenue. **(74)** Suitable for

houses, that style was really intended to organize large buildings with long corridors and multiple rooms. The city halls in Boston, Providence, and Philadelphia and great hotels like the Palmer House in Chicago were modeled on this style. It was also a favorite architectural form for hospitals and asylums. The Executive Office Building has about two miles of corridors and more than five hundred rooms, enclosing more than fifteen acres of inside space. Interior designer Richard

74

von Ezdorf used cast iron, tile, and glass to create sumptuous meeting rooms and a gorgeous multi-tiered library for the State Department.

Though an architectural misstep in many ways, the Executive Office Building manifested two very important ideals of post–Civil War Washington. First, the building declared without equivocation that there was to be no turning back. As logical as it might seem for a newly reunited country to reassert its common roots, official Washington had no desire to return to the spare Greek Revival style of the founders' era. It preferred the international, the opulent, and the expansive. Second, the building acknowledged that government bureaucracy had grown. To house the clerks of three departments in the postwar era, a structure on an unprecedented scale was required. Mullett recognized that government was now big and complex, and his design reflected this new reality.

The burgeoning growth of government that created the Executive Office Building eventually doomed it. In 1918 the Navy Department left the building and moved into new quarters along Constitution Avenue. The War Department moved out in 1938. It was housed in temporary quarters while the Pentagon—the first government building on the Virginia side of the Potomac—was under construction. In 1947 the army, navy, and air force were merged into a single Department of Defense. In the same year the State Department moved into new quarters bounded by Twenty-First and Twenty-Third streets. This area, known as Foggy Bottom, houses a mixture of private homes and apartments, private institutions like George Washington University, and government departments. In addition to the State Department, the largest of these are the Interior Department and the General Services Administration.

Interior—then called the Home Department—was added to the president's cabinet in 1849 as western expansion began to accelerate. Until 1917 its offices were in the Old Patent building. In 1937 its headquarters were moved to a massive new structure just north of the Mall between Eighteenth and Nineteenth streets. Covering nearly two city blocks, the building is composed of six seven-story structures running east-west that are connected by a central block running north-south. Three miles of corridors join more than two thousand rooms. The building was the first New Deal structure to be completed.

75

Like the nearly contemporary Folger Shakespeare Library, the formal vocabulary of the building is evidently neoclassical, but the elements of that style have almost lost their individual characteristics and dissolved into a common surface. (75) The two-story basement forms a deep pedestal broken by small widely spaced windows. A recessed entry at the center of the building gives access to five doors. The next three stories of the building are marked by an applied colonnade composed of square piers; the columns of the center bay above the entrance are free-standing. Each column frames three rows of double windows. An entablature and cornice at the top of the façade partially conceal an attic story with a frieze marked by state seals. The basement, the outer face of the columns, and the entablature form a single plane and can be thought of as a flat wall with recessed windows. From this viewpoint, the classical vocabulary of the structure becomes almost invisible in a façade that has the simple lines of 1930s Modernism.

The area that would become the Ellipse was originally part of the President's Grounds, south of Tiber Creek. Far from the house and close to that channel's suffocating stench, the site was cut off by a white picket fence in the 1850s. While the rest of the White House lawn was landscaped and planted with trees, this forlorn lot devolved into a public commons of no particular character or purpose. Andrew Jackson Downing created a design for the plot, with a large circular drive as its center-point, but the project was never carried out. His central figure, trans-posed to an ellipse—the emerging geometrical symbol of the president's office—would eventually became its defining feature.

When construction on the Executive Office Building began in 1871, contractors dumped dirt excavated from its foundations on the still empty lawn. In 1872, when the smelly Tiber was finally enclosed in a culvert, muck from this excavation also helped raise the level of the ground and dry it out. In the 1880s, money and talent were finally available to improve the long-neglected site. The grounds were sodded and cleared of odd trees; elms were planted and a pattern of walks laid out. Today, the Ellipse is best known as the site of the national Christmas tree.

Many offices of the Executive Branch are housed in a nearby wedge of buildings that begins at Fifteenth Street, just east of the Ellipse, and ends where Constitution and Pennsylvania avenues converge at Sixth Street. Now called the Federal Triangle, the area was singled out by the McMillan Commission as a key to redirecting city development along the lines laid out by L'Enfant. The commissioners recognized that in Wash-ington "a sentiment has developed both among the residents of the Dis-trict and also in Congress, that the area between Pennsylvania Avenue and the Mall should be reclaimed from its present uses by locating within

that section important public buildings." While recognizing that "imposing buildings devoted to business purposes have been erected on the
north side of the avenue," the commissioners were aware that most of
the avenue was "lined by structures entirely unworthy of the conspicuous
positions they occupy. The upbuilding of Pennsylvania Avenue, therefore,
must of necessity have consideration in any comprehensive plan for the
treatment of Washington."

What the commissioners proposed was a relocation of the old Central
Market and dedication of the wedge between Pennsylvania and Constitution Avenues to offices of the District government. Their inspired plan
would have given city government a monumental presence in the most
prominent part of the city. The plan survived, but its key components
were changed, and in the end only a small part of the complex was
devoted to District government. After massive relocation and ground-
clearing twenty-five years later, the bulk of the space was taken over by
offices of the Executive Branch, an act that sealed the federal government's monopoly over the city's symbolic center. The only building representing the District was erected in 1904 along the south side of Pennsylvania Avenue between Fourteenth and Fifteenth Streets. Now formally
called the John A. Wilson Building, the old District Building is a richly
ornamented variation on neoclassical and Second Empire themes.

Article I, Section 8 of the Constitution authorizes Congress "to exer-
cise exclusive legislation in all cases whatsoever, over such District (not
exceeding ten miles square) as may, by cession of particular states, and
the acceptance of Congress, become the seat of the government of the
United States." During the city's more than two-hundred-year history, this
authority has taken many forms. For most of the nineteenth century,

Washington's government was a hybrid. A mayor selected by the president shared power with a twelve-member council elected by DC citizens. In 1871, in evident reaction to the dramatic increase in the city's African American population, the long-standing arrangement was reversed, and President Grant chose both the mayor and an eleven-member council. Citizens were allowed to vote only for members of a House of Delegates and for their one nonvoting congressman in the House of Representatives. Three years later, when the city became bankrupt, the federal government seized complete control and governed the District through a three-member appointed commission.

Until the Twenty-Third Amendment to the Constitution was ratified in 1961, DC citizens did not have the right to vote for president and vice president of the United States. Many residents thought that enfranchisement in national elections would be the prelude to home rule. These hopes were disappointed when Lyndon Johnson replaced the three commissioners with a single mayor-commissioner and an appointed nine-member council in 1967. Home rule finally came in 1973, but widespread graft and repeated fiscal crises led to increased congressional oversight. In 1997 a compromise between city and federal officials preserved a limited form of local control.

Aside from the District Building, the rest of the land that the McMillan commissioners had identified was given over to federal offices. Andrew W. Mellon, secretary of the Treasury under Harding, Coolidge, and Hoover, was the leading figure in the development of the seventy-acre patch south of Pennsylvania Avenue that would become the Federal Triangle. A Pittsburgh banker and financier, Mellon amassed a sizable fortune through investments in oil, steel, shipbuilding, and construction.

During his decade in Treasury, he lowered the national debt and reduced taxes. Until 1927 his office was responsible for enforcing Prohibition.

Mellon's responses to the stock market crash of 1929 and the Depression were ineffectual, his financial dealings while in office came under suspicion, and Hoover was forced to replace him in the last year of his administration. But in 1926, just after Congress passed the Public Buildings Act, Mellon was the man who oversaw the appointment of a Board of Architectural Consultants to design the Federal Triangle. The board projected and eventually carried out a complete clearing of the site, which closed the Central Market. A coherent complex of buildings, impressive from the outside and laced with inner pedestrian passages and plazas, was designed to take their place.

The complex that was actually built is far different. A jigsaw puzzle of interlocking agencies, hedged in by a phalanx of gray façades, its planned amenity was quickly surrendered to the demands of the automobile. Pedestrian walkways gave way to roads, and an open plaza at the western end of the complex was immediately cannibalized as a parking lot; that space was not reclaimed until the 1980s, when it became the site of the Reagan Building. Some of the architectural inventiveness of the original design for the complex was recaptured at that time, along with a pedestrian walkway.

But many of the problems of the Triangle were beyond the board's control. The height of Washington buildings is limited in order to preserve the Capitol's towering dominance over the city. Skyscrapers, which by the 1920s were the main building form in America's great cities, were never an option in Washington. The ever-growing federal bureaucracies that

would have been well housed in urban towers had to be placed in buildings that hugged the ground. Horizontal skyscrapers create a surprisingly
monotonous urban fabric, and their thousands of offices—connected by
pedestrian corridors, rather than fast-moving elevators—discourage integration and promote inefficiency.

The expanding federal government of the 1920s required assembly
rooms far larger than anything then in existence. One of the more imaginative structures in the Federal Triangle—the Andrew W. Mellon Auditorium on Constitution Avenue at Fourteenth Street—filled this need. With
its two connected buildings, the complex that houses the auditorium
forms an impressive Capitol-like structure. Its central pavilion has a massive temple front with a fully decorated pediment raised on a rusticated
basement. (76) Short colonnades link it to two similar pavilions at each
end of flanking buildings, which now house the
Environmental Protection Agency.

The main EPA building, called the Ariel Rios
Federal Building, was originally designed to
house the Post Office Department. The building's
curious footprint—a rectangle deeply cut into on
its long sides by two back-to-back parentheses—
testifies both to the ambition of the original concept and the forces that blocked its completion.
In Mellon's original plan, the Ariel Rios Federal

76

Building was to be mirrored by a structure on the opposite side of Twelfth
Street. Like so many Washington projects, that plan, which required
demolishing the Old Post Office, was never carried out.

77

Designed in the 1890s by Willoughby Edbrooke in the Romanesque Revival style pioneered by Henry Hobson Richardson, the Old Post Office is a great mass of brownish gray stone with turrets at its corners, a steep roof, and a soaring center tower. (77) Even after a series of costly renovations, the fate of the building remains uncertain. Its interior glass-roofed atrium features a food court, and the rest of the building currently holds a mix of corporate and government offices and retail spaces. (78) But with no local population to sustain them, the building's shops are mostly empty after 5 p.m. on weekdays and rarely visited on weekends except by tourists.

The Federal Bureau of Investigation is one of the largest agencies within the Department of Justice, and one of the most powerful. It has its own headquarters on Pennsylvania Avenue, across the street from the department's main building in the Federal Triangle. Dedicated in 1975, the concrete structure, named for the bureau's most controversial director, J. Edgar Hoover, fills the entire depth of the block between Eighth and Tenth Streets. Under Hoover's decades-long reign, the FBI transformed itself from an anonymous bureaucracy to a much-mythologized superagency. Known at first for bringing down celebrity crimi-

78

nals like Clyde Barrow, Baby Face Nelson, and John Dillinger, the FBI quickly realized that organized crime was its most suitable opponent. It targeted bootleggers, reputed Communists, and the Mafia, but it also homed in on civil rights leaders, including Martin Luther King Jr., campus radicals, and antiwar activists during the Vietnam era.

The J. Edgar Hoover Building is set back from the street on all sides and surrounded by a wide plaza. Concrete pillars frame a first floor originally intended for shops but now fortified with heavy wire grids. (79) The second story, inaccessible from the ground, is also well protected. Pillars support a five-story façade pitted with deeply recessed square windows. These cell-like structures of unfinished poured concrete link the building to a style called Brutalism. Not as harsh as it sounds, the name of the style reflects the use of what in French is called *béton brut*—raw or

unfinished concrete. The Swiss architect Le Corbusier was a pioneer of the style, which has been widely praised and widely criticized.

The corners of the FBI building do not meet at right angles, and the intersecting sides blend in a three-part pillar which on

79

the ground floor shelters the building's doors. Despite its many deviations from the norm of federal neoclassicism, the main structure is relatively compatible with its neighbors. It has columns, though from a neoclassical point of view they are in the wrong place. It is long and low like most government structures, and the verticals defining its window frames are just as pronounced as the long horizontals that link them. Even the color of the concrete is not completely out of tune with the limestone buildings of the Federal Triangle, though the concrete form-marks preserved on its surface add a willful crudity that is out of keeping with any classicizing sensibility. What is most disconcerting about the building and most aggressively anticlassical is the superstructure near the northern end. Supported on massive piers, it towers over the rest of the building like the bridge on a battleship.

The home of the National Archives, just east of the Justice Department, was designed by John Russell Pope. After studying architecture at Columbia University, in 1896 Pope was awarded the first fellowship from what would become the American Academy in Rome. Founded by Charles McKim and a handful of other like-minded architects and financiers, the academy offered architects the chance to visit and study classical buildings in Greece, Rome, and Renaissance Italy. It became an American equivalent of the French Academy in Rome that had trained architects, painters, sculptors, and musicians in the neoclassical tradition since the eighteenth century. After his academy residence and tours through Greece and Italy, Pope, like McKim before him, completed his education at the École des Beaux Arts in Paris. Trained at the end of an era, Pope practiced the nineteenth-century traditions of Beaux Arts classicism until World War II. By the time of his death in 1941, Pope and the style he championed had become a favorite whipping boy of architects brought up on the dogmatic functionalism of High Modernism.

Like the Corcoran, the National Archives occupies an irregularly shaped Washington block, but this building makes no concession to its site. A massive rectangular prism made from Tennessee marble, Pope's building has the weight and carriage of a national treasure house. Its center block sits on a wide base; its elevation is divided into three parts, each topped by a cornice and set back from the mass below. Near the corners of the main block, Pope designed isolated blind windows. Porticos stand out from each end of the building; their Corinthian columns support an entablature. A temple front projects from the center of the main façade, which faces Constitution Avenue and is highly visible from the National Mall. (80) Sculpted eagles mark the peak and corners of its roof, and an ornamental frieze fills its pediment.

The allegorical scene sculpted by James Earle Fraser represents the transfer of historical documents to a personification called The Recorder of the Archives. Seated figures on the plinths at the sides of

80

the stairs, also by Fraser, represent Heritage and Guardianship. The bronze doors under the portico are among the largest ever cast. The images on and around the portico are meant to enrich the building and define its purpose. But like the nearly contemporary sculptures on the Supreme Court building, they are more or less mute.

The research collections of the National Archives are especially strong in genealogy, American Indians, the New Deal, the District of Columbia, the Federal Courts, Congress, and military history through World War II. The entrance for researchers is on the north side of the building. In this age of high security, the main entryway to the exhibits is beneath the south side stairs and through the basement. Romans typically stored valuables in the substructures of temples, so in this case security has inadvertently added a note of authenticity. Exhibition areas are on the main floor. These include the Lawrence F. O'Brien Gallery, where temporary exhibits are hosted, and the Public Vaults. These exhibits offer an inside look at the range of collections that make up the national record.

The main attraction of the building is the solemn, dimly lit Rotunda for the Charters of Freedom. The rectilinear outside of the building offers no hint that its central space is either curved or domed. The so-called rotunda, moreover, is only half circular and resembles the oldest meeting rooms in the Capitol—D-shaped rooms based on Roman theaters and apses. Pope, like Latrobe and Bulfinch, combined these shapes with reminiscences of the Pantheon. The oculus, the five-layered coffering of the vault, and the patterned marble floor reflect that building. In a miniature temple front framed by marble columns—another allusion to the Pantheon—the Constitution is displayed.

To its left, in a simple display case, lies a copy of the Declaration of Independence, probably written out by the Pennsylvanian Timothy Matlack and signed by all the delegates on August 2, 1776. Printed copies of the Declaration were in circulation as early as July 5, but this official handwritten version was not completed and signed until a month later. The document traveled with the Continental Congress and reached Washington with the new government in 1800. The State Department looked after it until 1841, when it went on display in the Patent Office. Hundreds of thousands of people saw the document at the centennial

celebrations in Philadelphia in 1876. Its deterioration was evident to all
of them. For the next fifty years, commissions argued techniques of
restoration while official facsimiles were produced and widely dissemi-
nated. During this era, the Library of Congress was the document's home.
Throughout World War II it was stored in Fort Knox. Finally, in 1952 it
was enshrined in the National Archives. Alongside the Declaration is a
copy of the Bill of Rights.

Two large mural paintings by Barry Faulkner celebrate the signers of
the Declaration and the members of the Constitutional Convention.
Faulkner's murals are an idealized group portrait of the men who created
the documents on display. On the left margin of the *Declaration* mural, a
neoclassical temple façade stands at the top of a short flight of stairs.
(81) Four columns that evidently support its pediment rise out of the picture frame. A balustrade behind the steps continues across the full
length of the mural. A large oak fills the left background. A small
sumac—a symbol of adaptability and rapid growth—stands in front of it.
The clouds begin to break in a stormy sky; in the right middle-ground a
stand supports a multitude of flags. The spare imagery of the mural is a
faithful representation of democratic symbols common in the early nineteenth century.

The *Constitution* image is
a complement of the *Declaration* mural. The temple
front—now on the right—
partially hides a spreading
oak. The small sumac visible

81

in the *Declaration* is absent, as are the stormy skies; the group of banners is different and larger. The men who converge in two unequal groups on the figure of John Hancock in the *Declaration* mural are now focused on the central figure of George Washington.

These murals recall Trumbull's paintings in the Capitol Rotunda, which also associate neoclassical architecture with the founding of the republic. In his painting of the *Declaration,* military banners are part of the trophies on the wall of Independence Hall. Storm clouds in the *Surrender of Lord Cornwallis* represent the calm after the storm of revolution. The portraits of individual signers in the National Archives owe a great deal to Trumbull as well. The *Declaration* group led by the redheaded Jefferson is the mirror image of the men who stand in front of Hancock's desk in the Capitol painting.

On the north side of Pennsylvania Avenue, directly across from the National Archives, two curved buildings designed by Hartman-Cox Architects form a broken exedra that embraces the Navy Memorial. (82) A Postmodern version of 1930s Federal Triangle neoclassicism, this mixed-use development sits on either side of Eighth Street and frames a vista of the Old Patent Office just up the hill. The buildings are fronted by massive colonnades set above a rusticated first floor. The street-level arcade and square windows of the mezzanine present the Renaissance formula of Raphael and Bramante on an inflated scale, while a second colonnade, above, shelters open balconies behind square columns.

A short walk up Eighth Street leads to the Old Patent Office. L'Enfant designated the block between Seventh and Ninth streets and F and G streets as the site for his national church. It was never built, and during

the Jackson administra-
tion William P. Elliott and
Ithiel Town were hired to
design a building for the
Patent Office at this site.
Built of sand-colored Virginia freestone, the structure was completed in

82

sections between 1837 and 1868. Its exterior, like Thornton's Capitol,
combines a rusticated lower story with two upper stories in which classical elements predominate. A porch shaped like a Roman temple front
juts from the center of each of the four slightly different façades. These
porches, enclosing the building's second floor entries, were originally
approached by flights of stairs that were removed in the mid-1930s. Six
Doric columns support an entablature decorated with triglyphs and a low
pediment. On either side of the porches, Doric pilasters outline a double
row of undecorated windows.

The Constitution gives the federal government control over the grant-
ing of patents and enforcement of patent rights. As George Washington's
secretary of state, Thomas Jefferson was the first recorder of patents; his
interest in novelty and invention made the job pleasurable. The Patent
Office was created during his own presidency, and William Thornton
became its first director. By a law enacted in 1836, the informal examination of patents was replaced by a more rigorous researching of the util-
ity, practicability, and novelty of inventions. Applicants for patents were
required to provide paperwork and scale models of their inventions. Over

time, the models, stored in glass cases, took up more and more space in the ever-expanding building. A handful are still exhibited on the second floor.

The south half of the Old Patent Office was for many decades home to the National Portrait Gallery, a division of the Smithsonian Institution. After extensive renovation, the gallery and the other occupant of the building, the Smithsonian's American Art Museum, have reopened as the Donald W. Reynolds Center for American Art and Portraiture. The portrait collection displays images of "men and women who have made significant contributions to the history, development and culture of the people of the United States." This mission is a combination of the roles that L'Enfant assigned to his national church and to the squares throughout the city that were to be decorated by the states with memorials to their outstanding citizens. Like the Library of Congress, the Senate offices, and the Supreme Court, it is also a building that extends a role played in part by the Capitol. But neither the memorials displayed throughout the Capitol or even the conversion of the Old House of Representatives chamber into Statuary Hall could fully represent America's heritage of individual achievement. The National Portrait Gallery provided an additional space for exploring that tradition, and a different climate for preserving and presenting it.

Like many branches of the Smithsonian, the National Portrait Gallery is a shrine with a didactic cast. Its role goes beyond preservation and presentation to the active examination and discussion of the men and women whose likenesses are preserved and the modes in which their images were recorded. One of the most significant and hard-won treasures in the museum's collection is a portrait of George Washington by

Gilbert Stuart. In April 1796, after much urging, Washington posed for a portrait commissioned by the marquis of Lansdowne, a British aristocrat who supported the American Revolution. Stuart's painting, known as the Lansdowne portrait, was loaned to the gallery in its inaugural year, and in 2001 it was purchased outright with a thirty-million-dollar grant from a private foundation. The portrait duplicates one that has hung in the White House since the beginning of the eighteenth century.

Washington wears a long black coat, black stockings, and black shoes; there are touches of lace at his neck and wrists. (83) His open hand extends in the Roman gesture symbolizing eloquence. Beneath his fingers, quill pens stand in a silver inkstand engraved with his coat of arms. On the table top beside the inkwell are a closed book labeled *Federalist* and scrolled up documents. Beneath the table and leaning against its leg are books labeled *American Revolution* and *Constitution and Laws of the United States.* The gilded front leg of the table is decorated with images of an American eagle and a Roman fasces. The gilded chair behind Washington, reminiscent of a throne, features the stars and stripes in a medallion above its embroidered back. Along with the rainbow in the sky—symbol of the calm after the storm of revolution—the columns and drapery are fictions of the painter; they do not represent any real place. While the portrait is meant to show the president as he addresses Congress in Philadelphia, Washington is alone. Though his gesture suggests speech, no one seems to

83

hear. The neoclassicism that in American painting generally evokes Roman republican virtues is replaced here by gilded symbols that suggest an aristocratic or imperial vision. Painted for an English nobleman, the scene transforms Washington from a rebel into an emperor.

Other images in the gallery include a portrait of Benjamin Franklin painted in Paris in 1785 by Joseph Duplessis, and portraits of every American president. Writers, inventors, and artists from the eighteenth century to the present are also represented. Many of Alexander Gardner's photographs of Lincoln are in the collection, which also houses more than five thousand glass negatives from the studio of Mathew Brady.

The other collection housed in the Old Patent Office has a closer historical connection with the building than its neighbor. In 1836 John Varden, a Washington resident, opened an art gallery in his home near the Capitol. In 1841 his collection was transferred to a newly formed National Institute for the Promotion of Science. Along with many other historical objects—the Declaration of Independence and Benjamin Franklin's printing press among them—Varden's paintings were displayed in the Old Patent Office alongside models of the cotton gin and the walking beam engine. In 1862 the charter of the National Institute expired, and its art collection passed to the Smithsonian Institution. Many of the paintings were destroyed in a fire at the end of the Civil War. In 1903 an American collector of pictures, Harriet Lane Johnston, died, and in her will she left her collection to "a national gallery of art." In 1906 the Supreme Court of the District of Columbia ruled that the Smithsonian, as successor to Varden's National Institute, was indeed America's "national gallery of art."

Johnston's collection of American art, along with many other works,
including an enormous wealth of art sponsored by the Depression-era
Federal Art Project, makes up the Smithsonian American Art Museum. In
a somewhat haphazard way, this section of the Reynolds Center presents
key works from each period in the growth and expansion of the United
States. The colonial and revolutionary eras are represented in portraits by
John Singleton Copley, Charles Willson Peale, and Gilbert Stuart, and in
landscapes by Thomas Cole and sculptures by Horatio Greenough—works
that, according to the gallery, "trace the transformation of the thirteen
colonies into a nation." The landscape painters of the early nineteenth
century, including masters of the Hudson River School, "drove and documented Western expansion."

The end of the nineteenth century posed more of a conundrum for the
museum's organizers. The "American Impressionism and the Gilded Age"
gallery binds together an era of political corruption, explosive industrialization, and immigration with an art that disengaged itself from social,
political, and economic events and concentrated on atmosphere. In the
twentieth century, when abstraction and realism parted company, the
social link became even harder to find. Despite the didactic, historical
framing of the collection, many remarkable works from every period are
on display.

Albert Bierstadt's luminous and surreal *Among the Sierra Nevada* is
the sole occupant of a shrinelike alcove fitted with a bench at the proper
viewing distance. A herd of deer emerge at sunset from a tangled wood to
drink from a mirror-smooth lake glazed with mist. In the distance, broken
peaks rise to a crescendo of ice and rock among glowing clouds. In a

84

scene of similar magic, the northern lights glow above an icebound ship in Frederic Church's *Aurora Borealis,* painted in 1865. George Catlin's gallery of majestic Indian portraits, in full dress and paint, includes Osceola, who led Seminole resistance to forced relocation in the 1830s. (84) Numerous small landscapes and village scenes supplement Catlin's Indian portraits, many still in their original numbered frames.

A walk eastward along F Street leads from the Old Patent Office to the Old Pension Office. This building was designed by Meigs in 1883 to house the agency that distributed funds to almost three million veterans. Recipients included a few men who had served in the War of 1812 and a larger number who had fought in the Mexican War. A handful of widows whose long-dead husbands had served in the Revolution were also beneficiaries. But the bulk of the Pension Office's business was with Union veterans of the Civil War. Administrators disbursed more than eight billion dollars altogether, a staggering amount of money in the nineteenth century.

Loosely based on the Palazzo Farnese in Rome but built entirely of red brick, this unique structure is now home to the National Building Museum. Vast and high from the outside, it is a hollow rectangle with four stories of offices surrounding a roofed inner court. The most striking exterior feature is the transverse roof topped by a clerestory that runs the length of the structure, between gables at each end. An intersecting peaked roof one story higher with a glazed arcade at its base and slim Romanesque windows of various sizes in its gable stands above the south-facing main façade of the building. **(85)** This unusual roof design led detractors to describe the structure as three red barns piled on top of one another. General William Tecumseh Sherman, on the other hand, reportedly found nothing to criticize in the building except that it was fireproof.

The exterior is elaborately and skillfully enriched with neoclassical ornaments that represent the full range of nineteenth-century terracotta castings. The building's ground story windows are crowned by heavy lintels supported on curving brackets. Alternating curved and peaked pediments top

85

the second and third story windows. A complex cornice separates the floors, and another tops the walls; improbable free-standing brick columns are set into each corner.

But the most engaging feature is an entablature with a pictorial frieze that runs around the entire building. Seen from a distance, the figures in

86

the frieze are like an endless line of marching men broken here and there by cavalry, supply wagons, and sailors in boats. What appears to be a continuous narrative is actually an ensemble of twenty-nine cast terracotta panels with a total length of only seventy feet. Multiple copies of these panels are arranged to create the impression of novelty. At Meigs's insistence, the designer, Caspar Buberl, included an image of an African American freed by war in the panel representing the quartermaster's wagon. (86)

The dominant interior feature of the Old Pension Office is an exploded courtyard far beyond the dimensions of any Italian palazzo. Roughly the size of a football field, the wide space was used for presidential inaugural balls from the 1880s until 1909. The practice was resumed in the 1970s. This indoor piazza is broken into three sections by groups of

Corinthian columns, built of brick, stuccoed, and faux-painted, that soar more than seventy feet to an arcade supporting the roofs and buttressing the walls. (87) On the second and third levels, interior balconies are closed by more conventional arcades.

Though the building that houses the National Building Museum is vast, the museum itself consists of a relatively small suite of exhibition spaces. It hosts lectures and mounts exhibits of architectural details, photographs, and models. Fittingly, a long-term exhibit focuses on the planning and development of Washington DC.

87

Chapter Seven

PUBLIC WALKS

The open greensward stretching west from the Capitol
that we now call the National Mall was part of the
ideal plan for the federal city from the very beginning.
Jefferson drew it on his rudimentary map and labeled
it "public walks." In his conception, the space would
recall the Roman Forum, that most democratic of ancient political institutions. In the eighteenth century, the Forum as Jefferson knew it was in a
state of decorative abandon—a picturesque sheep's meadow or cow pasture
dotted with ruins and rimmed with churches.

In his expanded plan for the new city, L'Enfant transformed Jefferson's
public park into something more dynamic. On his map, the space became a
long and exceptionally broad avenue—a great axis that formed a symbolic
link between the Capitol and White House. The hinge of that axis was a
monument to the first president. Along its edges were theaters and exhibitions for public enrichment and delight, but also home sites for dignitaries
and foreign ambassadors. The expanse would become Washington's Champs
Elysées—the grand corridor that was just being laid out in Paris on the eve
of L'Enfant's departure for the United States.

Like the Rotunda of the Capitol, L'Enfant's avenue was both symbolically
important and a pragmatic waste of time and space. The capital that was

striving to pull itself together in time to welcome the national government in 1800, or the city that twenty years later was struggling to rebuild after the British invasion, had no time to think about a French-style boulevard, and no money to establish it. As the L'Enfant plan receded in importance during the middle decades of the nineteenth century, the ideal represented by this space more or less disappeared from view.

Andrew Jackson Downing, the brilliant but short-lived landscape architect who designed the White House grounds, drew up schemes for the area, but they were never carried out—the Civil War interrupted. Soldiers were billeted or hospitalized in every available government building in the city, including the White House, the Patent Office, and the Capitol. When practically every free space in the District was becoming an army camp, an open field so close to the center could not be ignored. Ordered rows of canvas tents appeared on the future Mall, along with stables, pastures, and slaughter-houses for the army's livestock.

After the Civil War, the field was again vacant. In the absence of a clear vision of what to do with it, the area became a casualty of unplanned development. Streets and street-level rail lines ran across it; the train station where President Garfield was assassinated stood on top of it. The space might have been overtaken completely by commerce and the burgeoning postwar government, except for the fact that the site itself made development difficult. Rimmed on the north side by the Tiber until its enclosure in 1872, the Mall consisted of low-lying mucky soil, not impossible to build on but expensive to consolidate and shore up.

Ultimately, it was the 1901 McMillan Commission that saved the Mall from development and cleared it of those few invaders who had successfully colonized it. Their plans called for an open, unpaved green axis that would not only carry out L'Enfant's project but extend it to newly

reclaimed land west of the Washington Monument. (88) With some reluc-

tance, the commissioners agreed to preserve the one nineteenth-century

building of historic significance that had already been placed on the

Mall—the Smithsonian Institution.

In 1835 the United States ambassador to Great Britain learned that a

man named Henry James Hungerford, the nephew and heir of James

Smithson, had died without
issue. Smithson, a member
of the Royal Society of London who dedicated his life
to the study of chemistry,
was unknown to the general
public but well known in

88

scientific circles. Smithson's estate had passed to his nephew with a

default clause that would become effective only if the first heir died leav-

ing no children. In this curious clause, which an accident of fate sud-

denly activated, Smithson bequeathed the "whole of [his] property" to

the "United States of America, to found at Washington, under the name

of the Smithsonian Institution, an establishment for the increase and dif-

fusion of Knowledge among men." The estate was valued at a hundred

thousand pounds, a little more than half a million dollars, which was

delivered in gold to the United States Mint in 1838. A millionaire was an

exceedingly rich man in 1838. Today, when the richest Americans meas-

ure their wealth in tens of billions, Smithson's bequest would have the

buying power of five billion dollars or so.

Smithson's motives have been debated since his gift was first made public. An illegitimate son of the duke of Northumberland, Smithson wrote that "every man is a valuable member of society, who, by his observations, researches, and experiments, procures knowledge for men." Smithson lived much of his life in self-imposed European exile; and as receptive as the Royal Academy had been of his work—publishing more than twenty of his papers—he may have felt that America was an even more congenial intellectual climate. Perhaps he took to heart the story of the English chemist and discoverer of oxygen, Joseph Priestley. Nearly killed by a mob and ultimately hounded out of England because of his unorthodox religious and political views, Priestley found refuge in Pennsylvania.

American legislators were just as confused by Smithson's will as anyone else. Research to them seemed abstract and impractical. Most congressmen thought a college or teacher training school would give better value. A national library was proposed; so was a national agricultural station with a small faculty to teach navigation, animal husbandry, and house-building. Former president John Quincy Adams, elected to the House of Representatives in 1830, had his own pet project—a national observatory that would increase knowledge through new discovery. While Congress did not fund Adams's observatory, his argument helped his colleagues to understand the difference between research and teaching, and to begin to imagine the Smithsonian as an organization that would not just store and disseminate knowledge but create it.

In 1846 Congress passed legislation recommending that the new institution be housed in the Old Patent Office, where a national collection of historic documents, art and artifacts, scientific specimens, and

curiosities already existed. Failing that, the legislation authorized construction of a building "with suitable rooms or halls, for the reception
and arrangement, upon a liberal scale, of objects of natural history,
including a geological and mineralogical cabinet; also a chemical laboratory, a library, a gallery of art, and the necessary lecture rooms."

The enabling legislation also created a board of regents that included
the vice president and chief justice of the United States, along with six
members of Congress. Their political muscle would ensure the institution's survival. The regents in turn would appoint a secretary of the
Smithsonian whose scientific interests and abilities would guide research.
One hundred men applied for the job, and the final candidates were narrowed down to two: Francis Markoe, a scientific amateur with a job in the
State Department and political ties to President Polk, and Joseph Henry,
a professor of natural philosophy (the nineteenth-century name for
physics) at the College of New Jersey, which at the end of the century
would become Princeton. Henry was an internationally respected
researcher in the emerging field of electromagnetism, and many saw him
as the successor to America's most famous scientist up to that time,
Benjamin Franklin. Though a theorist, Henry outlined principles that led
to the invention of such basic devices as the telegraph, transformer, and
electric motor.

The regents found that, of the two finalists, only Henry was "capable
of advancing science and promoting letters by original research and
effort, well qualified to act as a respected channel of communication
between the institution and scientific and literary individuals and societies in this and foreign countries; and, in a word, a man worthy to repre-

89

sent before the world of science and of letters the [Smithsonian] institution." Henry's example and his continuing advocacy defined the Smithsonian. The organization he headed would produce new knowledge through research in science, human culture, and the arts, and it would disseminate that knowledge through publication and displays of specimens and artifacts in its building.

James Renwick, soon to be the architect of William Corcoran's first gallery on Pennsylvania Avenue, was hired to design a structure to house the new scientific institution. The architectural style he chose was very different from the neoclassicism of the Old Patent Office. The material was red sandstone quarried near Seneca Creek, Maryland, and carried in barges down the C&O canal to Washington. The site chosen by the regents was within the area that L'Enfant had set aside for informative public exhibits, but it cut deeply into grounds that the designer had intended to remain open. (Map 7)

Renwick's building was a fusion of late Romanesque and early Gothic elements, with historical links to Anglo-Norman architecture. This picturesque style suited a building that would stand alone, far from the built-up high ground north of Pennsylvania Avenue, with its two anchor points, the Capitol and White House. (89) The medieval style underscored the separation of the Smithsonian's building (and perhaps also its mission) from that of the rigorously classicizing Patent Office, and looked forward

to the emergence of Gothic Revival architecture as the major style not
just for American churches and public buildings but for research universities such as Georgetown, Princeton, and Chicago.

Towers project from the corners of the main block and the west wing;
a square tower at the center of the south wall with a tiny tower at its side
provides a second entrance. The windows range from narrow slits to wide
openings, but all have arched tops; some have internal ribs that divide
them into sections. Pensile arches—ornamental friezes made up of
unsupported arches that appear to hang down like stubby icicles—decorate rooflines and cornices. On the side facing the Mall, a porte-cochere
projects from a grand façade. With its buttresses, its three-part vertical
division, central rose window,
and flanking towers, this façade
resembles a cathedral front.
Crenellations top the porte-
cochere and run along the walls
of the linking corridors at either
end.

Despite a complex profile
that bristles with turrets and
towers (90), the ground plan of the building is simple and nearly symmet-

90

rical. From the entry, a short corridor leads to a two-story transverse hall.
At each end of the hall, corridors connect winglike rooms at right angles
to the center line of the building. The room on the west has an apse at
its north end. With its beautiful Gothic ribbing, it appears to be modeled
on the private chapels that a chateau might normally include.

Commonly called the Castle but actually named the Smithsonian

Institution Building, this structure originally housed the entire staff and collections of the Smithsonian. It is now used for administrative offices and a visitor center. In 1858 the complete collection of the museum that was open to the public could fit into the main hall. But when the objects that had been on display in the Patent Office were transferred, the collection multiplied, and by the 1870s the exhibit space had expanded dramatically. The main hall was reserved for biological specimens. Geology and fossils were exhibited in the west corridor and wing. The large hall on the second floor (now closed to visitors) displayed a collection of American Indian artifacts. Anthropology, which in the nineteenth century was linked with the new theories of Charles Darwin, was another of Joseph Henry's intellectual interests, and the Smithsonian was active in the collection and preservation of objects that documented the rapidly disappearing life-ways of America's native peoples.

It soon became evident that Renwick's castle was too small to house the institution and its growing collection. A second building, based on plans by the versatile Montgomery Meigs, was constructed under the oversight of Adolph Cluss, who created the Eastern Market, and his partner, Paul Schulze. The new building, located just to the southeast of the Castle, was square in plan and more than three hundred feet on each side. Its structure of pavilions and connecting corridors was Second Empire in inspiration, though the ornamental vocabulary was not. Its iron framework was faced with multicolored brick and tiles. Its four identical façades each had a central entryway flanked by square towers, two long wings, and a pavilion at each end. Arched windows subdivided by ribs filled each long wall. Corridors reached from every entryway toward a central sixteen-sided pavilion. (91)

While the building echoes many of the
features of the original Smithsonian, its
design is most indebted to the pavilions created for the Philadelphia Centennial Exhibition of 1876. That celebration of the hun-
dredth anniversary of the Declaration of
Independence put on public display for the
first time the pioneering achievements of
American industry. When the exposition
closed, many of those exhibits were transferred to Washington and reinstalled in the

91

new Smithsonian building. It was called the National Museum Building
when it opened in 1881, but it is now generally known as the Arts and
Industries Building. The Smithsonian Guide for 1889 summarized its
purpose and what it displayed: "All specimens of natural history, geology,
mining, metallurgy, objects of aboriginal workmanship, ancient or modern, etc., belonging to the United States are contained in this collection.
The museum, however, is not merely a place of deposit for scientific
material but, by means of a thorough classification and the illustration of
the history of human culture, it is destined to become the most comprehensive and instructive educational exhibit in the world."

By the mid-1890s, the Smithsonian had again outgrown its exhibition
space. The architectural firm of Hornblower & Marshall was hired to
design balconies in the National Museum Building to create more room
for display. In the Renwick building, they contributed to the design of a
children's museum and a tomb for James Smithson, just inside the main
entrance. In 1904, under the supervision of Alexander Graham Bell,

92

James Smithson's body was disinterred from a cemetery in Genoa and brought to Washington.

In 1903 Congress appropriated funds for Hornblower & Marshall to design a new free-standing Smithsonian structure directly across the Mall from the Castle. Unlike Renwick's building, this expansion of the Smithsonian was sited to conform with L'Enfant's plan, as recently revived by the McMillan Commission, and its architectural style was in harmony with the neoclassicism that Renwick had ignored. The façade that faces the Mall and the Castle focuses on a central pavilion, where a wide span of stairs leads to a colonnaded porch with a square entablature. (92) Above the entablature is a gable with an arched window. Similar gables on each of the four sides of the center pavilion support a drum and a low dome. With its two wings extending to the sides, the museum's Mall façade resembles Thornton's original design for the Capitol. On the north face, along Constitution Avenue, a small pavilion encloses a secondary ground-level entrance. Additional wings were added at the east and west sides of the building in 1964, and its two interior courtyards were roofed in 1999.

Now called the National Museum of Natural History, this building houses—in addition to its public displays—enormous research collections open only to staff and specialists. The collections are especially strong in botany, entomology, vertebrate and invertebrate zoology, and paleobiology.

Resources in the physical sciences are limited to mineralogy. Among the
research materials are so-called type collections that represent standards
for identifying and defining organisms and minerals. These include vast
holdings of bird skins, fish, herbaceous plants, ants, and dragonflies. The
record of living or recently extinct species is supplemented by collections
of fossil plants, algae, and insects. Anthropology is represented by artifacts and a vast photo archive.

While we might think of a laboratory, an observatory, or a particle
accelerator as a place where basic scientific research takes place, in the
nineteenth century and through much of the twentieth the natural sciences were rooted in collections like those housed in the Smithsonian.
Mineral study required the identification and classification of rocks from
around the world. The same was true of the life sciences. Without a
knowledge of the diversity of animal and plant kinds that exist, it would
be impossible to achieve the goals of scientific taxonomy—the grouping
of life forms into species, genus, family, and phylum.

Darwin's own revolutionary work began with the collection of specimens. From adaptive changes in the beaks of finches that he discovered
in the Galápagos Islands, he conceived the grand idea of evolution
through natural selection that had eluded biological thinkers since Aris-
totle. Members of a given species are usually well-adapted to their habitat from birth. This conformity of heredity and environment suggests
either the existence of a craftsman who fits each bird or blade of grass to
its habitat, or some mechanism by which habitat molds the inherited
characteristics of a species over time. Darwin's answer to this conundrum
was "natural selection." Those individuals or varieties whose innate characteristics are best suited for the environment around them are more

likely to survive and to pass on to their offspring, with increasing preci-
sion, these favorable characteristics. When environments change, species
adapt quickly or die out.

In the isolated Galápagos, this adaptation was especially clear to Darwin as he observed differences in the beaks of finches from one island to
another. What Darwin could not explain was the source of the innate variation on which natural selection acts, nor the mechanism that preserves
these variations and passes them along to offspring. These questions
were answered in the early twentieth century by geneticists, drawing on
the experiments of an isolated Moravian monk, Gregor Mendel. By establishing a link between evolution and environment that accounted for both
the diversity of life and its taxonomic order, Darwin took the great leap
from collecting and systematizing data to creating theory. He set an
example for researchers in all the natural sciences, including the study of
humans.

Beginning in the last decades of the twentieth century, the analysis of
genetic markers rather than external characteristics has become the basis
for determining relationships among species. This advance has broken
the link between evolutionary theory and the accumulation of specimens;
and with that change, the model of biological research on which the
Smithsonian prospered has become somewhat antiquated. Nevertheless,
natural history is still a thriving scientific enterprise, and new specimens
are being described all over the world, including extreme environments
such as hydrothermal ocean vents. For a great many zoologists, the focus
of field research today is animal behavior and habitat, rather than body
form (morphology).

The Mall entrance of the Museum of Natural History leads to a vast

rotunda, which is the hub of the collections on public view. The
unadorned central dome with its glazed oculus is met by four intersecting
coffered vaults with demilune windows at their ends. Beneath each vault,
the building's main floors are visible behind Ionic colonnades. (93) The
corners between the colonnades are treated as square openings framed
by great piers and crowned with pediments. The effect is a little like the
crossing of a great Baroque cathedral. Since 1958, the area underneath

the rotunda has focused
on an installation of an
enormous African elephant
raised on an artificial
ground and surrounded by
grasses and birds that suggest its savanna habitat.

Just as the enabling
legislation of the Smith-
sonian ordained, the

93

exhibits of the museum illustrate and explain the research associated
with its specimen collections. To the right of the elephant, the museum's
east wing houses its paleontology collections. Three-dimensional recre-
ations in the surrealistic style of Tanguy or Miró represent the earliest life
forms of the ancient seas. Fossil plants display the varieties of terrestrial
life. The center of the exhibit and the museum's major attraction is a
large room two stories high filled with recreated dinosaurs and other
extinct reptiles. Specimens include an enormous Diplodicus skeleton, its
neck and tail spanning almost the full length of the hall, and a fiberglass
cast of Tyrannosaurus Rex facing off against a fossilized Triceratops. Next

to the exhibit is a glassed-in laboratory where conservators can be seen unpacking bones from their plaster wraps and preparing them for study or installation.

Fossil mammals—the squirrelly nocturnal creatures that coexisted with the great reptiles while they waited for a chance to rule the world— are relegated to a side gallery. In the depths of the east wing are installations that represent the fauna of the Ice Age, especially mastodons and mammoths, and dioramas illustrating the imagined life of premodern hominids. These exhibits combine real artifacts with reconstructions. An exhibit called African Voices replaces earlier ethnographic installations that characterized African civilizations as subordinate steps on the ladder of human progress.

On the west side of the museum's main floor, mammals take center stage. The Kenneth E. Behring Family Hall of Mammals is a dramatic presentation of skeletons and nearly three hundred mounted specimens. Its centerpiece is a two-story installation that makes dynamic use of the museum's spaces. Animals at eye level are protected but not enclosed by glass. Specimens are carried upward on plinths and steel beams. A cheetah sleeps on the branch of a mounted tree trunk; the corpse of a gazelle hangs further out on the same branch. Two female lions chase down a water buffalo. Though the posture of all the animals reflects an understanding of the dynamics of motion that only a high-speed camera could capture, the scene is as familiar as nineteenth-century paintings—and as old as the cylinder seals of the Mycenaeans.

The second floor exhibit spaces are shared by mineralogy, nonmammalian zoology, and anthropology. The geology exhibits are among the most popular. Spectacular specimens of rocks and minerals, giant quartz crystals, coral-like masses of mineral that glow under blacklight, blobs of gold and fool's gold are beautifully displayed. The centerpiece of the collection is also a mineral, but the Hope Diamond is more treasure than scientific specimen. What draws visitors is the romantic history of the stone, not its crystalline properties. Of the nonmammalian zoology collections, the newest and most appealing is a small insect zoo where living bugs of all shapes, sizes, and degrees of creepiness are exhibited under glass and liberally handed around by docents. A hive of honeybees works tirelessly behind plexiglass in one corner. In warm weather they communicate with flowers in the outside world through a clear tube much like a clothes dryer vent. The northwest corner of the wing is filled with exhibits that illustrate the foundations of Western culture in the life-ways of Mesopotamia, Egypt, and Greece.

To the east of the Natural History Museum is the National Gallery of Art. It was established as a division of the Smithsonian by legislation passed in 1937. Before that time the nation's art collection was itinerant. At one point or another it was housed in the Old Patent Office, the Smithsonian Castle, and on the second floor of the Natural History Museum. The gallery's prime mover was, once again, Andrew W. Mellon, who began to collect paintings in the early years of the twentieth century. He quickly developed from a conventional collector of popular European artists to a discerning and bold acquirer of major works.

His fellow Pittsburgh industrialist, Henry Clay Frick, offered some guidance, and the art impresario Joseph Duveen procured many works for him, as he did for other American industrialists of the era. Mellon specialized in paintings by the Old Masters and in British portraits. In 1931 he bought twenty-one choice paintings from the Hermitage Museum in St. Petersburg, offered for sale by the cash-strapped Soviet government. By the time he left the Treasury Department in the last year of the Hoover administration, he had the largest art collection in America. In 1935 Mellon commissioned architect John Russell Pope to design a building to exhibit his collection. And one year later, he wrote to President Roosevelt offering it to the nation, along with a ten million dollar endowment. Mellon died soon after Congress accepted his gift.

The building Pope designed for Mellon's collection reflects both the classical tradition in general and the central monuments of the nation's capital. Pope, who had already designed the National Archives building, admired and imitated many of the same buildings that had inspired Jefferson, Latrobe, and Bulfinch; the most important of these for his

National Gallery project was the Pantheon. The centerpiece of Pope's south-facing façade is a pavilion with a pedimented porch rising above a monumental flight of stairs; behind it is a hemispherical dome. (94) Two unadorned wings with blind openings lead to large blocks

94

that jut out on both faces of the building. The two ends of the building are capped by extensions of the narrower wings.

If the Pantheon is the building's Roman birthparent, its godfather is the Capitol six blocks to the east. The three-part structure of the building

is very similar to the completed Capitol, with its
domed center block, narrow extensions, and prominent House and Senate wings. But instead of Meigs
and Walter's massive dome, Pope reflected Thornton's low dome and pediment and the steps added
by Latrobe. In keeping with the modernists' disdain
for ornament and with the spare neoclassicism represented by the Folger Museum, Pope created a
structure that is mostly wall, subtly divided by shallow moldings, cornices, and pilasters. There are no
applied columns, no rustication, no aedicules, and
only a few ornamental windows. It is a remarkably harmonious building,
very well suited to its job of foregrounding the paintings on display rather
than trumpeting its own artistry.

95

The interior of the building, by contrast, is very rich. Behind the entryway a vestibule orients visitors and sends them directly into a surprisingly
dark rotunda. Windowless, its oculus veiled, the circular room has black
marble floors and black marble columns supporting a coffered dome. (**95**)
A fountain in gray stone and a bronze Mercury fill the center space.
As beautiful as the rotunda is, the visitor is almost immediately drawn
away from it by the bright light streaming in from the east and west galleries.

Arranged chronologically, the gallery exhibits Italian, Spanish, French,
German, Dutch, Flemish, British, and American painting. Highlights
include Hals, Rubens, Van Dyke, and Vermeer, along with Ribera, Zur-
barán, Velázquez, and Murillo. The French nineteenth century is represented by significant works of the most celebrated painters: Manet,

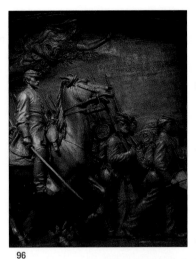

96

Monet, Van Gogh, Gauguin, and Cézanne. The great British and American landscape painters are also strong. There are significant and beautiful paintings by Homer, Eakins, Whistler, and Sargent and compelling portraits of the urban scene at the turn of the twentieth century by Robert Henri and George Bellows.

All the American works on exhibit chronicle the development of the nation, but in some works history is a more immediate presence. The Civil War inspired Augustus Saint-Gaudens' *Memorial to Robert Gould Shaw and The Massachusetts 54th Regiment*. A bronze cast of the memorial, completed in 1897, stands opposite the State House in Boston. The National Gallery acquired Saint-Gaudens' gilded plaster cast of the monument in 1997. The 54th was a regiment of African American troops raised in the aftermath of the Emancipation Proclamation. Shaw, the son of abolitionists and veteran of the Antietam campaign, was appointed to lead it. A few months after its formation, the unit, which included volunteers from many northern states, was dispatched to Hilton Head Island in South Carolina. Their first assignment was a land assault in support of naval bombardment of Confederate Fort Wagner, which guarded the harbor of Charleston. Shaw led the assault and was killed on the ramparts of the fort. One third of the regiment died at the same time, and the men were buried in a common grave.

The memorial sculpture in high relief shows the troops of the 54th marching in ranks led by drummers and flanked by Shaw on horseback.

An angel, her drapery billowing in complex folds, floats above them. Though the three inscriptions on the monument all refer to Shaw rather than the troops, the representations of the men of the regiment are anything but routine. Saint-Gaudens modeled a number of the most visible soldier's heads in clay, and they are strikingly individual. (96) A few casts are displayed in a niche on the wall to the left of the memorial. Despite this attention to detail, the monument remains less a tribute to the men of the regiment than to their leader; it is he, not they, the Latin inscription describes as having "sacrificed everything to preserve the Republic." So while the monument records a turning point in African American history, it also reflects the assumptions of racial inequality that plagued America long after the Civil War.

Early and significant donations by Samuel H. Kress, Joseph Widener, and Lessing J. Rosenwald magnified the Mellon collection. While each contribution brought new strengths to the gallery's holdings, the major thrust remained unchanged. The National Gallery, like the Library of Congress and the Smithsonian before it, was never intended as a repository of purely American work. It was not a representation of the nation to the world but just the opposite—a triumphant assembly of the art of the world placed before the American public as a free resource. Whatever the motivations and the private benefits to men of wealth, the creation of the National Gallery and its magnificent collection represents a democratic triumph. Access to this gorgeous temple of art is open to everyone at no cost.

As the number of works in the National Gallery grew, it became clear that more space would be needed for exhibition and research. I. M. Pei

97

was hired to design a new structure on a piece of land just east of the gallery. Transected by Pennsylvania Avenue, the site set aside for the new museum is a blunt wedge with two parallel sides of unequal length and two long sides that are oblique. With its intersecting grid of roads and radiating avenues, the L'Enfant plan produced many blocks with tight corners where walls were destined to meet at odd angles. Thornton's Octagon House was one of the first responses to the city's unique dissection. Pei's design not only accommodated the site, it made this unique geometry the basis for the building's design. The footprint roughly duplicates the shape of the block. A gap that mimics the diagonal thrust of Pennsylvania Avenue separates the building into two triangular masses, which are joined by a bridge. (97) A subterranean passage beneath Fourth Street links the old and new galleries, which are faced with the same stone.

From the plaza between the two buildings, the East Wing façade reveals its structural principles. The angled inner faces of the towers at each end of the main entryway apparently converge on a triangular tower at the building's far end. The low horizontal between the towers represents the bridges between the structures and within the two parts of the East Wing. The narrow end of the second building protrudes beyond the gap that separates the two.

Wide doors open on a multistory atrium lit by skylights and spanned by multiple bridges. Unlike the dark rotunda of the old building, this is a light-filled space with interesting architecture and a few massive and

compelling works on display. A giant Calder mobile hangs from its ceiling, and other Modernist sculptures are perched in niches or at odd corners of the floor. (98) The galleries house a large permanent collection of
Modern and Contemporary American art, including generally large, wonderful works by the titans of High Modernism—Jackson Pollock, Mark
Rothko, Jasper Johns, Willem de Kooning, Robert Motherwell, and David
Smith, among others. While these objects are very much at home in the
building, its unusual geometry does not overpower works from other periods. The large exhibition spaces are reconfigured with temporary barriers
in a variety of shapes that suit the temper of works
of the most disparate kinds.

Despite its uncompromising Modernism in a part
of the city more resolutely neoclassical than any
other, the Pei building has been a success from the
beginning. The careful choice of materials and the
novel and inventive ways in which the old and new
buildings are interconnected have played a large
part in that success. The translation of the local
geometry into a visible and tangible presence in the
knife-edge of the East Wing is magical. Touching
that edge transforms the building from a structure
into a sculpture.

98

The National Museum of the American Indian, which opened in
2004, was conceived by architect and project designer Douglas Cardinal,
a member of the Blackfoot tribe. Unlike the traditional ethnographic displays of the Smithsonian that viewed cultures progressively and from the

outside, this museum is a continuing exposition in which Native Americans present those aspects of their culture that they wish to explore and share with others. Like the East Wing of the National Gallery, this museum speaks an architectural language that is almost entirely out of temper with the buildings around it. Pei's building finds its place through creative adaptation of L'Enfant's geometries. The American Indian Museum explores the very ground on which L'Enfant inscribed his grid. Rooted in the geometries of rock forms, the museum is surrounded by a meandering plaza and streamlike fountains that both incorporate and mimic organic forms.

Visitors who enter the site from the west follow a walkway that traces the irregular outline of the building, passing by boulders that mark the route. Stones in the waterway along the path form waterfalls and pools. As visitors approach the main entrance on the eastern side, the boulders recede, and both the path and the waterway become more abstract. At its end the water swirls down into a circular well. This is a very unusual climax for any artificial watercourse in the Western tradition, which typically emphasizes cascades and towering jets. It is a wonderful representation of the entry to the various underworlds and points of emergence that play a part in many Native American creation stories.

Just beyond the low walls of the round plaza at the entrance, landscape designers created a marsh fringed with indigenous plants and a pond with many varieties of local waterfowl. (99) This installation recreates the wetland environment of the undrained and unimproved lowlands on which this part of the federal city was built. From the marsh side, Jenkins Hill and the gentle uplift of land across the Mall toward Pennsylvania Avenue are suddenly visible as terrain as well as cityscape. This

recreated prospect makes the
newest building on the Mall seem
the oldest—and a ground-level
point of view from which to
observe and assess the rest.

The building is an artful combination of organic and geometric
forms. Its undulating façades are
made of carefully fitted rectilinear
blocks of dolomitic limestone

99

with perfect corners and rough faces. Thin string courses of smooth stone
divide each face into horizontal layers that correspond to the divisions
between rock strata in natural outcroppings as well as to the conventional
marks that distinguish one story of a building from another. The rows of
windows that peek out here and there from between the layers look as
though they have been fitted into cave openings; they are an image of
technology grafted onto the natural.

The entryway to the museum is one of its most striking features. The
doorway is set deep in a space that cantilevers out floor by floor above it.
The jutting stories are supported on a curious and ingenious series of
brackets that combine rock forms with columns. The suggestion of a cliff
dwelling like Canyon de Chelly in Arizona is unmistakable. Less obvious
is the form of a shelter rock, a massive boulder with an inward slanting
face that many Indians in the eastern United States used for temporary
camps.

The interior of the museum combines the meandering forms and
recurrent circles that mark the exterior. The multistory central hall has

space for changing exhibits at its base. This wood-floored theaterlike area is surrounded by a beautiful and comfortable stone bench that traces the irregular contour of the hall and mimics the path and watercourse leading into the building. Directly overhead is one of the most striking features of the museum. Concentric expanding bands, like ripples in water, create a circular dome with a glazed oculus. Enormous prisms mounted in a long slit in the southern wall of the building refract sunlight, which plays around the room; the fragmentary rainbows it creates are especially remarkable on the white surface of the dome.

Neoclassical Washington is a city of domes, all of which trace their ancestry to Hadrian's Pantheon in Rome. It is a wonderful tribute on the part of the builders of this organically inspired museum that they included such a structure here. In a remarkable example of collaboration—or probably more accurately of cultural convergence—the dome in the American Indian museum brings to life a feature of Hadrian's dome that no other neoclassical imitation captures. With its oculus open to the sky, the vault of Hadrian's dome is always marked by the image of the moving sun, and at night the stars are visible from inside. Hadrian made the celestial a living presence in his structure, and this museum has done the same.

The most popular and crowded Smithsonian gallery is the National Air and Space Museum—indeed, it claims to be the most visited museum in the world. Designed by Gyo Obata, the façade of the vast building is composed of alternating positives and negatives. Blocklike marble-paneled sections are counter-pointed by areas with floor-to-ceiling glass. The general effect is roughly similar to the rhythm of a colonnade, and the surface material harmonizes well enough with the neoclassical buildings on the Mall. For decades before the museum was opened in 1976, its treasures hung from the ceiling of the Arts and Industries Building. In the late 1950s the artifacts of early American space flight—the increasingly massive Vanguard, Jupiter, and Titan rockets—stood outdoors along the northwest wall of the building.

The national aerospace collection has since grown to such proportions that the Smithsonian has been obliged to open a new museum beyond the Beltway and a few miles from Dulles Airport. Called the Steven F. Udvar-Hazy Center in recognition of a multimillion dollar gift from the airline magnate, this hangarlike facility exhibits hundreds of flying machines, from the modest scale of a crop duster to an Air France Concorde and the space shuttle *Enterprise.* The gallery also exhibits the controversial *Enola Gay,* the B-29 Superfortress that dropped on Hiroshima the first atomic bomb ever used in warfare.

The heart of the downtown museum is the second floor gallery devoted to the Wright brothers. Their kitelike bi-wing, with its elevated box tail, chopped off propellers, and bicycle chain drives, is the supreme treasure of the museum and the Rosetta Stone of manned flight. The Wrights first offered the plane to the Smithsonian in 1910. For many decades the institution refused to accept the airplane or to acknowledge the Wright brothers' achievement. Instead, the Smithsonian touted the rival claim of a former secretary, Samuel P. Langley, who successfully flew a steam-powered drone in 1896. A few weeks before the Wrights' historic flight, Langley launched a large-scale piloted version, which he called the Great Aerodrome. Though it crashed immediately after take-

off, the Smithsonian exhibited it anyway and asked the Wrights to provide one of their later planes to fill out the exhibit, which they refused to
do. Finally, in the decade that plunged the United States into World War
II, the Smithsonian relented, and in 1948 the Wrights' heirs were finally
able to hand over the plane.

On May 21, 1927, Charles A. Lindbergh landed his single-engine
Ryan strut-braced aluminum monoplane, *The Spirit of St. Louis,* at Le
Bourget Airport outside Paris. Nearly a hundred thousand people
thronged the field, and Lindbergh quickly killed the engines to avoid
slashing well-wishers with his propeller. The young pilot and his St. Louis
backers won a $25,000 prize for the achievement, which boosted com-
mercial airline development in the United States. Lindbergh donated the

100

plane to the Smithsonian a year
after his triumph. (100) In 1929
Calvin Coolidge presented him with
the Medal of Honor, and he
remained an international celebrity
for the rest of his life. An outspoken
opponent of Franklin Roosevelt,
Lindbergh and his family were also
the victims of the most highly covered crime of the 1930s, the kid-
napping and disappearance of their baby on March 1, 1932.

Among a number of early space capsules, the atrium gallery displays
the Apollo 11 Command Module *Columbia* in which astronauts Neil Armstrong, Edwin "Buzz" Aldrin, and Michael Collins returned from the moon

on July 24, 1969. The *Breitling Orbiter 3* gondola, in which Bertrand Piccard and Brian Jones were the first to circumnavigate the globe in a balloon, is the only nonpowered exhibit in the room. The most recent acquisition is *SpaceShipOne,* which on June 21, 2004, made the first privately funded manned spaceflight.

Like the East Wing of the National Gallery, the Hirshhorn Museum was designed for the exhibition of modern art. The core of the collection—some twelve thousand works—and an endowment to construct and maintain the museum were donated by the financier Joseph Herman Hirshhorn. Hirshhorn was born in Latvia in 1899, the twelfth of thirteen children. His father died soon after Joseph's birth, and the remaining family immigrated to the United States. His mother worked in a purse factory, and the older brothers and sisters helped to maintain the family. Joseph left school at age twelve and began selling newspapers; by age fourteen he found a job in a brokerage house.

When he was seventeen, Hirshhorn established himself as a broker and was immediately successful. He was among those legendary investors who took all their money out of the stock market before the 1929 crash. In the 1950s he invested in Canadian gold mining and later in uranium, which yielded enormous profits. Like the industrialists and financiers whose collections formed the core of the National Gallery, Hirshhorn began collecting art as soon as he was making money. During the 1950s, when his collection already numbered more than five thousand objects, he hired the art dealer Abram Lerner as curator. Hirshhorn died in 1981, seven years after the opening of his museum. The Hirshhorn collection features paintings primarily by American modernists, while the sunken sculpture garden just in front of the museum includes international works.

The building was designed by the firm of Skidmore, Owings & Merrill. A stubby concrete cylinder with a wide slitlike window and shallow balcony, this uncompromisingly modern structure looks at first glance like the pillbox gun emplacements of World War II. It stands on its own plaza supported on widely spaced concrete pylons. Inside, the hollow center of the museum is open to the sky, and the view is considerably friendlier and more appealing. The interior façade encircles an open courtyard with entrances and exits in all four directions. The inner wall of the museum is formed of three stories of concrete cells with deeply recessed windows. While the building materials and the exterior form are at odds with the prevailing architectural styles of Washington, the inner courtyard embraces the same model with which the American Indian Museum finds common ground. It is not entirely fanciful to think of the courtyard as an outdoor rotunda; the window cells are like coffers and the opening to the sky an enormous oculus.

Though it encroaches on the Mall, the sunken sculpture garden is an appealing blend of works in all styles, from the abstract to the realistic. (101) Set in small formal lawns at various levels and sheltered by overhanging trees, the garden and its choice collection are appealing from above or within.

The Enid A. Haupt Garden, directly behind the Smithsonian Castle, opened in 1987. The garden reflects nineteenth-century ideals in its symmetrical design, formal parterres, and period iron benches. Pavilions at its back corners lead visitors into the underground galleries of the

National Museum of African Art, the Arthur M. Sackler Gallery, and the
S. Dillon Ripley Center. The African Art collection, drawn in part from the
ethnographic collections of the Smithsonian, includes sculptures, tex-
tiles, architectural elements, and decorative artifacts representing nearly
one thousand African cultures. The Sackler Gallery was built to house
Asian art objects donated by its namesake, a renowned physician, medical researcher, and philanthropist who also endowed galleries in New
York, at Harvard and Princeton, and in Beijing. The permanent collection
includes works of art from China and
others representative of the Silk Road
and South and Southeast Asia.

101

An underground passage links the
Sackler to the much older Freer Gallery
of Art. Charles Lang Freer was a manu-
facturer of railroad cars and an early
American collector of Japanese art.
Freer also put together the largest col-
lection of works by James McNeill
Whistler. As a painter, Whistler is deeply rooted in Western traditions; but
as a designer, his work, which is represented by the magnificent Peacock
Room, shows a kinship with a Japanese aesthetic. Buddhist Art, Islamic
Art, and Ancient Near Eastern Art are well represented in the Freer collection.

The Department of Agriculture is the only representative of the Executive Branch with a presence on the Mall. And its building, next door to
the Freer Gallery, was one of the first tests of the government's will to

carry out the recommendations of the McMillan Commission. In the early nineteenth century, American agriculture was overseen by the Patent Office. In the second year of the Civil War, when food production became vital to the war effort, Congress voted to grant land for the creation of agricultural colleges throughout the states, and it established a separate Department of Agriculture. In 1889 the department achieved cabinet status.

After much debate and the direct intervention of President Theodore Roosevelt, the building that would house the department was built on the Mall, but it was pushed up against the margins, and its façade was cast in Classical Revival style. Designed by Rankin, Kellogg & Crane of Philadelphia, the structure combines a large central block with interior courtyard and two long wings that step back from the Mall. At the rear of the structure, two bridges span Independence Avenue and link the elegant front building to a seven-story complex housing more than four thousand offices. Designed in a stripped-down classicizing style, that second building is one of many utilitarian structures that mark this area on the south side of the Mall.

When the National Museum of American History opened in 1964 across the Mall from the Agriculture Department, it was called the Museum of History and Technology. The building was designed by Walker Cain of Steinman, Cain & White, the successor firm to McKim, Mead & White. It sits on a high windowless plinth that encloses its two lower stories. Its superstructure is a long and low rectangle faced with marble. The façade is divided into vertical panels that push forward or step back in a pattern suggesting the rhythm of a colonnade. The spaces separating adjacent panels are glazed. The windows are virtually invisible head on, but from an angle they give the façade a sense of depth. A small attic with tiny square windows sits atop the main structure.

For decades the fifteen star and fifteen bar United States flag that hung over Fort McHenry throughout the British bombardment during the night of September 13–14, 1814, hung on the back wall of the atrium. In recent years it was replaced by the flag that flew above the Pentagon on September 11, 2001. If any modern Smithsonian museum preserves the character of the Old Patent Office collection, it is the American History Museum, which proudly bills itself as the national attic. The range of curators gives some idea of the nature of the over three million objects in its collection. Curators specialize in home and community life; information technology and communications; medicine and science; military history and diplomacy; music, sports, and entertainment; politics and reform; work and industry. The museum's overall aim is to represent American communities and their particular ways of life and values. Popular culture is exceptionally well represented. The studio set in which the pioneering "French chef," Julia Child, filmed her television programs in the 1960s is part of it. The ruby slippers Judy Garland wore in *The Wizard of Oz* have been an especially popular exhibit.

The grim side of American communal history is also represented. In 1839 Joseph Smith founded Nauvoo, Illinois, as a refuge for the persecuted Mormon sect, and under his leadership the population of the city grew to some twenty thousand. The Nauvoo Mormon Temple featured thirty carved folk-art capitals at the tops of columns. The one in the Smithsonian collection represents a personified sun with pursed lips and puffy cheeks rising over stylized waves; above his spiky hair two hands holding trumpets reach down from the sky. Bitter experience led the Mormon community to form its own militia, and anti-Mormon groups armed themselves in turn. An incident within the community led to demands for the arrest of Smith and other members of the City Council. Under a promise of protection from the governor, Smith, his brother Hyrum, and two others surrendered and were jailed. Smith and his brother were shot in Carthage jail on June 27, 1844, by the armed mob.

The museum also displays the Woolworth's lunch counter from Greensboro, North Carolina, which in the era of "separate but equal" was reserved for whites only. On February 1, 1960, four black students from North Carolina Agricultural and Technical College sat down and refused to budge when they were denied service. Their action sparked a sit-in that lasted for months and eventually succeeded at integrating eating establishments. Along with Rosa Parks's refusal to give up her seat on the bus five years earlier, this spontaneous challenge to Jim Crow laws gave birth to the modern civil rights movement.

The newest museum to be constructed on the Mall is the National Museum of African American History and Culture, just west of the National Museum of American History. After years of campaigning by the museum's supporters, Congress acknowledged in 2003 that "there exists no national museum within the Smithsonian Institution that is devoted to the documentation of African American life, art, history, and culture on a national level." House Bill 3491 created "a National Museum of African American History and Culture . . . dedicated to the collection, preservation, research, and exhibition of African American historical and cultural

material reflecting the breadth and depth of the experiences of individuals of African descent living in the United States." In 2006 a site on
empty land near the Washington Monument was officially assigned to the
new museum.

In 1978 President Jimmy Carter established a commission focused on
Holocaust remembrance. In its report, issued in 1979, the Carter Commission recommended "that a National Holocaust Memorial/Museum be
erected in Washington, D.C., that would present the Holocaust through
pictorial accounts, films, and other visual exhibits within a framework
that is not merely reportorial but analytic, encouraging reflection and
questioning . . . Special emphasis would also be placed on the American
aspect of the Holocaust—the absence of American response . . . the
American liberation of the camps, the reception of survivors after 1945,
the lives rebuilt in this country . . . the development of a new sensitivity
to the Holocaust, and the growing respect for the multi-ethnic, multi-
dimensional aspects of American culture."

The government provided a building, an unused annex of the Treasury
Department located on Fourteenth Street SW, directly south of the Washington Monument. In 1984 permission was granted to raze the building
and erect a new one in its place. After much give and take, a design by
James Ingo Freed—a partner of I. M. Pei—was selected. The façade of
the United States Holocaust Memorial Museum is composed of blocklike
masses with a neoclassical cornice and a central exedra with rectangular
openings at street level and gridded openings above. The labyrinthine
interior of the building is designed to simulate the fear and uncertainty
that inmates of the camps confronted. (102)

102

Random itineraries weave through the harrowing collection. Each culminates in the Hall of Remembrance, a hexagonal shrine overlooking the Tidal Basin at the far end of the complex. Its commemorative rotunda is crowned by a faceted diamond-shaped skylight. The red granite floor, reminiscent of broken flesh, is ringed by a double wall. A narrow walkway passes between the inner and outer walls. In the inner wall, triangular windows offer partial views of the Tidal Basin and green space at the base of the Washington Monument. Wider openings suggest funeral chapels or the furnace doors of crematoria. Behind them, black walls inscribed with the names of the death camps can be seen. A sooty yellow flame burns in front of the westernmost recess, which is inscribed with a verse from Deuteronomy warning of the dangers of forgetting.

As early as 1783, while British troops were still being evacuated from the newly liberated colonies, Congress resolved "that an equestrian statue of General Washington be erected at the place where the residence of Congress shall be established." The legislators even went so far as to describe how the statue would look. According to the notes on L'Enfant's plan, it "shall be supported upon a marble pedestal on which should be represented four principal events of the war which he commanded in person." In designing the federal city, L'Enfant chose a place for the equestrian monument at the right angle of a triangle, with Pennsylvania Avenue as the hypotenuse and the President's House and Capitol at its other two vertices.

Repeated attempts to fund the monument failed. President John Quincy Adams sponsored legislation in 1825 that was voted down. In 1832, at the centenary of Washington's birth, the prominent and powerful senator Henry Clay introduced a monument bill that was also rejected. Convinced that Congress would never carry through with a project now fifty years on the drawing board, George Watterston, librarian of Congress, formed the Washington National Monument Society and enlisted prominent political figures to serve on its board of directors. In 1836 the society announced a competition to plan the monument.

The winning design by Robert Mills would have astonished the men of Washington's generation. True to the original commission, Mills designed an equestrian monument. Thirty feet tall, the first president stood in a Roman chariot driven by a winged Victory and pulled by four Arabian horses. This Ben Hur ensemble was to stand a hundred feet above ground on the attic of a round colonnaded temple some two hundred feet in diameter. Rising above and behind Washington to an astonishing height of six hundred feet was an obelisk in the Egyptian style. The four-horse chariot and its supporting substructure were never attempted. Mills's design serves mainly to explain how an equestrian monument was transmogrified into a giant stone needle.

Even after the competition, money came in slowly and Congress failed to grant the society a site for its extravagant project. Finally, in 1848, they relented. But the site L'Enfant had chosen for Washington on horseback was too unstable to support Mills's megalith, and the monument was moved to higher and more stable ground nearby, which put it off axis with the White House and Capitol. On July 4, 1848, the grand master of American Masons laid the cornerstone using the trowel with which Washington himself had set the Capitol cornerstone in place. Funds came in abundantly after this, then just as rapidly dried up. In lieu of money, Alabama citizens offered to cut and dress a stone for the monument and ship it to Washington. Hundreds of organizations and many foreign governments followed suit.

Newly elevated to the throne of Saint Peter, Pope Pius IX sent a block from the ruins of Rome's Temple of Concord. Given the Masonic sponsorship of the monument and the American stand on separation of church and state, this was a bold and generous act by a pontiff whose liberal views contrasted with the authoritarian and reactionary policies of his immediate predecessors. While Catholics welcomed the gift, members of the Native American Party, popularly called the Know-Nothings, were outraged. Anti-immigration and fiercely anti-Catholic, the group organized a raiding party that on the night of March 6, 1854, overpowered the watchman at the monument site and made off with the papal gift. The stone was never recovered. The notorious and shameful theft put an end to donations.

A year later the Know-Nothings seized control of the monument itself. Breaking into the headquarters of the Monument Society, they seized the group's records and voted themselves its overseers. They remained in legal control until an act of Congress on the brink of the Civil War ousted them and restored the monument to the legitimate society. While construction of the Capitol Dome went on throughout the war, the Washington Monument remained an unfinished stub 176 feet tall, topped by a decaying derrick and surrounded by sheep and cattle pens. Nearby was a slaughter-house where beef and mutton were prepared for the Union troops encamped throughout the city.

In the burst of energy that marked the postwar period, the government assumed full responsibility for the monument. Congress appropriated adequate funds. Army engineers who surveyed the foundations of the structure found it one and a half inches out of plumb and determined that its substructure could not support an obelisk now projected to reach a final height of 555 feet. They burrowed under the existing foundations in sections to correct the tilt, then filled the excavations with concrete; they extended the base outward in all directions.

Given the new building techniques available in the 1870s, it is surprising that construction continued along old-fashioned lines. A granite inner core was substituted for the rubble reinforcement of the first section, but the building continued as a pure masonry structure. It remains today the tallest such structure in the world. From 1880 on, the monument went up at a regular and rapid pace, with blocks lifted through the center of the shaft in a steam-powered elevator. On December 6, 1884, the final block of marble was set in place and a tiny pyramid of aluminum—an exotic and costly metal in the nineteenth century—was set on its tip. Preparing the inside of the monument for the public took another four years.

The areas west and south of the Washington Monument were swamp or river in L'Enfant's day and played no part in his plan. By the time the McMillan Commission began its work in 1901, much of the area had been transformed to solid ground. Commercial and residential development was slow to take hold, however, and when the commissioners looked at this area, they saw open land that suited their twin goals of reinvigorating L'Enfant's plan as a guide to development and creating more green space for the residents of the tightly urbanized city center. As they considered this new area, they saw an opportunity, even an obligation, to extend L'Enfant's grand avenue. "Where L'Enfant dealt with a composition one and a half miles in length, the Commission is called upon to deal with an area two and a half miles long, with a maximum breadth of about one mile."

The commissioners proposed to enlarge the center of the District to embrace a kite-shaped swath of land that took in "the space between Pennsylvania and New York avenues on the north, and Maryland Avenue and the Potomac River on the south." Dense commercial development downtown made land north of Pennsylvania Avenue unaffordable, however, and their plan had little effect there. Leaving this area aside, the space they planned to organize had as its central feature an ideal intersection in the shape of a Latin cross. This area was defined "from east to west by the axis of the Capitol and from north to south by the White House axis. Regarding the Monument as the center, the Capitol as the base, and the White House as the extremity of one arm of [the] cross, we have at the head of the composition on the banks of the Potomac a memorial site of the greatest possible dignity, with a second and only slightly less commanding site at the extremity of the second arm."

While the commission's recommendations did not finally determine how the spaces they laid out would be used, their general ground plan

and the axes they identified did take concrete form. Monuments of the
kind they described eventually assumed the places they designated. In
their view, the minor axis anchored in the White House was to be quite
different from the major east-west axis. South of the Washington Monument, the Commission envisaged "a place of recreation." They noted with
some dismay that "the positive dearth of means of innocent enjoyment
for one's leisure hours is remarkable in Washington, the one city in this
country where people have the most leisure."

To meet this need, the commission projected "a great stadium
arranged for athletic contests of all kinds and for the display of fireworks
on festal occasions. Ball grounds and tennis courts, open-air gymnasiums
for youths, and sand piles and swings for children, all should be provided, as they are now furnished in the progressive cities of this country.
The tidal basin should have the most ample facilities for boating and for
wading and swimming in summer, as well as for skating in winter. To this
end boat pavilions, locker houses, and extensive bath houses should be
constructed with all the conveniences known to the best-equipped institutions of like character."

Many decades later, the great stadium, named in honor of Robert F.
Kennedy, was actually built in a different but equally prominent place, on
the eastern end of a line that begins at the Lincoln Memorial and passes
through the Washington Monument, the Capitol, and Lincoln Park. South
of the Washington Monument, tennis courts, a pool, and a golf course
were added to the ball fields the commission proposed, and they are still
in use in East Potomac Park between the Tidal Basin and the river. Created in 1882 to control water levels in the Potomac, the Tidal Basin was

103

soon transformed into an amenity and an ornament. Swimming in the Potomac has been a
risky business for decades, but paddleboats can
be rented between March 15 and Columbus Day
weekend from the northeast shore of the Basin.

The commissioners did not foresee the landscape element that has become not only the
defining attraction of the area but a living symbol of the city itself. In 1909 first lady Helen
Taft proposed that Japanese cherry trees be
planted along the river. Through the efforts of
Jokichi Takamine, a Japanese chemical
researcher living in America, the mayor of Tokyo then presented three
thousand specially grafted Yoshino cherry trees to the city. These trees,
planted in 1912, and their descendants line the Tidal Basin and both
sides of East Potomac Park. The city celebrates its annual Cherry Blossom Festival for two weeks in early April. (103)

The great monument on axis with the White House that the McMillan
Commission recommended remained unbuilt for many years. During the
Republican 1920s the site was set aside for a memorial to Theodore
Roosevelt. In 1934 a Democratic Congress usurped Roosevelt's spot and
dedicated it to Thomas Jefferson. Roosevelt's monument was moved to
an island bird sanctuary in the Potomac. Congress created the Thomas
Jefferson Memorial Commission, which chose John Russell Pope, architect of the National Archives and National Gallery, to design the monument. Pope had no difficulty coming up with an architectural language to

fit a man whose own architectural ideals were so well known and so close to his own, and the Commission agreed with his choice. The monument would be based on the Pantheon, surrounded by wide terraces, and set in a formal landscaped garden.

Problems arose when the United States Commission of Fine Arts, which held general control over monuments in Washington, objected. A compromise design was prepared based on the now-deceased Pope's original plan, with modifications by his former partners. This satisfied almost no one. Finally, President Franklin Roosevelt stepped in and gave executive approval to the Memorial Commission's original choice. Still, the controversy continued. Pope was already becoming a favorite target of Modernist critics, and his design received little but

104

professional scorn. Nature lovers entered the battle on behalf of the Tidal Basin, which, they claimed, might be compromised. A few Japanese cherry trees would have to be cut, and they also had their champions.

The memorial, dedicated in 1943, is an adaptation of Jefferson's beloved Pantheon to suit a 360-degree exposure. (104) Pope broke through the walls so that the colossal image of Jefferson inside could be seen from a distance. An open colonnade around the entire building gives the memorial interest from any angle and also ties it to a tholos, the ancient Greek shrine whose form underlay Mills's unbuilt monument to George Washington. The inner walls of the memorial were inscribed with quotations from the Declaration of Independence, Jefferson's *Autobiography,* and his *Notes on the State of Virginia.* There were also passages from personal letters to George Wythe, George Washington, James Madison, and others. The statue of Jefferson, nearly twenty feet tall, was installed in the monument in 1947. Shortages of metal during World War II had delayed its casting.

On the western rim of the Tidal Basin, surrounded by century-old cherry trees, is a meandering memorial to Franklin Delano Roosevelt. The long and narrow monument, designed by Lawrence Halprin and dedicated in 1997, is a string of open-air half-rooms, the central four representing Roosevelt's four terms as president. Free-standing sculptures and bas-reliefs represent both the president's accomplishments and the great challenges of his long presidency, especially the Great Depression. A continuous plaza marks the boundaries of the monument.

Individual rooms within it are outlined by huge rusticated red granite blocks, often marked with inscriptions, that are piled one atop another in a way suggesting both a structure half-built and one on the verge of falling down. Trees and bushes sprout from the walls' tops. Unused blocks stand in piles and lie scattered in a corner fountain. (105) Sculptures and sculptural groups in the monument, many of which are based on photographs, are near ground level and easy to touch. One group by sculptor George Segal represents a bread line; another, a man listening on his radio, presumably to one of Roosevelt's Fireside Chats. Eleanor Roosevelt stands alone in a sheltered niche with the symbol of the United Nations behind her. A seated figure of Franklin Roosevelt, his body swathed in his naval cape, is the only representation of the presi-

dent. The president's Scotch
terrier, Fala—blown up to New-
foundland proportions—sits near
his feet.

The northwest rim of the
Tidal Basin, on a direct line
between the Lincoln and Jefferson memorials, is the future site
of a monument dedicated to the

105

memory of Martin Luther King Jr. Similar in conception to the FDR
memorial, its nearest neighbor, the King monument combines landscape,
architectural, and sculptural elements in an ensemble symbolically linked
to King's achievements and his philosophy of nonviolence.

Nearby, the Korean War Veterans Memorial commemorates the more
than fifty-four thousand American soldiers killed or missing during the
United Nations action to stop the invasion of South Korea by troops from
the Communist North. The footprint of the monument is a triangle intersecting a circle. The triangular area, flanked by a black granite wall
etched with images from contemporary photographs, is meant to be a
landscaped representation of the field of battle. It combines granite
strips and juniper shrubs. Within this simulated field a platoon of soldiers, heavily armed and carrying full backpacks, with windswept pon-
chos draping their bodies, makes its way forward. (106) The group was
sculpted in stainless steel by Frank Gaylord. At the apex of the triangle
the framing wall ends in a shallow circular pool. The monument, dedicated in 1995, was designed by Cooper-Lecky Architects.

The McMillan Commission had a very specific idea in mind for the endpoint of their primary axis running through the Capitol and the Washington Monument and westward through the long green strip of reclaimed marshland to the edge of the river. They imagined "a memorial erected to the memory of that one man in our history as a nation who is worthy to

106

be named with George Washington—Abraham Lincoln."

Ground was broken for the Lincoln Memorial on February 12, 1914, just six months before World War I began in Europe. The design corresponds closely to the McMillan Commission's suggestions. A traffic circle (its eastern half now closed) rings the monument, which stands upon a large platform, or stylobate. It recalls a Greek temple, such as the Parthenon in Athens, except that the monument lacks pediments and a sloping roof and its interior is visible not from the end but from one of its long sides. (107) A cascade of steps leads to its grand portico of thirty-six columns, the number of states in the Union at the time of Lincoln's death. Separated by wreaths, the names of these states are inscribed in the frieze above the portico. An attic projects above the building, decorated with forty-eight swags to represent the states of the union at the time the monument was built.

From inside the monument's central chamber, a seated figure of Lincoln looks out on the Reflecting Pool, the Washington Monument, and the distant Capitol. Sculpted by Daniel Chester French, who based his design on careful study of the many surviving photographs of Lincoln, the massive figure is true to life and realistically dressed. (108) This historical Lincoln sits on an entirely symbolic throne decorated with Roman

fasces—the symbol of strength in
union. Looking out from between the
columns of a Greek temple, such a
seated figure has to recall the image of
a god. The deity French evokes is
Olympian Zeus, the figure on which
Greenough's controversial seated figure

107

of George Washington, sculpted for the Capitol Rotunda, was also based.

Inscriptions from the Gettysburg Address and Lincoln's Second Inaugural emphasize themes of sacrifice and the renewal of the union. A
mural by Jules Guerin above the text of the Gettysburg Address shows an
"Angel of Truth" between two emancipated slaves. This is the only
explicit reference in the memorial to what has become one of the dominant themes in its history.

On Easter Sunday 1939, in a highly symbolic event, the African-
American diva Marian Anderson sang for seventy-five thousand people
from the memorial's long cascade of steps, having been turned away from
performing in Constitution Hall because of her race. In protest of its

white-artists-only policy, Eleanor Roosevelt
resigned her membership in the Daughters of
the American Revolution, who owned the hall.
Soon after, A. Philip Randolph and Bayard
Rustin began to plan for a great march and rally
to take place on July 1, 1941. The focus of the
march on the Mall would be discrimination
against African Americans in industries that
were receiving huge federal contracts for war

108

materiel. Randolph was the founder of the Brotherhood of Sleeping Car Porters, the first majority black labor union of national importance. Rustin was a key activist in the African American struggle for civil rights. President Roosevelt felt the march would be embarrassing to his administration and urged the organizers to call it off. When they refused, he issued Executive Order 8802, which established the Committee on Fair Employment Practice and required government agencies issuing contracts to enforce equal opportunity. The march was cancelled.

Over twenty years later, Randolph and Rustin returned as organizers of the August 28, 1963, March on Washington for Jobs and Freedom. More than a quarter of a million people participated in what is remembered as a defining moment in the civil rights struggle of the 1960s. On that day, Martin Luther King Jr., leader of the Southern Christian Leadership Conference and an outspoken champion of nonviolent protest against racial inequality, gave his famous "I have a dream" speech from the steps of the Lincoln Memorial.

Throughout the 1960s a number of marches on the Mall were directed against the growing violence and futility of the Vietnam War. On November 15, 1969, as many as half a million people filled the grounds between the Capitol and the Lincoln Memorial to demand an end to the conflict. There were further demonstrations after the Cambodia incursion and the Kent State shootings in 1970. The March on Washington for Lesbian and Gay Rights was held in 1979, with upwards of one hundred thousand marchers. A second march in 1987 that focused both on rights and on the need for government to address the AIDS crisis drew half a million. In 1995 Louis Farrakhan, at that time the leader of the Nation of

Islam, organized the Million Man March. Its focus was registration of African American voters and increased political and community involvement by black men. On every January 22—the anniversary of the Supreme Court's decision in *Roe v. Wade* that legalized abortion—opponents have held a March for Life. This is now the largest regularly recurring protest demonstration in Washington.

The highly regarded Vietnam Veterans Memorial was conceived by a private nonprofit group organized by Jan Scruggs. The group wanted a monument that commemorated American soldiers killed or missing in action but ignored the divisive politics that still surrounded the war. Maya Ying Lin, while an undergraduate architecture student at Yale, won the design competition. (109) In 1982 the memorial opened to the public.

It is a boomerang-shaped granite wall that digs into the earth at its center and rises to the surface at both ends. The name of each man and woman lost in the war is etched into the stone in the order in which they died. The names begin in the middle and move in sequence to the eastern wall, then resume at the western tip and climax again at the center. Alphabetical guides to finding an individual name are available at the monument, which is always attended by docents who are for the most part veterans themselves. The wall is meant to be touched, and rubbings of names can easily be made. The polished surface of the memorial reflects visitors and the surrounding monuments as a ghostly presence within the endless list of dead.

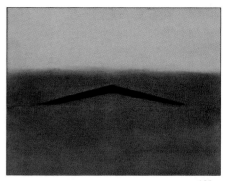

109

The Franklin D. Roosevelt, Vietnam, and Martin Luther King Jr. memorials were all designed to harmonize with their settings. The Korean War Memorial is less successful, and the World War II Memorial, placed near the base of the Washington Monument in a more formal part of the Mall, makes even less effort to accommodate itself to its surroundings. Completed in 2004 at a cost of some two hundred million dollars, the elliptical monument is set on an elevated platform; its fountain is ringed with standing stones hung with bronze wreaths that commemorate the war dead from each state. A partially enclosed pavilion at each narrow end is dedicated to the Atlantic and Pacific theaters of war. Inside the pavilions, four bronze columns support a victory wreath and two eagles with outstretched wings. Gilded stars on a blue field commemorate the four hundred thousand Americans lost in the most extensive conflict of a war-torn century.

Chapter Eight

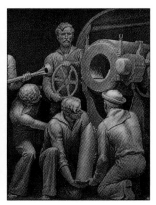

CITIZENS OF DC

North of Pennsylvania Avenue and the White House,
the land rises in just a few blocks to a modest height,
generally about eighty feet above sea level. The well-
drained soil rests on substantial bedrock, and no special site preparation is necessary to create secure
foundations. Pre–Civil War Washington developed in this area, and in areas
at similar elevation beyond Capitol Hill to the east and at the junction of the
two rivers to the south. (Map 8) The more or less even and solid terrain
throughout this intermediate zone was well suited to the grid of streets
L'Enfant laid out, and easily adaptable to horse-drawn transport for goods
and passengers. But beyond the line traced by the curve of Florida Avenue,
the steep rise of the piedmont was hard going for horses. That difficulty,
added to the distance from the city center, made urbanization of these areas
impractical before the age of mass transit.

After the Civil War, urban growth followed the horse car and streetcar
lines up country roads that fanned outward to the farm towns and villages
beyond the District boundary. Some of these roads had been in use before
L'Enfant sketched his design and were joined up with the diagonal avenues
traced on his map. Others were connected in a more haphazard way.
Between these avenues, the city was less completely built up. By the last

quarter of the century, neither L'Enfant's plan nor the neoclassical architecture that gave coherence to government buildings retained the prestige and power they once held. The lines of the city's expansion were driven by a combination of opportunistic housing development and the spread of public transport.

This unplanned growth embraced the architectural eclecticism of the Victorian age in America. All the major styles of late nineteenth-century domestic and commercial buildings were represented in the District. The region's steep rises, ravines, and valleys also contributed to the city's spotty development and polyglot architecture. While a small part of the District beyond the old boundary was designed with parallel streets and block after block of row houses, in most areas developers and architects took advantage of the dynamic contours of the land to create communities that reflected new thinking about urban layouts. Designers like the Olmsted Brothers (son and stepson of Frederick Law Olmsted) planned and publicized parklike communities where house types varied and streets meandered across hill and valley.

The city of Venice in Italy is an interesting counterexample to the pattern of development that prevailed in Washington. In the maritime republic, buildings surrounding the Piazza San Marco—especially St. Mark's Basilica and the Doge's Palace—influenced the styles of domestic architecture throughout the city's long history. In the Gothic period, arcades with four-lobed medallions between the points of successive arches distinguished both the ducal palace and the façades of great private houses. When Jacopo Sansovino introduced Renaissance High Classicism to the piazza in the early sixteenth century, the style quickly caught on in charitable institutions and in the palaces of wealthy families along the Grand

Canal. The result was a city in which civic and private structures spoke the same stylistic language.

In Washington, the overlaps between domestic and government buildings were few. Thornton's Octagon House was a rarity among Washington houses because it adapted a public style to a private residence. The Renwick Gallery and the Executive Office Building exhibited a common style too, but what they shared was a rejection of the neoclassicism that had harmonized government buildings in an earlier time. Architecturally, geographically, and ethnically, the nation's capital is two cities, a fact that is recognized in its dual name. The official city of government and the goal of most visitors is Washington. Most residents of the city call their home DC.

DC is a fragmented urban environment. The Anacostia River cuts both the southeast and northeast sectors of the city in two. Rock Creek and the wooded hills along it divide the northwest. Manmade features also break up the extended city. Fort Totten, which dates from the Civil War, and the once extensive grounds of the U.S. Soldier's Home create a void in the northeast. The rail lines and yards that stretch out behind Union Station like a comet's tail and the warehouse district that grew up around them further divide that part of the city. The Metrorail Red Line follows the railroad lines and creates an almost unbreachable barrier. Since the 1960s, multilane highways have diced the city into ever smaller pieces.

Developed at different times and broken by natural and artificial boundaries, the Washington street grid, which in theory extends evenly across each of the four quarters of the District, is pocketed with gaps. Street and avenue names mask this inconsistency. Avenues throughout the District are named for states, and north-south streets are numbered

110

just as they are in the center of town. Since the alphabet is too short to name all the east-west streets, the District has adopted a series of extended alphabets to supplement them. There are no X, Y, or Z streets in the original plan; W Street NW, the last on L'Enfant's grid, is immediately south of Florida Avenue. The first wave of streets added beyond Florida Avenue begins with Adams, Bryant, and Channing and runs through an alphabetical roll call of two-syllable names. After Upshur, Varnum, and Webster (not X-Ray, Yankee, and Zeno) come Allison, Buchanan, Critten-den, and on through a three-syllable alphabet. Running obliquely through this welter of named and numbered streets, the city's radiating avenues form the nuclei of its distinctive neighborhoods.

Wisconsin Avenue is the westernmost artery linking the interior of the District with the Maryland suburbs beyond. It intersects M Street—the continuation of Pennsylvania Avenue—in the center of Georgetown. This town was founded on the fall line of the Potomac at the site of an aban-doned Indian village called Tahoga. The Anacostan Indians who had inhabited the village controlled trade between the upper and lower stretches of the river, and throughout its early history Georgetown did the same. The first land grants were made in the area at the beginning of the eighteenth century. Ninian Beall was the first recorded resident.

On the land of Beall's neighbor, George Gordon, a tobacco inspection station was established. Scottish refugees from the unsuccessful upris-

ings of 1715 and 1745 fled to the city. In 1751 a town was incorporated
and laid out in an irregular grid on sixty acres of Beall and Gordon land
along the river. A multitude of tobacco roads converged on the port, and
warehouses for tobacco and flour—the city's chief exports—crowded the
waterside. Modest stone houses lined the nearby streets, while mansions
overlooked the town and river from the heights. Washington's oldest
house, built in 1765, is still standing at 3051 M Street. **(110)**

Commerce continued to drive growth until the early decades of the
nineteenth century, when steam-powered ships requiring a deeper harbor
than Georgetown could offer began to bypass the town. The Baltimore
and Ohio Railroad, which ended in Baltimore rather than Washington,
deprived Georgetown of much of
its domestic market. Only the
Chesapeake and Ohio Canal, completed alongside the Potomac in
1850, kept Georgetown trade alive.
When volume declined on the
canal in the late nineteenth century, the town went into a steep
decline. Then, during the 1930s,

111

Georgetown houses were rediscovered by congressmen and government
workers, and the area began to recover. The small streets north of M
Street still boast brick sidewalks and beautiful row houses **(111)**, and the
Georgetown Market has been preserved. Just south of Wisconsin Avenue,
joggers run tirelessly along the tow path of the murky C&O Canal—now a
threadlike national park that traces the Potomac from Georgetown to

Cumberland. (112) Mules move along it far less frequently, pulling the canal boat *Georgetown,* which offers short scenic trips.

Under the overpass and through the maze of riverside restaurants at the end of Thomas Jefferson Street, a short boardwalk provides public access to the Potomac. The once-notorious Watergate complex and the surprisingly graceless John F. Kennedy Center for the Performing Arts are both visible along the water to the east. Directly across is tree-covered

Theodore Roosevelt Island, a favorite birding spot today, as it was when the nation's most energetic president was in office. But the main attraction is the river itself, which still rolls down from the interior on its way to the sea. This is one of very few spots in the District where the city maintains even a fingertip grip on its ancestral bloodline.

As the weekend approaches, Georgetown becomes a rowdy college town, its bars drawing students from the many DC colleges and from nearby towns in Maryland and Virginia. Founded in 1789, Georgetown University is the oldest institution of higher education in the federal city. As a colony

112

dedicated to religious toleration, Maryland attracted large numbers of Catholic settlers, and for many years Baltimore served as the episcopal seat of the country's only bishop. Even before ascending to that office, Father John Carroll began planning an academy at Georgetown and established a fund-raising committee. In 1815 Congress chartered the college, which was staffed by priests of the Jesuit order. It grew rapidly in the first half of the nineteenth century, and a medical school was opened in

1850. During the Civil War, most Georgetown students returned to their southern homes and to service in the Confederate Army. Union troops took over the campus, and after the Second Battle of Manassas, college buildings and the medical school hospital housed the wounded. The college recovered quickly after the war, adding a law school in 1870.

Transforming the institution from a small Catholic college to a major teaching and research university became the goal of Father Patrick Healy. The biracial child of a plantation owner and a slave, Healy was educated in the North in Quaker schools and at the College of the Holy Cross in Massachusetts. Since postgraduate education in the United States was closed to African Americans, Healy earned his Ph.D. at the Catholic University of Louvain in Belgium. He joined the Georgetown faculty at the end of the Civil War and became its president in 1874.

The campus today reflects the institution's long history. Its earliest building, called Old North, was in use by the end of the eighteenth century. Smithmeyer & Pelz, the architects of the Library of Congress Jefferson Building, designed Healy Hall while its namesake was still president of the university. A four-story building in the Romanesque Revival style, it anchors the buildings of the Main Quad.

On L'Enfant's plan, Massachusetts Avenue runs parallel to Pennsylvania Avenue a few blocks to the north. Dupont Circle, at the intersection of Massachusetts Avenue with Connecticut, was once the center of Washington's wealthiest community. Because it stood on the western rim of the city until about 1880, the intersection was originally called Pacific Circle. It was renamed in 1884 to commemorate Civil War Admiral Samuel Francis Du Pont, whose fleet captured Port Royal, South Carolina, in a brilliant naval attack in November 1861. The victory was one of the first Union successes in the war, and it made Du Pont a hero. A first statue erected in 1884 by the Du Pont family—major suppliers of gunpowder to the Union Army—was replaced in 1921 by a fountain with allegorical figures designed by Daniel Chester French.

113

In 1881, at 2000 Massachusetts Avenue just west of Dupont Circle, the prominent Maine politician James Gillespie Blaine built a mansion in Second Empire style, richly ornamented with Gothic and Romanesque details. A few blocks off the circle at 1307 New Hampshire Avenue, the owner of the Heurich Brewery built Heurich House in 1892–1894. Designed by John Granville Myers in a modified Romanesque style with some affinities to the Old Post Office building, it is one of the best preserved Victorian houses in the country. (113) The Patterson House (now home of the Washington Club) at 15 Dupont Circle was built for the owner of the *Washington Times-Herald* newspaper in 1901. Designed by Charles McKim's partner Stanford White, the building is an Italianate mansion with two projecting wings and a porticoed central block. (114) In a conventional design of this type, the wings would meet at right angles, but here they meet obliquely to fit their wedge-shaped site.

The majority of the families who transformed this area into Washington's most prestigious neighborhood were industrialists. Nearby at 1600 Twenty-First Street, Duncan Phillips, heir to one of the founders of U.S. Steel, lived in a Georgian Revival mansion built in 1897. An avid collector of art, Phillips opened his home as a museum in 1921. The gallery

features nineteenth- and twentieth-
century paintings alongside works
from earlier periods that inspired
them. The length of Massachusetts
Avenue west of Sheridan Circle
attracted equally prominent families,
and by the early twentieth century it
was known as Millionaires' Row. The

114

Depression ruined many of the fortunes that had sustained these homes,
but as financiers and industrialists left the area, foreign embassies
moved in.

Eclecticism is the dominant mood of Embassy Row. The Embassy of
Haiti at 2311 Massachusetts Avenue occupies a building derived from a
Parisian mansion. The Pakistani Embassy a few doors away combines
Mansard roofs and silolike towers. The Embassy of Cameroon is housed
in a transplanted chateau. Among the many grand houses that line Sheridan Circle, the mansion at 1606 Twenty-Third Street stands out. (115) Its
improbable combination of neoclassical and craftsman-style detail is surprisingly successful. With a basement swimming pool and gold-plated

doorknobs, the
house suited the
tastes of Edward
Hamlin Everett, the
Cleveland inventor
of the fluted bottle
cap who commis-
sioned it in 1910.

115

Its designer, George Oakley Totten Jr., worked for a brief time as an architect in Turkey, and today the mansion is the Turkish ambassador's residence.

After crossing Rock Creek further west, Massachusetts Avenue swerves around one edge of the circular grounds of the old Naval Observatory in its steady climb up the piedmont. The observatory was established to coordinate celestial astronomy and the accurate measurement of time. Both were essential to navigation before the development of the Global Positioning System. Built on one of the highest points within the District and insulated as well as possible from light pollution and vibrations caused by traffic, the buildings on the site housed telescopes and the most accurate chronometers. Gradually, population growth in the area, combined with Washington's high humidity, made the telescope useless for serious astronomy. Advances in the calculation of time in the late twentieth century have been less of a threat. While the Naval Observatory no longer establishes standard time for the United States, it continues to be the official time-setter for the Department of Defense and for GPS satellites.

The mansion built in 1893 to house the superintendent of the Naval Observatory became the official residence of the vice president of the United States in 1974. Because of Richard Nixon's resignation, Gerald Ford rose to the presidency before he had a chance to occupy the mansion. His vice president, Nelson Rockefeller, used the residence only for entertaining. Walter Mondale, in the Carter administration, was the first VP to call Number One Observatory Circle home.

At 3101 Wisconsin Avenue, only a block from the point where Massachusetts Avenue intersects Wisconsin at the height of land, stands Wash-

ington National Cathedral. L'Enfant's plan called for a national
church near the Capitol that was
never built, and over time many of
the ceremonial and commemorative
tasks he imagined were taken over
by the Capitol Rotunda. In 1893
Congress granted a charter to the
Protestant Episcopal Cathedral
Foundation, and in 1907 construction of a national cathedral began
on a commanding site overlooking

116

downtown and Georgetown. In 1912 Bethlehem Chapel in the crypt of
the vast structure was completed and daily services begun. Construction
continued throughout most of the twentieth century. The nave was dedicated in 1976. In 1990, with the completion of the west towers, the
building campaign ended.

The outspoken architecture of the cathedral firmly declares its alle-
giance to the English Gothic and to the spirited revival of that tradition in
American churches and universities at the turn of the twentieth century.
The building, which is cruciform in plan, is over five hundred feet long
and soars three hundred feet in the air. A crypt of the same extension
runs beneath it. Its entryway on the west is divided into three bays with a
mammoth doorway in the center and smaller ones to either side. A blind
arcade above the doorways is surmounted by a rose window in the central
bay and pairs of tall arches on each side. (116) Twin towers with multiple
pinnacles at their corners flank the peaked roof, which is partially hidden

by a tall balustrade. Secondary entryways open at the ends of each apse. A tower is incorporated into the north entryway.

The nave is divided into nine bays by piers that separate it from the lower side aisles. (117) Two rows of windows illuminate the aisles; each section of the nave is lit by small pointed-arched windows with enormous Gothic windows above them. Beyond the transept, with its shallow arms, are two pulpits and a raised choir. The main altar of the church is behind the choir in a deep apse. The extensive grounds shelter a wonderful walled garden as well as two well-known preparatory schools, the National Cathedral School and St. Albans.

Before the new federal government moved to Washington, General Uriah Forrest built a country house in the rolling hills just west of Rock Creek, which he named Rosedale. He sold a quarter of his original plot of nearly a thousand acres to Judge Phillip Barton Key, who created his own estate called Woodley nearby. While both estate houses survive, their extensive grounds have been fractioned into ever smaller parcels to create the adjacent communities of Woodley Park and Cleveland Park. The community that should have been named Rosedale became Cleveland Park when newly elected President Grover Cleveland bought a house there which he later used as a summer White House. Key's mansion, Woodley, had been borrowed as a summer White House by presidents Van Buren, Tyler, and Buchanan; Cleveland himself stayed at Woodley while his own home was being remodeled. After he failed to win re-election in 1889, the disappointed ex-president sold the house, which was torn down in 1927.

A few years after Cleveland's defeat, electric street cars running along Wisconsin and Connecticut Avenues reached the area. By the mid-1890s

the in-town suburb of Cleveland Park began to fill
up with grand houses on large lots. As the neighborhood continued to expand throughout the early
decades of the twentieth century, smaller lots and
simpler houses became the norm. With its winding
streets, hills, and valleys, parklike plantings, and
variety of housing styles, Cleveland Park remains
one of the most congenial neighborhoods in the
city.

117

Rock Creek Park, which runs from the Maryland
line to the Potomac River, is the largest and most
widely used natural amenity in the city. It is
threaded by a twisting avenue that connects the center of the city with
the District's in-town neighborhoods and the Maryland suburbs. At the
end of the Civil War, when Congress began to consider setting aside some
land in Washington for public recreation, the serpentine hollow through
which the narrow creek flowed on its way to the Potomac was an obvious
choice. Recreation was not a sufficient argument to get Congress to act,
however; nor was the beauty of the area or the positive effect on property
values of its protection. In 1890 Congress finally agreed to buy the
watershed when it became clear that pollution was turning it into an
open sewer.

The valleys of Rock Creek's tributaries were added to the park in the
early twentieth century. The surrounding hillsides remain, even today,
more or less in their natural state, with most improvements confined to
the flood plain. Picnic areas—in almost continuous use during three seasons of the year—are scattered along the drives that trace the course of

the creek. (118) Packed with commuter cars morning and evening, the avenues that give access to the park also threaten to poison it.

As Connecticut Avenue climbs the piedmont beyond Dupont Circle, it skirts the entrance to the National Zoological Park. Established in 1889 and placed under the umbrella of the Smithsonian the following year, the zoo occupies two hundred acres of land that slopes down from Connecticut Avenue to the Rock Creek valley. Laid out and landscaped by Frederick Law Olmsted, the site features meandering, tree-lined pathways that connect a diverse group of animal exhibits from around the world.

118

The zoo is a far cry from the Smithsonian's first menagerie, which was housed in a corral on the Mall. That zoo was sponsored by the Smithsonian's taxidermist, who hoped to increase the accuracy of his installations by observing live animals. His dream of seeing those animals in approximations of their habitats led to the formation of a national zoo, with its naturalistic exhibit spaces. The establishing act passed by Congress imagined a center that would foster not just animal study but public recreation as well. Olmsted's design merged animal exhibits with a pleasant, parklike setting.

Since animal behavior was not a significant research interest during most of the zoo's early history, and comparative anatomy was better observed in skeletons than in living animals, the scientific mission of the zoo was initially limited. This changed dramatically in the mid-1950s when it became startlingly clear that the wild animal populations of the world faced significant, immediate threats. The zoo, which had relied on animal collectors to replenish its exhibits, began to nurture and breed species threatened by hunting and habitat destruction. As animal behavior became an object of important scientific study, the zoo expanded its mission and became a laboratory for observation. Exhibits that had once favored the exotic and curious now taught conservation and the interaction of animals with their environment. Wherever possible, the old brick animal houses and square cages were replaced with large spaces that placed animals in their natural habitat and removed barriers to observation.

Rock Creek divides the residential city not just geographically but sociologically as well. Residents of communities to the west of Rock Creek Park are generally affluent and predominantly white. Residents of neighborhoods to the east are for the most part poorer, less educated, underemployed, and predominately African American. How Washington came to be divided in this way is a complex and, in many ways, a frustrating and tragic story. The racial divide reflects the history of a city which, like many others in the North, served as a mecca for African Americans from the Civil War onward. But paradoxically, it also reflects a history that distanced Washington from these northern industrial cities and placed it within the cultural orbit of the American South.

European immigration transformed nineteenth- and twentieth-century

America. The effect was felt nationwide, but the impact was greatest and most visible in cities. In 1900 more than one third of New Yorkers had come to the city as immigrants. The proportions in Chicago, Cleveland, and Detroit were about the same. In small industrial towns like Lowell or Fall River, Massachusetts, the numbers were closer to fifty percent. Millions of immigrants filled the floors of newly created textile mills, foundries, steel mills, and factories. Similar millions crowded tenements, and ethnic neighborhoods were a fact of life in most American cities. Beginning in the second half of the nineteenth century, the immigrant saga replaced the American Revolution and the emancipation struggle as the most up-to-date dramatization of American democracy at work.

Washington DC was by no means immune to the political and ideological influence of immigration, but as a city it largely missed out on this event—the most important mass movement of the era. In 1900 only one in fourteen residents was a first-generation immigrant. The absence of a foreign-born population had several implications. For one thing, it signaled that Washington was not an industrial city. And for another, it highlighted the very important and tangible link between Washington and other cities with very small immigrant populations—primarily cities of the South.

Fewer than three percent of Atlantans in 1900 were foreign born; Richmond's numbers were about the same. In Nashville, the most diverse city in the region, fewer than four percent of residents was born outside the United States. The South's immigrant profile in the late nineteenth century was different from the rest of the nation because of the Civil War and because of the absence of industrial jobs to attract workers. To a remarkable degree, Washington DC shared the southern cultural experi-

ence. African Americans were the most important minority in Washington, as they were throughout the South.

A lack of industrialization and immigrant workers meant that white
urban dwellers in Washington did not have to compete for centrally
located housing. Like other southern cities, the capital sprawled and mid-
dle-class housing was relatively inexpensive because there was no pre-
mium on compactness. But laced into this city of wide avenues and
uncluttered homes was a second, vastly inferior city for blacks. Alleyways
were cut through the backs of the grand blocks on L'Enfant's plan, and
these unpaved, undrained secondary arteries were lined on both sides
with shanties thrown together at little cost. By the turn of the century,
more than three hundred such alleyways, housing a predominately black
population of nearly twenty thousand, were scrawled on top of the city's
formal grid. Domestic labor was the major source of income for most
freed blacks, and many black families—though by no means all—lived in
the alleys behind the major streets. In nineteenth-century New York,
African Americans clustered in homogeneous communities on the edges
of the Irish ghetto in lower Manhattan. While they were more often the
victims of violence and discrimination than other ethnic groups, their
physical place in the city was like the ethnic enclaves of other minorities.
Washington and cities of the South were organized differently. Race, not
ethnicity, was the most significant social category. Social codes defining
black and white ways of life were so complete, so inflexible, and so well
understood by both groups that physical separation was unnecessary.
And, in the general absence of cheap and efficient public transportation,
it was impractical.

Washington's back-alley solution to its post–Civil War housing crisis was not finally eliminated until Franklin Roosevelt's presidency. But even then, the racial mix of the city remained unchanged. Though the District population nearly doubled between 1910 and 1940, two thirds of DC residents were white and one third were black. African Americans lived for the most part within the old city limits, but even in areas with the largest concentrations of blacks, the population was at least half white. All of this changed in the aftermath of World War II. The war flooded the city with tens of thousands of bureaucrats, specialists, and military personnel. As comfortable housing within the District became scarce and increasingly expensive, real estate developers created vast tracts of cheap homes in the farmlands that surrounded the city. Despite the inconvenience of a long commute to work, the new housing at the periphery was affordable. And since many Americans had rural or small-town roots, the suburbs were more like the homes they remembered than were tightly packed urban neighborhoods.

Planners as well as developers presented low-density neighborhoods with wide lawns and frame houses as the ideal way of life. Boosted by GI bill mortgage assistance and income tax deductions for interest payments, home ownership became the bedrock of individual wealth. Black as well as white families left center-city neighborhoods when they could afford to do so. Generally speaking, wealthier families with better education and stable jobs were the first to go. The people who remained behind or moved in to take their place were likely to be poorer, less educated, less skilled, and less frequently employed, and they crowded into smaller and smaller spaces.

In addition to the positive pull of the suburbs, the negative push of race prejudice had a devastating effect on DC communities in the 1950s. After the 1954 Supreme Court decision in *Brown v. Board of Education* outlawed school segregation, many whites worried that their children would be forced to attend integrated schools and that black families would move into neighborhood enclaves long closed to them. Some in the real estate industry exploited these fears by buying houses on all-white blocks and selling them at reduced prices to black families. White families panicked and were willing to sell below market in hopes of recouping at least part of their investment. As the District's housing stock declined in value, in-town residences that the middle class once competed to rent or own were transformed into housing for those at the bottom of the economic ladder.

In the period between 1940 and 1970, the District of Columbia, with a population approaching three quarters of a million, flipped from being two thirds white to being more than two thirds black. The northeast and southeast sectors had even higher concentrations of African Americans. Whites remained an overwhelming majority in Georgetown and in the area of the northwest moated by Rock Creek Park. But by 1970, hundreds of thousands of the city's workers commuted from counties in Virginia and Maryland, and ninety percent of them were white.

In many cases federal action accelerated the disruption rather than easing it. In 1945 Congress established the Redevelopment Land Agency to "provide for the replanning and rebuilding of slum [and] blighted . . . areas of the District of Columbia," and in 1949 the National Housing Act provided federal funding for urban redevelopment. By redevelopment, the planners of that era meant wholesale "clearance" of what they labeled as inferior buildings and their replacement by structures that met the aesthetic and utilitarian criteria of the time. Planners were required to provide housing for those displaced by the destruction, but it was never a requirement that replacement housing be in or even near the original neighborhood.

Southwest Washington was once a working-class neighborhood near the city's port, but by 1946 it had become one of the District's most crime-ridden and impoverished areas. Yet resistance to urban redevelopment in the southwest was strong and widespread. Residents complained that they were being exiled from their homes and driven away from church, family, and friends. Landowners protested that the government was condemning their property and taking it without adequate compensation. In 1954 the Supreme Court, in a unanimous decision, found that the federal government had the right to seize property on public-welfare principles that were "spiritual as well as physical, aesthetic as well as monetary." As a result, fifteen thousand people in southwest Washington were displaced, and "cleared" blocks were taken over by government agencies and commercial structures. Graceless public housing towers replaced dilapidated row houses, and a historic DC neighborhood laid out by L'Enfant and inhabited since the early days of the republic was systematically destroyed.

The scale of community disruption in the decades after World War II and the physical, social, and political dislocation it created are difficult to overestimate. The city reversed its entire demographic history within a single generation. Voluntary or forced, directed or spontaneous, the movement had tumultuous and long-lasting consequences. Deprived of leadership in economic, social, and political life, DC's in-town communities foundered during the 1950s and 1960s. Black-owned businesses all but disappeared. Poverty became the norm in neighborhoods marked by increasing divisions between residents and the absentee owners of businesses and real estate there. Tensions accelerated during the civil rights era, and areas of the city once open to both blacks and whites became off-limits to outsiders.

On Thursday, April 4, 1968, at 6:01 p.m. James Earl Ray fired a single rifle shot that struck and killed Martin Luther King Jr. as he stood on the balcony of his room at the Lorraine Motel in Memphis, Tennessee. King was pronounced dead an hour later, and the news rapidly spread throughout the nation. African Americans in more than sixty cities began protests that quickly grew into riots. Washington was among the most volatile. News of Dr. King's assassination brought DC residents into the streets of Shaw in the early evening. This neighborhood, just northeast of the White House, was the center of African American political and cultural life in DC. A small crowd gathered outside the office of King's Southern Christian Leadership Conference at Fourteenth and U streets. The DC headquarters of the NAACP and the Student Nonviolent Coordinating Committee were located nearby.

SNCC's former leader, Stokely Carmichael, who had recently disavowed King's philosophy of nonviolence in favor of "black power," became de facto head of the unruly crowd. Carmichael seemed stunned and purposeless as he led his followers up and down Fourteenth Street, stopping at each open business and asking the owners to close in recognition of King's death. After an hour or so, Carmichael left the area. The crowd, however, grew larger and more reckless, and Fourteenth Street businesses, whether closed or open, remained their focus. While some of these were chain stores, others were small retail businesses on which the neighborhood depended. A decade before, their owners had lived and worked in the neighborhood; in the flight from the center, they had moved their homes but held onto their stores as the neighborhood became more impoverished and its economy declined.

The People's Drug Store at the corner of Fourteenth and U was one of the first buildings to be attacked. Rocks were thrown through its windows early in the evening. Later, rioters pushed inside and began looting its shelves. What began as unfocused mourning for Dr. King and anger over his assassination morphed within a few hours into mass robbery, vandalism, and arson. In other cities, riot police had fired on looters and rioters, and many people had been killed and wounded. Determined at all costs to avoid bloodshed, the DC precinct police and special forces were ordered not to draw their weapons. With clubs and shields, they herded the crowd along U Street and up Fourteenth while other officers arrested those who failed to move along. Late at night the crowd dispersed and the city grew quiet.

Riots typically happen after dark, so in consultation with the White House, District officials decided that schools would open Friday morning as usual. The Cherry Blossom Festival, which had drawn crowds of tourists to the city, would go on as planned. Few students attended school that day, however, and many teachers called in sick. By noon young people had again gathered along Fourteenth Street and Seventh Street, and not long afterward the Safeway market on Fourteenth was set on fire. When firemen responded, they were attacked. More fires erupted, set by gangs undeterred by volleys of tear gas coming from the over-matched police force. Two boys burned to death in a clothing store they were robbing.

H Street in the northeast—another business strip in a black neighborhood—and many parts of Anacostia were also the scenes of roving crowds, who harassed business owners and threatened commuters. The police response gradually accelerated, and over the next two days the combined force of National Guard troops, special units, and precinct police stopped the rioting throughout the city. By Sunday, the many fires had been brought under control.

Loss of life was minimal, but the cost in every other way was enormous and long-lasting. Nearly a thousand stores in African American sections of the city were damaged or destroyed. Many of these businesses, which had provided not only food and clothing but the only economic infrastructure in their communities, never reopened. Though commercial property was the main target, nearly seven hundred houses and apartments were also damaged; in one of them, a handicapped woman had suffocated. Striking out at the nearest targets they could find, the rioters ripped apart their own neighborhoods.

A second disaster struck Washington's black communities in the late 1980s. Throughout the United States, powdered cocaine use and addiction steadily increased in the 1970s, but it did not reach epidemic proportions until the 1980s, when crack cocaine flooded the market. Because this form of the drug could be smoked and inhaled rather than snorted, it produced a stronger and quicker reaction. And because of its potency, crack could be sold in smaller quantities at lower prices.

The drug crisis in DC and elsewhere drew overwhelming media attention, and some commentators have argued that the epidemic was more a media event than a social reality. But most observers agree that crack addiction devastated Washington's black neighborhoods. Cocaine-related deaths and injuries increased dramatically. Thousands lost their jobs, and petty crime rose as users stole to pay for their addiction. Infants born to crack-addicted mothers were at grave risk. Crack dealers became heroes to boys, though their short careers typically ended in homicide or prison. In 1993 the District recorded 454 murders and nearly seventy thousand major crimes.

The response of the judicial system to the crack epidemic was swift, and many have argued intemperate. Because crack was believed to cause more volatile and violent behavior than powdered cocaine, sentencing guidelines for distribution of the two forms of the drug were, and remain, very different. A first conviction for crack possession carried a mandatory prison sentence, while possession of powdered cocaine did not. Possessing a pound of powder brought a five-year sentence; possessing five grams of crack earned the same prison time. The longer and more frequent sentences for crack possession and distribution fell disproportionately on African Americans. A lasting effect of the epidemic was the imprisonment of tens of thousands of young black men.

Mass criminal activity cannot thrive without political protection, and during the worst periods of the city's history the local government in Washington was self-indulgent, callous, and corrupt. At the cost of some local control, the DC government entered a partnership with federal agencies—a recurrent feature of DC history, but this time the two groups worked effectively to produce a local government responsive to citizens' needs and alert to opportunities for economic recovery. Today, some twenty years after the height of the drug crisis, Washington's in-town neighborhoods have resumed normal daily life. Communities on the periphery of L'Enfant's city that were most strongly affected by social and economic turmoil have become quiet and pleasant places to live and visit once again.

The reasons for this recovery are multiple; and to a greater or lesser degree every part of the community has contributed to it. In the 1990s, political stability in the city and years of positive economic growth in the nation led to a boom in development, commerce, and housing in the District. Dotcom startups along the Dulles Airport corridor and near Tysons Corner, Virginia, were the most visible bellwethers of prosperity, but the city as a whole shared in the bounty, which has continued more or less uninterrupted. Targeted development in communities that were hardest hit also played a role in reversing the decline. A convention center built at the edge of downtown in 1980 drew some commerce to the area but proved too small to be successful. The completion of what is now called the Verizon Center at Seventh and F Streets NW had a more significant and longer lasting effect.

Since opening in 1997, the complex, with shows on more than two hundred days per year, has drawn over twenty million patrons. This steady stream of customers has sustained a wide range of businesses in the blocks around the center, and these hotels, shops, and restaurants employ members of the local community. In 2003 another 2.3 million square foot convention center opened a few blocks north of the Verizon Center, adding to the cumulative effect of concentrated development in this key area between the historic downtown commercial district and the hardest hit inner-city neighborhoods.

Economic opportunity for those neighborhoods increased dramatically when the Washington Metro Green Line was created. Construction of the Metro subway system began in 1969, and the first trains were in operation in time for the nation's Bicentennial celebration. The original lines of the system—the Red, Orange, Blue, and Yellow, all open by 1983—served the needs of commuters coming into the city from Virginia and Maryland suburbs more adequately than they served in-town residents. In 1991 when the long-awaited Green Line finally opened, it ended the isolation of central city neighborhoods and allowed residents to travel to jobs virtually anywhere in the District and surrounding areas.

This dramatic history of nineteenth-century growth, twentieth-century disruption, and recent recovery is repeated in each of Washington's historic in-town neighborhoods. Just one year after the Civil War ended, members of Washington's First Congregational Church met to create a theological seminary whose graduates would serve America's newly emancipated blacks. During their extended discussions, the group expanded its original focus to include teaching. In 1867 Congress granted a charter to Howard University, and land was set aside on the Seventh Street horse car line. Congress recognized that the university's mission would be to educate African Americans and other young people in liberal arts and the sciences. The university's first board of trustees was composed of eighteen white men who were all members of the Congregational Church. The first black trustee, Henry Highland Garnet, was elected within the year. Two years later another African American began to serve on the executive board.

The institution was named for Civil War General Oliver Otis Howard,

who headed the Freedmen's Bureau, the organization responsible for
integrating former slaves into national life. Since the university's mission
was central to the bureau's task, Howard was able to fund much of its
early activity while also serving as its president. Howard Hall, a home
with Mansard roof and square tower in the Italianate style, was built for
the president in 1869; it is the oldest building on the university's campus. (119)

On forty acres of land purchased from Howard University, a former
trustee, Amzi L. Barber, laid out a new neighborhood in the picturesque
style of Andrew Jackson Downing. Barber named the area for his father-
in-law, LeDroit Langdon, a successful real estate broker. In the 1870s
James McGill, an architect and engraver, adapted house plans from contemporary model books in a variety of popular "romantic" designs, ranging from Second Empire to Gothic Revival to Italianate. LeDroit Park,
now designated a historic district, was one of
the first housing developments made accessible
by the Seventh Street horse car line.

Despite Barber's associations with Howard,
his new community was reserved for whites
only. An iron and brick fence on its public side
and a broad board fence around the back of the
enclave enforced its exclusiveness. The all-
white community did not propose to do without
black servants and laborers, however. Black residents of nearby Howard Town did the yard
work, cooked, and looked after LeDroit Park

119

120

children. The fence, which forced blacks to walk around the perimeter rather than cut through the subdivision, was a source of anger and frustration.

In 1888, in an unusual act of protest, African Americans stormed the fence and broke it down. Some five years later the first black families moved into LeDroit Park homes. In the early twentieth century the neighborhood was home to some of the most prominent African Americans in the nation. But as the easing of segregation opened neighborhoods farther from the city center in the late 1950s, LeDroit Park began to lose its prominent residents. The area went into an economic decline that was reversed only at the end of the twentieth century. Howard University now owns a number of the houses in LeDroit Park, which it has renovated and made available to faculty and staff. Some fifty of the original McGill houses have been preserved; they are especially well represented in the three and four hundred blocks along T and U streets. (120)

Like LeDroit Park, Petworth was a by-product of the Seventh Street car line. The subdivision was laid out between Georgia Avenue and Second Street NW north of Rock Creek Church Road and south of Hamilton Street. The land on which Petworth was built combined two former estates. One was property that John Tayloe, the owner of Octagon House, bought in 1803. Unlike other Washington developments north of Florida Avenue, Petworth followed L'Enfant's grid. Its streets ran north-south, and

its avenues intersected in traffic circles. The Brightwood Railway Company took over the horse car lines in the late 1880s and speeded up
service by substituting electric cars. In 1930, ninety-nine percent of Petworth's residents were white. By 1980, whites made up only one percent
of its population. Today, Petworth is one of Washington's most charming
neighborhoods. Bungalows built to a standard pattern on generous lots
are scattered throughout it. Brick row houses run along many of the
streets, their uniformity muted by abrupt changes of trim or surface
paint, and by awnings or ornaments in the tiny yards. (121)

 Shaw, the largest and most significant of Washington's historically
black neighborhoods, took its name from Robert Gould Shaw, the white
commander of the Massachu-
setts 54th regiment who led
black troops against Confederate strongholds guarding
Charleston, South Carolina.
The name of the neighborhood
was first adopted by a black
community that formed around
a Civil War Union encamp-
ment. In the early twentieth century, U Street between Sixth and Six-

121

teenth Streets was the center of black-owned businesses in Shaw. Duke
Ellington, born and raised in the community, began playing in local jazz
clubs at an early age. (122) The greatest African American performers of
the era—Cab Calloway, Louis Armstrong, Art Tatum, and Pearl Bailey
among them—could also be heard there. The YMCA on Twelfth Street

122

was reserved for African Americans. The nearby Whitelaw Hotel was the only luxury hotel in Washington open to blacks. Shaw was the black neighborhood hardest hit by the riots of 1968, but today this multi-ethnic community near downtown is thriving once again. (123)

Aside from blacks, Washington's ethnic population continued to be small until about 1980. One of its oldest communities, an enclave of Chinese immigrants, experienced its own variation on the theme of prejudice, displacement, and crime. Directly north of the Old Patent Building, at the corner of Seventh and H, is the gateway to Washington's Chinatown. In the nineteenth century this area was a small German neighborhood. Its transformation into a Chinese community was the result of an earlier forced dislocation. From the 1880s until about 1930, Pennsylvania Avenue was the main street of a Chinatown that stretched from near the foot of Capitol Hill to the Public Market at Sixth Street. Estimates of its population vary. Some sources suggest that three thousand people may have been crammed into single-family houses or flats above stores along this brief stretch of the avenue. More conservative estimates place the population at six hundred, or even three hundred. Most residents were employed in wholesale businesses centered on the market and in restaurants or laundries nearby.

From the eve of the Civil War and well into the twentieth century, capital lawmakers viewed Chinese immigration with fear and distaste. As early as 1858 the Chinese government agreed by treaty to prohibit permanent emigration. A federal district court decision in 1878 declared

Chinese to be "nonwhite" and therefore ineligible for naturalization under a 1790 law that restricted citizenship to "free white persons." In 1882 Congress passed an immigration law that suspended Chinese immigration for ten years and outlawed naturalization. In 1889 the Supreme Court found that the provisions of this so-called Chinese Exclusionary Act were enforceable. A similar sequence of discriminatory acts and rulings continued into the 1950s.

In 1850, the first year in which the U.S. Census asked about country of origin, over two million people in the nation said they had been born in Europe, while only a thousand identified China as their home country. In 1930 over fourteen million Americans were first-generation immigrants from Europe; the number of first-generation Asian immigrants in America in that year was less than a quarter of a million. Because of immigration restrictions,  the Chinese community along Pennsylvania Avenue was, like most American Chinatowns of the time, almost entirely male. Few Chinese women were allowed to enter the country, and miscegenation laws prevented intermarriage with non-Chinese. Since the Chinese could not become U.S. citizens, the community had no power at the polls.

123

Traditional Chinese self-help organizations, called tongs, looked after the welfare of their members. In Washington, wealthier and more prominent members of the community belonged to the On Leong tong, while waiters, laundry workers, and other laborers joined Hip Sing. When it became clear that the buildings along Pennsylvania Avenue were to be destroyed in keeping with the McMillan Commission's recommendations, members of On Leong tong bought space along H Street to relocate the businesses of its members.

When the migration of Chinatown's businesses became known, opposition all along H Street was immediate and vocal. Many people continued to fear and look down on the Chinese, especially in the late 1920s and early 1930s when Chinese tongs throughout the nation were caught up in open warfare. Some of them were active in prostitution, gambling, opium trafficking, and bootlegging. Tong wars between rival Chinese gangs led to a handful of murders in Washington, but the newspapers of the period were full of lurid stories of mayhem in the Chinese communities of Los Angeles and San Francisco.

Today, Chinatown's seventy-foot-wide free-standing Friendship Archway leads to a short section of H Street lined with Chinese restaurants and second-floor apartments that house a dwindling Chinese American population. Many older members of the neighborhood live in Wah Luck

124

House at the corner of Sixth Street, which was built for residents displaced by the Verizon Center. The arch itself was designed by Alfred Liu in 1968 and built on site by Chinese craftsmen using traditional materials. At its top are seven sloping roofs; nearly three hundred gilded

dragons twist and twine across its red, green, and blue-lacquered sur-
faces. (124)

   The community of Adams Morgan, centered at Columbia Road and
Eighteenth Street, is the city's largest Hispanic neighborhood. It began as
a streetcar suburb of modest row houses whose skewed grid reflected both

the terrain and the developers'
disdain of L'Enfant's orthogonals.
This area passed from single-
family to multi-family housing
as early as the 1930s. By the
1950s, as affluent residents
fled to the suburbs and were
replaced by Cuban immigrants,
the neighborhood became eco-

125

nomically depressed. In the 1980s immigrants from Central America followed. Today, Adams Morgan's colorful murals, busy restaurants, and
lively clubs reflect the neighborhood's rejuvenation. (125)

   Northeast of Adams Morgan, between Fifteenth and Sixteenth streets,
is Meridian Hill Park, also called Malcolm X Park, a quiet twelve-acre
green patch in one of the most thickly settled areas of the city. In 1819
David Porter, a successful privateer during the War of 1812, bought the
acres now included in the park and built a mansion, which he called
Meridian Hill. The site was sold to the government nearly a century later,
and on the brink of World War I the landscape architect George Burnap
was commissioned to design a formal park and garden in the Italian Renaissance style. Gardens of this type were typically designed for the

grounds of palaces; the intention was to offer the same grandeur and formality to all the people of the city. The Italian theme of the garden may be responsible for the double-life-size figure of the poet Dante, who glowers over the lower park from a plateau on its eastern edge.

At the height of land on the steeply rising piedmont, the site looks due south toward the White House and Mall. The garden, which is divided into two parts, is well suited to this hilly terrain. Its upper expanse combines open lawns and walkways sheltered by trees. At its lower end is a grand terrace with views of the city that were once spectacular but are now blocked by apartment buildings. A figure of Joan of Arc looking skyward from the back of her horse stands near the edge, though the sword she once held in her hand has been broken off. Below the terrace, a seasonal fountain flanked by steps cascades down the center of the sloping hillside gardens.

During the 1980s, Meridian Park was an open-air mart for drug dealers, and dangerous to visit at any time of day. Though a little worse for wear, the park, like the surrounding neighborhood, has in recent years regained some of its former amenity and charm.

National history has been made in Washington since the beginning of the nineteenth century, but the city itself often has seemed a backwater in the surge of national events. With the exception of a few days during the Civil War when the capital threatened to become a battleground, and a long weekend in the 1960s when riots tore through its central neighborhoods, the city has scarcely felt the exhilaration of great national movements or the cold breath of disaster. It has always been a policy-maker's

city, where great events are investigated and their significance weighed—
a place where action is contemplated but seldom undertaken.

As it has eluded history, Washington has also lived beyond the reach
of art and literature. Though it is a city of great collections, no art movements developed there, as they did in New York, Boston, or San Francisco. Henry Adams was the most important American author to live and
write in the capital. His history of Jefferson's presidency and his own
autobiography bear the mark of long and close familiarity with a place he
loved. More typically, writers have passed through the city and recorded
fugitive and generally unflattering impressions of its layout and
prospects. Mark Twain and his collaborator, Charles Dudley Warner, pillo-
ried the capital in their 1873 book *The Gilded Age.* Virtually alone
among American authors, Walt Whitman felt both its tragedy and its sub-
lime promise.

In its architecture, too, Washington is alienated from the main traditions of American building. Founded in the heyday of neoclassicism, the
capital has repeatedly rediscovered and reinvigorated that international
style throughout its history. The result is a city that is unlike any other in
America. An eighteenth-century plan spread out like the worst American
cities but resolutely ordered; a modern city dotted with neo-Roman structures; a city that has preserved the Capitol's monopoly over the skyline by
excluding the most representative of American urban buildings, the sky-
scraper—all these features make Washington more like Paris, Rome, or
St. Petersburg than Chicago or Los Angeles.

Many people deplore the city's divorce from history and from the common thread of American urban life, calling it another symptom of the dis-

engagement between the unreal zone inside the Beltway and the real world beyond. But there is a more positive and truer sense of what makes Washington unique. While the rest of America has struggled with the day to day, its capital has been a city possessed by an ideal.

For two hundred years, the people of this peculiar place have been a nation's rulers. The city has evolved to accommodate with elegance and comfort a government that has steadily grown in size and complexity. Its equally important and far more elusive job has been to embody in every significant structure some fundamental truth about the democratic process. That is a difficult task at best, and in our era it is particularly challenging both to create and to appreciate.

Indeed, if Washington is hard for Americans to grasp, it is in part because democracy itself has become elusive. Over the generations since the nation's founding, we have lost a sense that democratic self-government is a historical creation, the work of individuals who struggled to articulate and put into action principles of shared power and responsibility. Throughout history, such an ideal has more often than not run against the main currents of political belief. Yet for reasons that are unclear, contemporary Americans have evidently come to believe that democracy is the default setting of human communities. Remove the obstacles of poverty, ignorance, superstitious bias, intolerance, or autocracy, and democracy, we confidently assert, will spring out of nothing into full maturity.

This conviction that democracy is the natural state of human societies has led us to expect miracles from interventions in the affairs of other nations that more reasonable people have seen as doomed to failure. It has also led us to undervalue the realization of democratic ideals in our own history and their embodiment in our institutions. Our era is uninformed about the nature of democracy and about the necessity of discovering new and satisfying expressions of it. And we are hard-pressed to decode the surviving expressions that articulated the hopes of our grandparents. As a nation, we are in danger of becoming mute on the subject and inarticulate in the face of its greatest incarnation.

American democracy is an artifact, and Washington DC is its concrete if imperfect realization. The city is an ideal that individuals have brought into being through imagination, energy, and endurance. The language of this democratic expression, like every other language, must be taught to each successive generation, and that is a task that the nation's capital has always carried on. The very fabric of the built city—the layout of its streets, the ornamentation of its government buildings, the design of its monuments, the elegance and accessibility of its libraries and museums—are meant to advocate and to articulate democratic ideals.

Today, the official keepers of the national capital preserve and present its history, but they are less attentive to its ideology and how that has been expressed. Overwhelmed by a clamoring public for the first decades of its life, the White House has become almost entirely off-limits to citizens in the twenty-first century. The Capitol, Supreme Court, and many other government sites share this apparently necessary but markedly undemocratic exclusiveness. Wary of the public but open to persons with influence, these structures are also fixed in their own histories. Renovation and preservation are their watchwords; within the predictable future they will not change or grow.

In this climate, the expression of democratic ideals has passed out of government hands, to a marked degree, and into the hands of the citizens of the capital themselves. The city that residents call DC was once a necessary adjunct to the national government—a larger-scale version of one of Jefferson's White House "dependencies." Today, DC has assumed a character, dignity, and power of its own. Its restored neighborhoods, its successful struggle for equality and justice, its recovery from decades of cynicism and neglect have transformed the national capital into one of America's most beautiful and successful expressions of the democratic spirit.

INFORMATION

This book chronicles the development of Washington in a series of chapters that cohere historically and geographically. Both a unified narrative history and a guide, it can be read alone or used as a reference on a visit to the capital.

The first chapter describes the regional and national forces that led George Washington to choose a site for the federal city on the Potomac River not far from his Mount Vernon home. It presents the layout of the federal district and the city within it. Chapters 2 and 3 are devoted to the two major stages in the design, building, and rebuilding of the national Capitol. The first section describes the building's history, growth, and repeated reconception from the end of the eighteenth century to the middle of the nineteenth. The following chapter describes the great expansion of the building in the Civil War era and its aftermath.

Chapter 4 looks more widely over Capitol Hill, taking in Union Station, the Supreme Court, the Library of Congress, and landmarks to the east and southeast. Chapter 5 recounts the history of the White House, and Chapter 6 traces the expansion and housing of a burgeoning bureaucracy, along with other noteworthy developments in Washington's historic downtown. Chapter 7 focuses on the National Mall, with its remarkable art galleries and museum collections, and on the memorials west and south of the Washington Monument.

These seven chapters range over the streets and avenues included in L'Enfant's plan. All are served by the clean, comfortable, and efficient trains of the Washington Metro system. Chapter 8 covers a broader field, ranging into the low hills that arc around the center city. The Metro covers most of this area, too. Georgetown, which is off the Metro map, is well served by city buses.

An urban landscape once blighted by crime, poverty, and racial tension, twenty-first-century Washington DC has become a city of broad tree-shaded avenues and charming, diverse neighborhoods, all set within a natural topography that Pierre L'Enfant might still recognize, if he could visit the city today.

FURTHER READING

ACKNOWLEDGMENTS

ILLUSTRATION CREDITS

INDEX

MAPS

FURTHER READING

Allen, William C. *History of the United States Capitol: A Chronicle of Design, Construction and Politics Prepared under the Direction of the Architect of the Capitol.* Washington, DC: Government Printing Office, 2001.

Federal Writers' Project Works Progress Administration. *Washington: City and Capital.* Washington, DC: Government Printing Office, 1937.

Gilbert, Ben W., and the Staff of *The Washington Post. Ten Blocks from the White House: Anatomy of the Washington Riots of 1968.* New York: Praeger, 1968.

Goode, James M. *The Outdoor Sculpture of Washington, D.C.: A Comprehensive Historical Guide.* Washington, DC: Smithsonian Institution Press, 1974.

Howard, Hugh. *Dr. Kimball and Mr. Jefferson.* New York: Overlook, 2006.

McGregor, James H. S. *Rome from the Ground Up.* Cambridge: Harvard University Press, 2006.

—— *Venice from the Ground Up.* Cambridge: Harvard University Press, 2006.

—— *Paris from the Ground Up.* Cambridge: Harvard University Press (forthcoming).

Moeller, G. Martin. *AIA Guide to the Architecture of Washington, D.C.* Fourth ed. Baltimore: Johns Hopkins University Press, 2006.

Monkman, Betty C. *The White House: An Historic Guide*, 21st ed. Washington, DC: White House Historical Association, 2001.

Passonneau, Joseph R. *Washington through Two Centuries: A History in Maps and Images*. New York: Monacelli Press, 2004.

Peatross, C. Ford, ed. *Capital Drawings: Architectural Drawings for Washington, D.C., from the Library of Congress*. Baltimore: Johns Hopkins University Press, 2005.

Protopappas, John J., and Alvin R. McNeal, eds. *Washington on Foot* Washington, DC: Smithsonian Institution Press, 2004.

Ryan, William, and Desmond Guinness. *The White House: An Architectural History*. New York: McGraw Hill, 1980.

Seale, William. *The President's House*. Washington, DC: White House Historical Association, with the Cooperation of the National Geographic Society, 1986.

Senate Committee on the District of Columbia. *The Improvement of the Park System of the District of Columbia*. Fifty-seventh Congress, First Session, Senate Report no. 166, 1902.

Temple of Liberty: Building the Capitol for a New Nation. http://www.loc.gov/exhibits/us.capitol/s0.html.

Whitman, Walt. *Specimen Days*. Boston: Godine, 1971.

Wolanin, Barbara A. *Constantino Brumidi: Artist of the Capitol*. Washington, DC: Government Printing Office, 1998.

ACKNOWLEDGMENTS

This book is dedicated to the memory of my parents, James Harvey McGregor (1907–1983) and Mary Twigg McGregor (1910–2005). While writing *Washington from the Ground Up*, I relived a lot of memories, both my own and those of my family. My father was in the War Department Office in 1932 on the day federal troops drove the Bonus Marchers out of the city; it was a scene he never forgot. My mother's father was running for the Senate that year on a third-party ticket. Thirty years later I stood on Pennsylvania Avenue and watched the funeral cortège of President Kennedy make its way to the Capitol. I believe in Washington as an expression of what democracy stands for; I acknowledge its repeated failure to live up to its own ideals.

In writing this book as in everything else, my wife, Sallie, has been both an inspiration and a strong support. My sons, Raphael and Ned, have joined me on many explorations of the city. I am deeply grateful to all of them. At Harvard University Press, Lindsay Waters saw the book safely through the needle's eye of review and acceptance; his advice was always sound and to the point. Jill Breitbarth and David Foss contributed design and production expertise. Susan Wallace Boehmer took the book on a test drive and pointed the way to many useful improvements. And finally, my debt of appreciation to Wendy Strothman and her capable staff continues to grow with each passing year.

ILLUSTRATION CREDITS

Achille Leclère (1813): 6

Architect of the Capitol: 21, 22, 23, 24, 25, 26, 31 (Thomas U. Walter); pp. 9, 37, 69, 111, 141, 181, 213, 261

Clifford Boehmer / Harvard University Press: 13, 14, 15, 16, 18, 19, 20, 28, 29, 30, 32, 33, 34, 35, 36, 37, 38, 39, 40, 41, 42, 43, 44, 45, 46, 47, 48, 49, 50, 51, 52, 59, 68, 69, 70, 71, 72, 73, 74, 75, 76, 77, 78, 79, 80, 81, 82, 83, 84, 85, 86, 87, 89, 90, 91, 92, 93, 94, 95, 96, 97, 98, 99, 100, 101, 102, 103, 104, 105, 106, 107, 108, 110, 111, 112, 113, 114, 115, 116, 117, 118, 119, 120, 121, 122, 123, 124, 125; pp. iii, 1, 299

Harvard Map Collection, Harvard College Library: 5 (detail after Giambattista Nolli's mid-eighteenth-century engraving of Leonardo Bufalini's 1551 plan of Rome)

Isabelle Lewis: Maps 2, 4, 5, 6, 7, 8

John W. Reps: Map 1

Library of Congress: 1 (George Beck), 3 (Francis Jukes), 4, 9, 10 (William B. Birch), 11 (William Strickland / George Munger), 12 (Robert P. Smith), 27 (E. Sachse), 54, 55 (William Strickland / George Munger), 56, 57, 60 (Anton Hohenstein), 109; Maps 9 (Currier & Ives), 10 (John L. Trout), 11 (H. H. Green)

Maryland Historical Society: 2 (Benjamin Latrobe), 53

Massachusetts Historical Society: 7, 8

INDEX

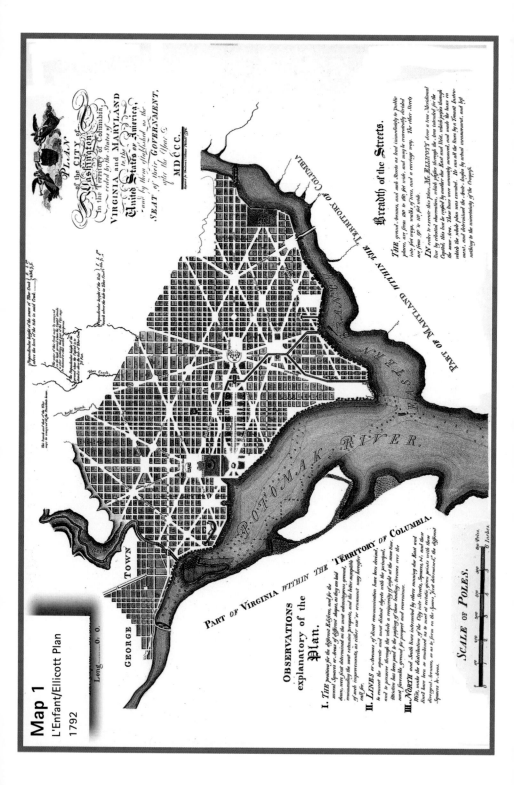

Map 1

L'Enfant/Ellicott Plan

1792

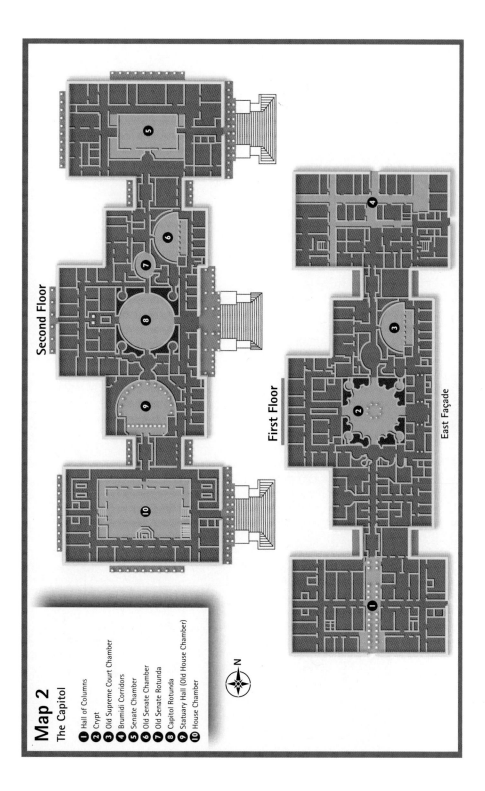

Map 2
The Capitol

1. Hall of Columns
2. Crypt
3. Old Supreme Court Chamber
4. Brumidi Corridors
5. Senate Chamber
6. Old Senate Chamber
7. Old Senate Rotunda
8. Capitol Rotunda
9. Statuary Hall (Old House Chamber)
10. House Chamber

Second Floor

First Floor

East Façade

N

Map 3
McMillan Commission Plan
1901–1902

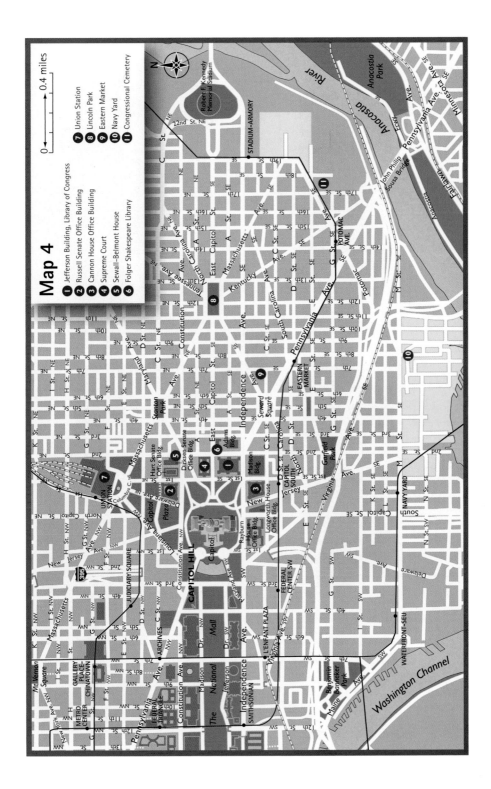

Map 4

1. Jefferson Building, Library of Congress
2. Russell Senate Office Building
3. Cannon House Office Building
4. Supreme Court
5. Sewall-Belmont House
6. Folger Shakespeare Library
7. Union Station
8. Lincoln Park
9. Eastern Market
10. Navy Yard
11. Congressional Cemetery

0 —— 0.4 miles

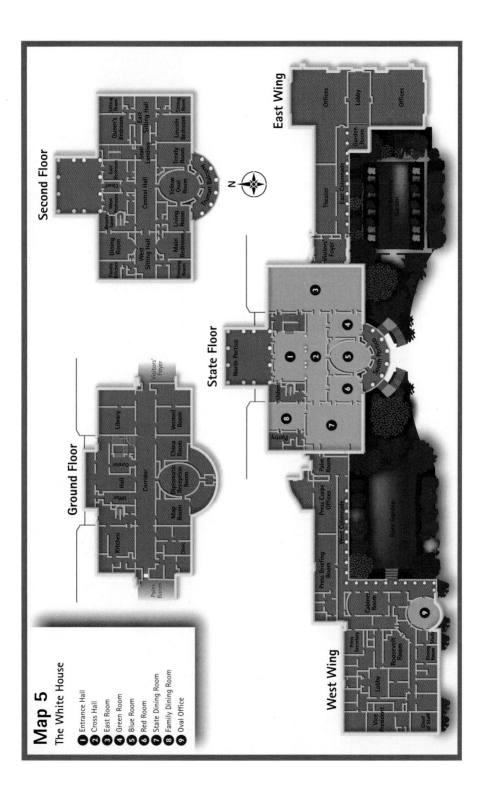

Map 5
The White House

1 Entrance Hall
2 Cross Hall
3 East Room
4 Green Room
5 Blue Room
6 Red Room
7 State Dining Room
8 Family Dining Room
9 Oval Office

Second Floor

Sitting Room
Queen's Bedroom
East Sitting Hall
Lincoln Bedroom
Lincoln Sitting Room
Treaty Room
Closet
East Bedroom
Stair Landing
Central Hall
West Bedroom
Beauty Salon
West Sitting Hall
Dining Room
Family Kitchen
Main Bedroom
Living Room
Yellow Oval Room
Dressing Room
Truman Balcony

N

Ground Floor

Library
Curator
Vermeil Room
Office
Hall
China Room
Corridor
Kitchen
Diplomatic Reception Room
Maps
Map Room
Palm Room
Visitors' Foyer

State Floor

3
4
1
2
5
6
8
7
North Portico
South Portico
Usher
Pantry

East Wing

Offices
Lobby
Offices
Garden Room
East Colonnade
Theater
Visitors' Foyer
Jacqueline Kennedy Garden

West Wing

Press Corps Offices
West Colonnade
Press Briefing Room
Cabinet Room
Press Secretary
Lobby
Roosevelt Room
Dining Room
Vice President
Chief of Staff
Palm Room
Rose Garden
9

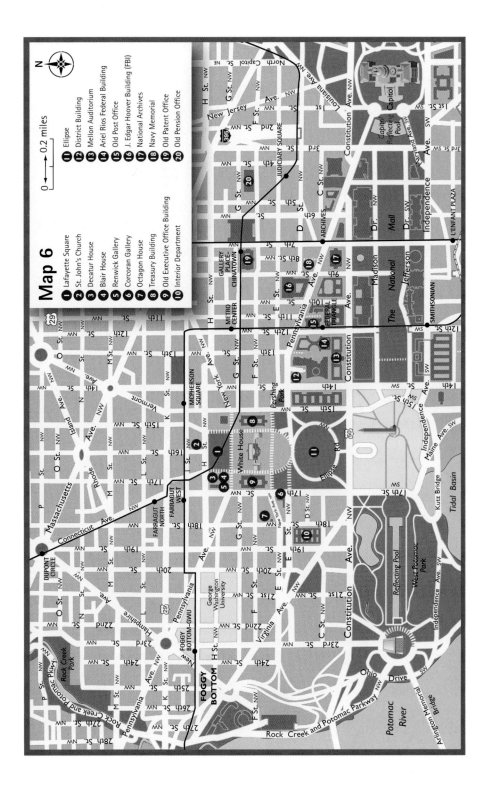

Map 6

1 Lafayette Square
2 St. John's Church
3 Decatur House
4 Blair House
5 Renwick Gallery
6 Corcoran Gallery
7 Octagon House
8 Treasury Building
9 Old Executive Office Building
10 Interior Department
11 Ellipse
12 District Building
13 Mellon Auditorium
14 Ariel Rios Federal Building
15 Old Post Office
16 J. Edgar Hoover Building (FBI)
17 National Archives
18 Navy Memorial
19 Old Patent Office
20 Old Pension Office

N

0 — 0.2 miles

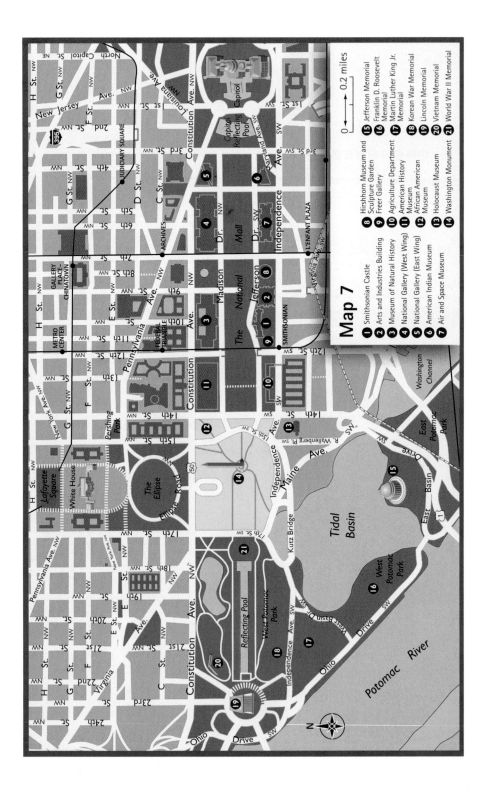

Map 7

❶ Smithsonian Castle
❷ Arts and Industries Building
❸ Museum of Natural History
❹ National Gallery (West Wing)
❺ National Gallery (East Wing)
❻ American Indian Museum
❼ Air and Space Museum
❽ Hirshhorn Museum and Sculpture Garden
❾ Freer Gallery
❿ Agriculture Department
⓫ American History Museum
⓬ African American Museum
⓭ Holocaust Museum
⓮ Washington Monument
⓯ Jefferson Memorial
⓰ Franklin D. Roosevelt Memorial
⓱ Martin Luther King Jr. Memorial
⓲ Korean War Memorial
⓳ Lincoln Memorial
⓴ Vietnam Memorial
㉑ World War II Memorial

0 — 0.2 miles

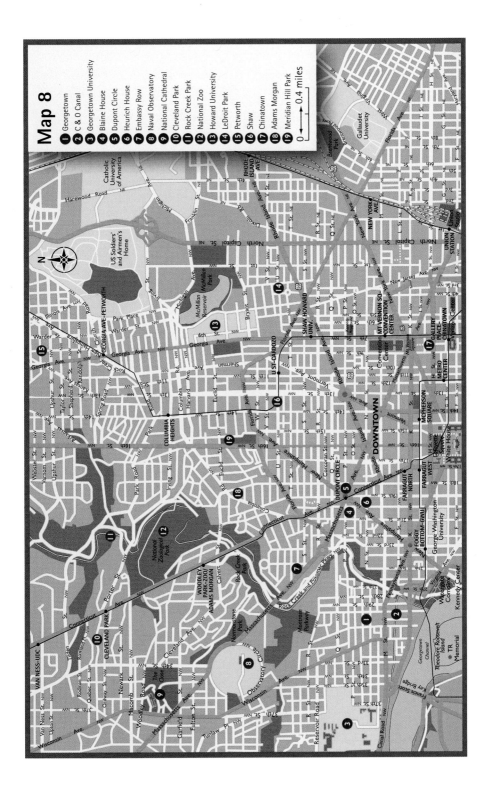

Map 8

1. Georgetown
2. C & O Canal
3. Georgetown University
4. Blaine House
5. Dupont Circle
6. Heurich House
7. Embassy Row
8. Naval Observatory
9. National Cathedral
10. Cleveland Park
11. Rock Creek Park
12. National Zoo
13. Howard University
14. LeDroit Park
15. Petworth
16. Shaw
17. Chinatown
18. Adams Morgan
19. Meridian Hill Park

0 ___ 0.4 miles

Map 9
City of Washington
1892

Map 10
City of Washington
1901

Map 11
City of Washington
1916